J.K. Lasser's
Invest Online

Do-It-Yourself and
Keep More of What You Earn

J.K. LASSER'S
INVEST ONLINE

Do-It-Yourself and
Keep More of What You Earn

LauraMaery Gold

Dan Post

Macmillan USA

MACMILLAN GENERAL REFERENCE
A Simon & Schuster Macmillan Company
1633 Broadway
New York, NY 10019-6785

Macmillan Publishing books may be purchased for business or sales
promotional use. For information please write: Special Markets Department, Macmillan Publishing USA, 1633 Broadway, New York, NY
10019

Publisher's Note: J.K. Lasser's *Invest Online* is published in recognition of the need for useful information regarding the establishment of
an online account, use of online research tools, and investment advise.
The views expressed by the authors of this book are solely their own.
Neither Christos Cotsakos, E*TRADE, nor Macmillan Publishing USA
gives express or implied warranties with respect to the information
contained herein. The publisher, E*TRADE, and the authors specifically
disclaim any responsibility for any liability, loss or risk (financial, personal, or otherwise) which may be claimed or incurred as a conse-
quence, directly or indirectly, of the use and/or application of any of
the contents of this publication. Reasonable care has been taken in the
preparation of this text. Readers are cautioned that this publicatonis
sold with the understanding that neither Christos Cotsakos, E*TRADE,
nor Macmillan Publishing USA provides investment, tax, legal, or accounting advice, nor recommends the suitability of any investment
strategy. Investors with specific investment questions are urged to seek
the advise of a professional broker, certified financial planner, certified
public accountant, or attorney.

J.K. Lasser Editorial and Production

Publishing Brand Manager	Maryam Banikarim
Editor	Elliott Eiss
Associate Editor	Connor Murphy
Title Manager	Kathie-Jo Arnoff
Acquisitions Editor	Jill Byus
Product Director	Lorna Gentry
Production Editor	Rebecca Mounts
Technical Editors	John T. Fakler
	Jeff Sengstack
Acquistions Coordinator	Michelle R. Newcomb
Cover Design	Paul Costello

MACMILLAN is a registered trademark of Macmillan, Inc.

International Standard Book Number : ISBN 0028623983
Library of Congress Cataloging Number: 97-80801

This book was formerly published under the title *Boot Your Broker* and
was sold for $29.99, packaged with a CD-ROM

ABOUT THE AUTHOR

LauraMaery Gold is an editor and financial columnist for Nikkei Business Press and other international business publications. She has worked as the business editor for a U.S. newspaper, and holds degrees in law and financial planning from U.S. and British universities. A former financial planner and tax advisor, she also has business reporting experience with *PC World*, the *Columbia Business Times*, the *China Economic News*, *The Industrialist*, and various other trade and business publications.

Dan Post is a professional software engineer and database designer. He works with Siemens Business Communications, and has been a consultant to Dow-Jones, MKD and other corporate technology and communications accounts. He is a long-time computing columnist for overseas editions of PC World and other publications. He and LauraMaery Gold are co-authors of two editions of the *Complete Idiot's Guide to Excel*.

ACKNOWLEDGMENTS

We're indebted to our good friend, financial guru William R. James. Bill's gift for teaching about investments got us through the rough patches. And now, if there are faults, they are the mistakes of the authors; any errors exist because we neglected to ask Bill's advice.

A long-neglected thank you to Dr. Jerry Mason, one of the finest financial planning professors ever and the inspiration behind all the wise parts of the financial advice found in this book.

Above all, thanks to the editorial team, past and present, at Que Publishing: Jill Byus, Lorna Gentry, Kathie-Jo Arnoff, Rebecca Mounts, Michelle Newcomb, and a crew of additional editors who were a pleasure to work with. We thank you all.

And last on the list, and first in our hearts, thanks to David, Price, Makai, Eric, Kole, and Maeja, the best "investments" we ever made.

Contents at a Glance

Foreword   1

Introduction   3

Part I   The Pregame Warm-Up

   1   Why Invest Online?   11

   2   Assemble the Tools   17

   3   Get Online   29

   4   Educate Yourself About Investing   39

Part II   Work Out Your Game Plan

   5   Develop a Portfolio Strategy   57

   6   Consider Investment Vehicles   77

   7   Use Expert Research Resources   95

   8   Investigate the Markets   109

   9   Talk to Smart Investors   123

   10   Use the Rest of the Internet as a Research Tool   133

   11   Search the Internet   145

Part III   Game Day

   12   Prepare to Invest Online   163

   13   Make an Online Trade   171

   14   Advanced Trading Techniques   183

   15   Locate Other Internet Investment Tools   195

Part IV The Postgame Show

16 Track Your Portfolio 207

17 Learn Analysis Techniques 215

18 Pick Your Analysis Tools 223

19 The Final Analysis 233

Index 243

Table of Contents

Foreword   1

Introduction   3

    Who This Book Is For   4

    A Growing Market   4

    About E*TRADE   4

    What This Book Contains   5

    How to Use This Book   5

Part I   The Pregame Warm-up

1 Why Invest Online?   11

    The Benefits of Online Investing   11
        The Cost Advantage   12

    The Control Factor   12

    The Information Age   12

    The Downside   12

    Security: Who's Minding the Mint?   13
        What's Being Done to Make it Safe   13
        Additional Protection   14

    Sites on Security   14
        Web Security   14
        Internet Security   15
        Open Financial Exchange   15

    Moving On   15

2 Assemble the Tools   17

    The Hardware Tools   17
        Mac versus PC   18
        Notebook PCs versus
        Desktop   19

    The Software Tools   19

Operating System   19

Financial Software   20
    Personal Finance   20
    Online Banking   22
    Tax Preparation   23
    Spreadsheet   24
    Analysis and Portfolio Management Tools   24

The Communications Tools   24

The Modem   25

Communications
Software   26

Internet Tools   27
    Web Browser   27
    Electronic Mail Reader   27
    Newsreader   27
    Chat Software   28

3 Get Online   29

Step One: Get an Internet Account   29

Commercial Online Services   29
    America Online   30
    CompuServe   31
    Other Commercial Services   31

Internet Service Providers   31

Step Two: Start Browsing   32

Surfin' Safari—Entering URLs   33

A Faster Surf: Hyperlinks   34

Back and Forth on the Web   34

Beyond the World Wide Web   36
    E-Mail   36
    Mailing Lists   36
    UseNet Newsgroups   36
    FTP Sites   36

4 Educate Yourself About Investing 39

Financial Planning Fundamentals 39

Get Your Finances in Shape 41
   Earn More 41
   Consume Less 42
   Stay Out of Debt 43
   Force Yourself to Save 44

Calculate Your Net Worth 45

Determine What You Can Invest 45

Investment Principles 46
   The First Rule of Interest 46
   The Difference Between Yield and Total Return 46
   Time Value of Money 47
   Dollar-Cost Averaging 47
   The Power of Compounding 48
   Tax Deferral 49

Investment Basics 50
   The Least You Need to Know About Securities 50
   Vocabulary 51
   Reading the Financials 52

Part II   Work Out Your Game Plan

5 Develop a Portfolio Strategy 57

Setting Goals 57

Investment Considerations: Risk vs. Reward 59
   Test Yourself 59
   Risk Assessment 60

Types of Risk 61
   Credit Risk 61
   Cyclical Risk 63
   Inflation Risk 63
   Interest Rate Risk 64
   Liquidity Risk 64
   Market Risk 65
   Opportunity Costs 66

Price Volatility Risk   66
Reinvestment Rate Risk   67

Mitigating Risk   68
Diversification   68
Term of Investment   71

Other Considerations in Creating a Strategy   72
Tax-free investing   72
Ethical Investing   73

Allocating Assets   74

6 Consider Investment Vehicles   77

The Basics   77

Stocks   78

Bonds   79
Corporate Bonds   80
Municipal Bonds   81

Government Securities   82

Mutual Funds   82
Index Funds   84

Alternative
Investments   85
Annuities   85
Certificates of Deposits   85
Collectibles   86
Commodities/Futures   87
Foreign Currencies   88
International Investments   89
Junk Bonds   90
Initial Public Offerings   90
Life Insurance   91
Money Markets   91
Collateralized Mortgage Obligations (CMOs)   92
Options   92
Real Estate Investment Trusts   93
Zero Coupon Bonds   93

7 Use Expert Research Resources 95

Online Business and Finance Publications 95
    Online Archive Searches 96
    Online Stock Quotes 96
    Reports 96

Feature Publications 96

News Publications 99

Newsletters 100

Electronic-Only Collections 102

Push the News 106

8 Investigate the Markets 109

Individual Companies 109
    Quotes Online 110
    Company Reports 113

Industry News and Analysis 115
    Industry News 115
    Industry Analysis 116

Economic and Market Trends 117
    Economic News and
    Indicators 117
    Economic Analysis 119
    Market News and
    Commentary 120

Combined Company, Industry, and Market News 121

9 Talk to Smart Investors 123

Find a Mentor 123
    The American Association of Independent Investors (AAII) 124
    CNBC 124
    Invest-o-rama 125
    Motley Fool 126

Reading the Fine Print 126

Interactive Web Sites   128
    Message Boards   128
    Silicon Investor   128
    Socialize   128
    Participate   129
    Bob'z   129
    Join Our Discussion   129
    Michael Campbell's Money Talks   129
    Mutual Funds Online   130
    Talk to Other Investors   130
    Bust the Tipster   130
    Conference Calls   130

Investment Clubs   130

10   Use the Rest of the Internet as a Research Tool   133
    UseNet Newsgroups   134

    Mailing Lists   138
        Mailing Lists of Interest:
        Participatory   140
        Mailing Lists of Interest: Read-Only   140

    Internet Relay Chats   140

    Netiquette   141
        Lower the Volume, Please   142
        The Personal Response   142
        The Public Response   142
        Ownership   143
        All the Other Rules   143

11   Search the Internet   145
    Search Engines   145

    A Few Words About Boolean Algebra   146
        The AND Function   147
        The OR Function   147
        The NOT Function   147

    How to Conduct a Search   147
        Unique Word Searches   147
        Combined Word Searches: Using the AND, OR, and NOT
            Operators   147
        Grouping Words   148

Spelling Counts—Somewhat   149
Filters   149

The Search Engines   149
AltaVista   149
America Online Mailing List Directory   150
Deja News   150
Excite   152
Infoseek   152
InfoSpace   153
LawCrawler   154
Liszt   154
Lycos   156
Magellan Internet Guide   156
SEARCH.COM   157
Starting Point   157
WebCrawler   159
WorldPages   159
Yahoo!   160

Part III   Game Day

12   Prepare to Invest Online   163

The Exchanges   163
AMEX: American Stock
Exchange   164
CBOE: Chicago Board Options Exchange, Inc.   164
CBOT: Chicago Board of Trade   165
CME: Chicago Mercantile Exchange   165
CSCE: Coffee, Sugar & Cocoa Exchange, Inc.   166
Minneapolis Grain Exchange   166
Nasdaq: National Association of Securities Dealers Automated
Quotations   166
NYCE: New York Cotton
Exchange   166
NYSE: New York Stock
Exchange   166
PHLX: Philadelphia Stock Exchange   168

Brokers: Traditional and Discount   168
Traditional Broker   168
Discount Broker   168

Cash vs. Margin Trading   169

13 Make an Online Trade 171

Why E*TRADE? 171
 Noteworthy Features 171

E*TRADE Security 172

Opening Your Account 172

The First Timer Primer 175
 Accessing Your Account 175
 About the Customer Main Menu 176
 Customize the Main Menu 177

Last Minute Information Before You Buy 177
 Check the Price 178
 Check Your Balance 179

Purchase the Stock 179

The Stock Order Page 181
 Transactions 181
 Number of Shares 181
 Stock Symbol 181
 Price 181
 Term 181
 The All or None Box 181
 Trading Password 182
 Preview 182

14 Advanced Trading Techniques 183

Selecting Transactions 183
 A Closer Look at Short Selling 184

Choosing the Price
Parameters 186
 Market Orders 186
 Limit Orders 186
 Stop Orders 186
 Stop Limit Orders 187

Coming to Terms 187
 All-or-None Order 188

Put It All Together 188

Placing an Options Order   188
    Placing Options Transactions   189
    Buy Open   189
    Sell Open   190
    Option Symbol   190
    Selecting Price and
    Term Options   191
    Preview Order   192

Making a Margin Trade   192

15   Locate Other Internet Investment Tools   195

Comparing Online Brokers   195

Other Signs of Life   196
    AccuTrade   196
    American Express Financial Direct   196
    Aufhauser   198
    Ceres Securities   198
    DATEK Online   199
    eBroker   199
    e.Schwab   199
    Fidelity Investments   201
    PC Financial Network   201
    Wall Street Access Online   201

Other Places to Look   203
    Daytraders   203
    Yahoo!   204

Part IV   The Postgame Show

16   Track Your Portfolio   207

Track Your Investments with Portfolio Management   207

Choosing a Portfolio Manager   208

E*TRADE Portfolio Manager   209
    Personal Portfolio   210
    Excite Business and Investing   210
    Galt NetWorth   210
    Infoseek Investor   212

InvestorsEdge   212
Market Watcher Version 1.10   213
Stock Smart   213

17   Learn Analysis Techniques   215

Fundamental Analysis   215
Get an Annual Report   216

The Least You Should Know About Financial Statements   218

Ratio Analysis   220
Measurements of Activity   220
Measurements of Leverage   220
Measurements of Liquidity   221
Measurements of Profitability   221

Securities Ratios   222

18   Pick Your Analysis Tools   223

Technical Analysis: The Theory   223
The Tao of Tau   224
Trend Watch   225
The Dow Theory   225

Technical Analysis: The Application   226
Moving Averages   228
Bollinger Bands   229
Moving Average Convergence/Divergence (MACD)   229
A Surfeit of Strategies   230

19   The Final Analysis   233

Data for Sale   234

The Data Store   234

Walking Through the Technical Analysis   234

Overview   235

The Quick Tour   235
The Focus List   236
To Calculate   236
Charting a Course   236
The Quick Out   238

Analyzing the Analysis   238

Value Line   240

The Value Line Analyzer   241

Value Line Online   241

Index   243

FOREWORD

Now is a great time to be an investor. Online investing has toppled the old ways of building wealth—and literally re-invented how you manage your assets. Unprecedented power and control has been given to you, the personal investor. Technology has put tools and information never available before right at your finger tips. And E*TRADE is proud to be leading this online revolution.

Every minute of every day, thousands of investors around the world open online trading accounts. They are tired of paying high commissions, fed up with inconvenient hours, and frustrated with limited research and analysis. Today, there are nearly 2 million online brokerage accounts, and in just four years, that number is expected to grow to 10 million.

Whether you're an experienced trader or just starting out, online investing can give you the edge you need to stay ahead of the game. Nowhere else will you find as much helpful information and guidance. You can get charts, research, financial analysis—whenever you want it. Up-to-the-minute news and market information is delivered to you free in seconds. All to help you invest with more intelligence and greater control. Equally important, you receive the tools you need to customize this information for your own personal needs.

Online technologies make it easier to invest and to track your portfolio. When you decide to buy or sell stocks, options, or mutual funds, you just click to the appropriate area and enter your order. Most transactions are executed electronically and confirmed in seconds. Your portfolio is automatically updated online, and you can review your holdings and account balances 24 hours a day. Never again will you be held hostage to market hours.

Perhaps best of all, online technology provides unbeatable value to the individual investor. In essence, the middleman has been cut out—allowing you to trade stocks at a fraction of the cost of traditional or discount brokers.

Online investing is safe and secure. It is tested day in and day out by millions of the toughest critics—investors like you. They trust us with billions of their hard earned dollars. And they'll trust us with more tomorrow.

15 years ago, we at E*TRADE created online investing with one goal: to give the individual trader more power and control. And now today, millions of trades later, we continue to put the tools of investing into your hands.

Someday, we'll all invest this way.

Christos M. Cotsakos

President and Chief Executive Officer, E*TRADE Group, Inc.

Introduction

Welcome to the exciting world of online investing, where the trades are faster, the information is better, and the financial planet is more evolved than ever before.

In the old world, you had to beg your broker for this kind of information. When it arrived, it was out of date, hard to digest, and probably biased. In that old world, you waited for your broker to get back from lunch, or from the Bahamas, when you wanted to trade. And you paid an outrageous commission for the privilege of doing so.

Life has suddenly gotten a lot better. The Internet opens a wealth of financial possibilities—and pitfalls—unlike anything you've ever experienced before.

Here you'll find up-to-the-second stock quotes, years of financial data on public companies, more (and better) analysis than you've ever dreamed of, tips, rumors, educational materials— it's nearly endless! You'll also meet reliable online brokerage services that execute trades for a fraction of the price you'll pay to traditional brokers.

Sweet on the broker you already use? Put this information to work and soon your broker will be calling you for advice!

Chapter 3: Get Online

While computer gurus may breeze through at a pace that would put Evelyn Woods to shame, there's plenty to learn for almost everybody else. Chapter 3 takes the hardware purchased in Chapter 2 and puts it to good use. This chapter explains how to get online, and introduces services from commercial providers, such as CompuServe or America Online, and from your friendly neighborhood Internet service provider.

Chapter 4: Educate Yourself About Investing

A significant responsibility that comes with online investing is educating yourself. Chapter 4 takes an in-depth look at financial planning principles and personal financial statements. Determining your own net worth is a necessary step in determining how much cash you need to invest. In keeping with the intent of this book, to serve and to guide, many helpful Internet resources are cited along the way. Included at no extra charge are introductions to different kinds of securities and an explanation of how to read the financial pages of your daily newspaper.

Chapter 5: Develop a Portfolio Strategy

Chapter 5 sets out to explain the goal-setting process. This is an extremely effective approach to investing, whether you're planning to purchase an automobile or a small tropical island. Identify the factors that influence your approach to investing and create a strategy for allocating your funds.

Chapter 6: Consider Investment Vehicles

Once the decision has been made to invest, the next step is determining what to invest in. The rundown of investment vehicles in this chapter is in itself a worthwhile investment of time. Descriptions, risk factors, and additional Internet resources are included for bonds, certificates of deposit, commodities/futures, indices, international investments, junk bonds, life insurance, mutual funds, stocks, and more.

Chapter 7: Use Expert Research Resources

What do the experts say, and where on the Internet do they say it? The focus here is on the Internet counterparts to some of the most respected financial journals in the nation. If knowledge equals power, then Chapter 7 may imbue a bit of Herculean financial strength.

Chapter 8: Investigate the Markets

Chapter 8 picks up where Chapter 7 left off. Here you'll dig a little further into the news, analysis, and summaries that are available for free on the Internet. Feel free to yell, "Hercules, you wimp," after you've digested the resources described here.

Chapter 9: Talk to Smart Investors

When experts like Motley Fool and the American Association of Individual Investors offer free advice, it pays to listen. In this chapter, you'll learn where to find them. The US government and other experts are also given their due.

Chapter 10: Use the Rest of the Internet as a Research Tool

Chapter 10 covers the mechanics and the rules for communicating on the Internet. The motive here is to get you into the thick of the discussions taking place across the Internet. Here you'll learn how to enter the world of UseNet newsgroups, mailing lists, and Internet Relay Chats. The basic rules of civilized online conversation are also covered.

Chapter 11: Search the Internet

The Internet is changing and expanding by the minute. Even as the ink dries on this page, new sites are appearing, and old ones are disappearing or undergoing such radical transformations as to be unrecognizable. Chapter 11 covers Internet search engines, the tools you'll use to find new financial sites on the Internet. In the increasingly transient world of the Internet, they are your only hope for keeping up with what's happening today.

Chapter 12: Prepare to Invest Online

Chapter 12 introduces you to the players you're likely to encounter when trading online: the major stock exchanges as well as descriptions of the key types of brokers. As an added bonus, there is a discussion concerning cash versus margin trading.

Chapter 13: Make an Online Trade

Chapter 13 is a step-by-step procedure for making a simple online transaction. E*TRADE is used as the model for a sample trade. Included is information on how to open an E*TRADE account.

Chapter 14: Advanced Trading Techniques

Once you've tackled the task of making that first purchase, it's time to move on to the more complicated transactions. Chapter 14 takes you to that next trading level. This is your basic "how-to" for short selling, limit orders, stop orders, terms, options, calls, puts, and margin trading.

Chapter 15: Locate Other Internet Investment Tools

In this chapter, we look at a number of other online brokers. No two are exactly the same. Rates, commissions, and services vary widely. That's actually a good thing since no two clients have exactly the same needs. So here they are: the good, the bad, and the ugly.

Chapter 16: Track Your Portfolio

Chapter 16 features the software tools that help manage your securities. Calculate your worth before, after, and even into the future. Most of the software featured here will display trading activity, portfolio history, and portfolio valuations.

Chapter 17: Learn Analysis Techniques

By the end of this chapter, you should be able to analyze the fundamental health of your securities. That factor, plus your personal temperament, will be the key in determining when it's time to buy or sell. Fundamental analysis will help incorporate the word *rational* into choices about your trades.

Chapter 18: Pick Your Analysis Tools

Technical analysis is all about charts, graphs, theories, and Ouiji boards—well, maybe not Ouiji boards. It's an attempt to plot the future based on all the parameters of the past. Chapter 18 will examine the theory and the practice of technical analysis.

Chapter 19: The Final Analysis

Once you've worked your way through the analysis, it's time to get practical. This chapter guides you through the practical application of the techniques you've learned. Follow along step by step and turn theory into application.

The Pregame Warm-up

1 Why Invest Online?   11

2 Assemble the Tools   17

3 Get Online   29

4 Educate Yourself About Investing   39

1

Why Invest Online?

"The money you would otherwise spend on broker commissions is better off working for you. Online investing can give you control of your investments, and—as an added bonus—make you a much smarter investor."

Online investing is not about get-rich-quick schemes. It's not about flash without substance. It is about bringing the financial resources of the world into your home. Trade faster, trade cheaper, get smarter, and take complete control over your investment options.

In this chapter, we explain the pros—and the cons—of online investing. We also discuss the issue of security in a manner that will, we hope, put your mind at ease.

The Benefits of Online Investing

As people who enjoy indoor plumbing know, technology constantly moves the world forward, and forces the human race beyond its tired old habits. That's why online investing isn't some anomaly reserved for the privileged few. It's the way business will be conducted in the centuries to come. This section describes the best reasons for turning to your computer for financial transactions.

The Cost Advantage

A Hall of Fame baseball pitcher was once asked to name the most important components of pitching. His answer: "Location, location, and location." Similarly, the most important reasons for investing online can be summed up in three words: Savings, savings, and savings.

If you've gotten into the habit of paying a huge commission every time you make a trade, now is the time to break that habit. Start trading online and pay those "commissions" to yourself. Across the board, brokers provide the lowest commission rates through their online services. We surveyed 18 large and small brokerages for trading prices and found, for our sample trade, astronomical price differences between online and traditional brokerages. For example, one large brokerage that provides both traditional over-the-phone sales and online trades quoted rate differences between the two services of more than 90 percent. The numbers can go much higher.

In Chapter 12, "Prepare to Invest Online," we provide a rundown of brokers old and new, and explain how they determine the cost of trades.

The Control Factor

Timing is everything. Online trading lets you conduct trading on your schedule, instead of the 9-to-5 hours of a broker.

Timing is critical when the hours most convenient to you— say, midnight to six in the morning—aren't necessarily the most convenient for others. Your online broker is always open.

■ N O T E
Although online trade orders can be placed all hours of the day or night, they'll still actually occur only after the market has opened.

Timing is also critical if you're a *day trader*— the kind of investor who likes to buy and sell frequently, trying to time transactions to coincide with market movements. If you're a day trader or a control lover, you're off with one tip in the morning, a few trades over lunch, and a quick sale in the afternoon. Trading online lets you do all that with precise control.

The Information Age

Online investing lets you take responsibility for your own decisions. The Internet's massive software and interactive features makes personal portfolio management an easy task. Graphic representations of stock activity can notify you of the right time to buy, or sell. In Part II, "Work Out Your Game Plan," we show you the best places on the Internet for researching all your potential investments.

The Downside

Managing your own investment portfolio is time-consuming, and it's hard work. It means staying on top of the news. It requires getting educated about the business world, financial principles, the economy, and various industries. Most of all it means educating yourself about the companies you're investing in.

Fortunately, the Internet's there to help. There is no shortage of reliable resources from which to extract data. You'll find online literally hundreds of quality locations from which to pull, and even exchange, valuable data.

Security: Who's Minding the Mint?

The world is full of honest people. But it has its share of scoundrels, some of whom have found their way online. Media hype to the contrary, their occasional presence is not a tremendous personal threat. The odd fellow in the cereal aisle at your local supermarket is a far greater menace than anything you're likely to encounter on the Internet. Still, the people who do business on the Internet—the brokerages, regulatory agencies, consumer groups, and the people who want you to buy their software—take your security concerns seriously.

The vast majority of the Internet community shares the same perspective on security: Everybody is working to ensure the security, reliability, and convenience of transactions that take place electronically. Online brokerages and other businesses need your continued patronage to survive. They know that without reasonable levels of security you're not likely to do business there. Similarly, they don't want unauthorized users prowling through their records. The incentive for security comes from all sides.

What's Being Done to Make it Safe

Corporations are investing heavily to assure that no unauthorized users enter their domain. The general consensus is that no single security system can keep *all* the hackers out, so many firms utilize three or more different security mechanisms. Still, no one will claim to have a 100-percent secure system; potential legal problems aside, the claim would simply create a challenge too great for hackers to resist. Nevertheless, your transactions are unbelievably safe.

Every trading site employs a safety measure called a *firewall*. A firewall is software designed to restrict outsider access. It's often the first line of defense. Firewalls may be several layers thick with each level having its own unique security mechanisms.

Another method of keeping sites secure is to monitor account activity. When something that could be defined as suspicious occurs, continued access is denied, and the perpetrator is removed from the system until the potential problem is sorted out.

Layers of firewalls and activity monitoring are transparent to most users. What you're more likely to notice as a customer is something similar to what

E*TRADE, the leading online investment services company, requires. Users of E*TRADE must use one of three pieces of extremely safe software—Netscape Navigator, Microsoft Internet Explorer, or the America Online 3.0 browser—to access the company's customer trading area. This requirement allows E*TRADE to employ the Netscape Secure Commerce Server for encryption and authentication of transmitted data.

The final line of defense? Every online broker requires users to enter a secure password before they transact any business.

Additional Protection

Online security is an important issue but ultimately it is one about which you will have little say. Online operators know that in order to survive, they must maintain secure communications and ensure against loss.

One security issue you do have control over is making sure your broker-dealer is a member of the National Association of Security Dealers. NASD members are required to carry, as a minimum, SIPC coverage, which insures the value of your securities if the broker goes bankrupt. The Securities Investor Protection Corporation provides up to $500,000 of securities insurance, limited to $100,000 for cash claims. Of course, this protection does not cover fluctuations in the market value of your investments.

Some brokerages will carry additional coverage. The securities of E*TRADE clients, for example, are provided an additional $9.5 million of coverage by a member company of AIG, the American International Group, Inc.

Sites on Security

The Internet carries a vast number of security-related *sites,* or locations, worth reviewing. Here are some of the best for individual investors. (If you haven't any idea how to get around on the Internet, don't panic. In the next two chapters we explain how to set up your computer to get onto the Internet, and how to get anywhere you want to go in the online world. Just bend the corner of this page and come back to it after Chapter 3, "Get Online.")

Web Security

E*TRADE's secure connection policies ensure that transmissions are authenticated and encrypted. This site explains how the security measures operate.

http://www.etrade.com/advantage/ sec.html

TECHNO-HERO OR PUBLIC ENEMY?

The following site offers a fascinating story of the raging battle over encryption technology. It features spies, espionage, gambling, and a cast of defiant software programmers.

http://pathfinder.com/ @@8RAH0AcAY7NBqMvn/fortune/ 1996/961111/rsa.html

◆

Internet Security

Advice for keeping your account secure. Part of a longer tutorial on many related subjects.

**http://www.sju.edu/WORLD/
roadmap.html#LESSON 10**

Open Financial Exchange

Educational material about a new technology from Intuit, Microsoft, and CheckFree that is expected to provide a secure environment for exchanging financial data.

http://www.intuit.com/ofx

Moving On

The remaining chapters will give the head start you'll want in locating online investment resources. Next up, Chapter 2, "Assemble the Tools," will give you a rundown of the hardware you'll need to make online investing a reality.

C H A P T E R

2

Assemble the Tools

"All the hardware, software, and equipment you'll need to get started."

Investing online doesn't require much more than a PC, a modem, and some software. If you're one of the 15 million or so people already online, with your own computer and your own Internet connection, you can skip ahead to Chapter 4, "Educate Yourself About Investing."

But if you're not sure exactly how to make it all happen, this chapter will tell you how to choose—and find—all the tools you'll need.

In this chapter, we'll tell you how to pick a computer, how to locate the best software, and how to acquire the communications tools that get you onto the Internet.

The Hardware Tools

If you've got the resources, get yourself a computer that looks as if it came straight off the Starship Enterprise.

We're assuming, though, that if you picked up this book, you're concerned with making wise investments. You can start that process by being wise about your computer investment.

When purchasing a personal computer, you're faced with essentially two choices: a Macintosh, or an IBM-compatible PC (which, ironically, isn't necessarily compatible with IBM's personal computers. You're more likely to purchase a machine that's Compaq, Dell, or Gateway compatible). In any event, all non-Macintosh home and business computers are classed together as PCs. (As always, there are some exceptions—but those are machines of the Star Trek class, called *workstations*; if you don't know what a workstation does, you don't need one.)

Mac versus PC

The authors of this book use PC software and hardware. While that's not necessarily a recommendation, it does put us in the broad majority of computer buyers. Approximately 80 percent of personal computers in use today are PCs.

If you don't already own a computer, you'll need to make a decision. Our recommendation: You should buy whichever machine you use at your place of employment. The particular brand of PC is not significant, but do consider the benefits of being able to use the same disks and data and computing conventions both at home and at the office. We think efficiency outweighs any other consideration in the Mac/PC war.

If you're genuinely starting from scratch, here's the simple breakdown of considerations.

PC	Macintosh
Less expensive.	Easier to use.
More software available.	Better software available.
Upgrades are cheaper.	Upgrades are easier.
Users are part of a larger community.	Users are part of an elite community.

Computer writers can and do argue about each of these points, but for the most part, that's the way the arguments break out.

Whether you already own, or are looking to buy, this is the minimum configuration you'll need for efficient online investing. In every category, higher numbers are better. Any computer purchased after 1994 probably meets these recommended minimums.

Component	PC	Macintosh
Processor (Chip)	80486—a "486" for short	75MHz PowerPC 603 RISC
Video adapter (card)	640 × 480	800 × 600 (built in)
Monitor	14" color, .28dp	15" color, .27dp
RAM	8M—"8 meg" for short	8M
CD-ROM drive	4x—pronounced "four speed"	4x
Hard drive	500M (1 gigabyte is better)	1 gigabyte

Concerned that your current setup is less-than-minimum? Not to worry. You can still have a rich and fulfilling online investing experience. You'll simply have to wait a little longer for software to load, search a little harder for usable software tools, and work on a more crowded disk.

PC users will find that most machines being sold today are of the Pentium—think of it as a "586"—class. Hard drives are generally 1 gigabyte (1,024M) and larger. CD-ROM drives are veering toward eight speed and higher. And video adapters are commonly 1,024 × 768. Rejoice while you can. In a few weeks, *whatever* you bought will be outdated.

Notebook PCs versus Desktop

We own a couple of each—and find that we use both kinds of machines for different reasons. While the notebook PCs are more expensive, their portability makes them a must-have if you travel, if you conduct business at multiple sites, or if you sometimes need to escape to another room to work. For commuting investors who need to stay abreast of market changes, a notebook makes some good financial sense.

The desktop machines have some real advantages over the notebooks, however. The most significant is that they're equipped with both CD-ROM and floppy drives. With most notebooks, you've got to give up one or the other, and when you're doing research, the CD-ROM drives can come in handy. The other advantage of the desktop—besides its lower price— is that when you're working for long periods of time at a stretch, the desktop is simply more comfortable and efficient. The screen is better, and the keyboard is larger.

As an investment choice, we recommend the desktop. The price going in is lower, the risk of destroying the thing by stepping on it is lower, the cost of replacing malfunctioning parts is lower, and you'll need that drive. On the other hand, if you're buying your third machine because the kids won't stop playing Carnage on your two desktops, get the notebook, hide in your closet, and don't come out until they leave home.

The Software Tools

Much of your software comes preinstalled when you buy your computer. In this section, we look at the software tools you should already have—or acquire if you don't—in four categories: your operating system, basic financial software, spreadsheet, and investment software.

Operating System

Macintosh users: You don't have much choice in the matter of operating systems. Take the latest version of System 7, and move along to the next heading.

PC users: You may have some decisions to make. Who do you love, Microsoft or IBM? If you buy your machine from IBM, chances are good that you'll get an *operating system*—the basic set of instructions that tell your computer it's a computer, and not a toaster oven—called OS/2 Warp. If you buy from anyone else, you'll probably find that you've got some version of Microsoft Windows. A few years ago, these two operating systems were virtually identical. Now, we reluctantly recommend against OS/2. Even though it's the better system, it's the Betamax of the computer world. Because it's not widely used, it's difficult to find software that runs well under OS/2.

Microsoft Windows comes in three flavors:

◆ The old 16-bit version called Windows 3.some-thing (and still based on DOS)

◆ The new 32-bit version called Windows 90-something

◆ The high-end network version called Windows NT 4.0

Windows 3.x continues to be a good solid operating environment with a large volume of useable software available. Expect this situation to change, though, as Windows 3.x software disappears forever from the shelves and is replaced by Windows 95 and subsequent versions.

If your PC is less than two years old, you probably own Windows 95. If you don't, do not run out and buy a copy. Microsoft was expected to release a new version of Windows at about the time this book is released. (For the full story on anticipated upgrades to Windows 95, see this *PC World* review (**http://www.pcworld.com/news/daily/data/1196/111796143110.html**). Chapter 3, "Get Online," explains how to access sites on the World Wide Web.)

Windows NT is the high-end corporate networking version of Windows 95. It's unlikely you'd be able to take advantage of its features as a personal investor.

Our recommendation: If you're currently using Windows 3.x or better, don't invest in a new operating system right now. Stay with whatever you have until at least six months after the release of the upgrade to Windows 95. That gives Microsoft time to work out the bugs, and leaves you with a perfectly viable operating system in the meantime. If you're stuck

with an older version of Windows—or, heaven forbid, a creaky old DOS system—it's past time to think about an upgrade. Give your old machine, and your old operating system, to a charity. Take the tax deduction, and invest in an inexpensive new computer. Your increase in productivity will compensate for the small expenditure.

Financial Software

Getting your personal finances in order is a necessary prerequisite to making investment decisions. This section describes the best financial software in several categories: personal finance, online banking, tax preparation, and spreadsheets, as well as a brief mention of portfolio tracking and analysis tools.

Personal Finance

Personal finance packages do everything from calculate your net worth to remind you of tax obligations. The better packages are particularly useful to online investors because they track your portfolio, provide a double check on your broker's reports, collect current market prices for items in your portfolio, and maintain complete tax records on your investments. (See Figure 2.1.)

Choose from among the four most popular personal finance programs. The World Wide Web addresses listed under each title direct you to more detailed descriptions, ordering information, and current suggested pricing for each product. (We explain how to use these addresses, or URLs, in Chapter 3.)

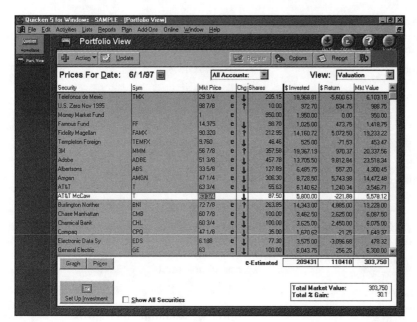

FIG. 2.1

Investment screen from a popular personal finance package.

◆ *Quicken Deluxe for Windows, Version 6.0 or Quicken Deluxe 7.0 for Macintosh.* The undisputed heavyweight champion of the personal finance industry is Quicken, from a California company called Intuit. For online investors, Quicken includes a wealth of features. Track investment activity in multiple portfolios, follow price histories and current prices, and analyze your investments. Use it to download stock quotes from the Internet free of charge.

http://www.intuit.com

◆ *Managing Your Money, Version 3.0.* Track stocks, bonds, and other investments, and read commentary from financial guru Andrew Tobias. Managing Your Money from MECA Software is second in popularity only to Quicken. For the investor, MYM includes portfolio tracking and tax planning tools. It's a time-tested program,

first introduced in 1983, and is available in Windows, DOS, and Macintosh formats.

http://www.mymnet.com

◆ *Microsoft Money 97, Version 5.0.* Microsoft's entry into the financial software arena. Microsoft Money has been loaded with "wizards"—Microsoft's interactive, online help. This program includes direct downloading of bank accounts from a growing list of banks. Personal financial planning features are extensive.

http://www.microsoft.com

◆ *Simply Money, Version 2.1.* Low-cost financial planning package. This former Kiplinger product is the most basic of financial planning packages. Available on CD for $15.

http://www.cdtitles.com

Most software packages can be ordered online. A very complete catalog of financial planning tools is available from Anderson Investors Software (**http://www.invest-soft.com**).

Online Banking

All of your banking chores—handling accounts, paying bills, and even applying for loans—can be done online. For investors, online banking gives you the ability to make automatic contributions to mutual funds and other investment vehicles (see Figure 2.2). Several of the personal finance packages, including Intuit's Quicken and Microsoft Money 97, offer direct links to a select number of banks. Even more institutions can be accessed through the World Wide Web or commercial online service providers such as America Online and CompuServe. See Chapter 3 for more information on service providers.

Some of the larger online-accessible banks, those with their own Web sites, are:

◆ *Bank of America*

http://www.bankamerica.com

◆ *First City Bank & Trust Company*

http://www.midirect.net/abcbanc/fcb/index.html

◆ *First National Bank*

http://www.firstnb.com/remote2.html

◆ *First National Bank of Baldwin County*

http://www.fnbbaldwin.com/homebank.html

◆ *Huntington Bancshares*

http://www.huntington.com/webbank.html

FIG. 2.2

Home page of bank offering online banking.

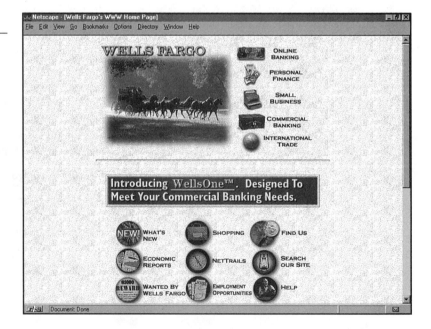

◆ *Security First Network Bank*

http://www.sfnb.com

◆ *Signet Bank*

http://www.signet.com/online

◆ *Union Bank of California*

http://www.tdmi.com/request/index.html

◆ *Wells Fargo Bank*

http://wellsfargo.com

◆ *Wilber National Bank*

http://www.wilberbank.com/online.htm

If your current bank is not one of those available through any of the these services, it doesn't mean you're shut out of online banking. Check with your local branch. Many banks offer online access via their own direct-connect line. The required software is generally free to customers. In most cases, data from

your accounts can be downloaded to your computer in a format compatible with the personal finance software package you use.

Tax Preparation

If you prepare your own taxes you should consider the tax preparation programs available for use in conjunction with your financial software. Tax preparation software is released yearly, implementing all the latest changes, and can take advantage of the records you're already maintaining with your personal finance software.

One of the most popular tax packages, Intuit's TurboTax (**http://www.intuit.com/turbotax**), includes help files, IRS publications, look-ahead planners, electronic filing, and online access to the latest tax information available (see Figure 2.3). The Macintosh version is MacInTax.

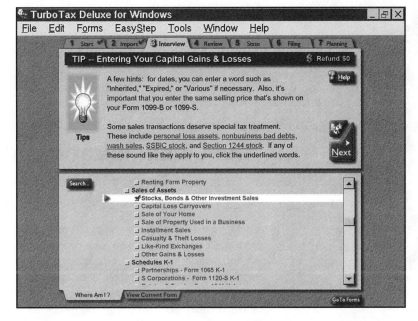

FIG. 2.3

Investment interview shot from TurboTax.

Also popular is Kiplinger TaxCut (**http:// www.conductor.com/cgi-bin/imagemap.exe/ homemap?147,71**), the program that competes head-to-head with TurboTax, and often comes out in front. Both packages use an "interview" format to collect information. TaxCut has the additional advantage of ties to Block Financial.

There are other tax-related Internet sites worth a visit. See Tax Logic for online tax preparation with free electronic filing: **http://www.taxlogic.com/ usatoday.html**.

Spreadsheet

An electronic spreadsheet is to an accountant what a blank canvas is to an artist. If you already own a spreadsheet, have some unique requirements, or just simply want to do things your way, a spreadsheet can be a viable alternative to commercial investment software. See Figure 2.4.

Users of the most popular programs, Microsoft Excel (**http://www.microsoft.com/msexcel/**), Lotus 1-2-3 (**http://www.lotus.com/123/**), and Corel Quattro Pro (**http://www.corel.com/products/ wordperfect/cqp7/index.htm**), will find many World Wide Web locations from which to download information directly. *Downloading*—geek-speak for "getting it from off the Internet"—is explained in Chapter 3.

Analysis and Portfolio Management Tools

Chapters 16, "Track Your Portfolio," and 18, "Pick Your Analysis Tools," explain how to locate and use the software you'll need for analyzing and tracking your portfolio.

The Communications Tools

To get from the inside of your wall to the outside world, you'll need a modem and some communications software. To make the best use of the Internet, you'll also need some special tools for tasks such as reading e-mail, visiting newsgroups, and browsing the World Wide Web.

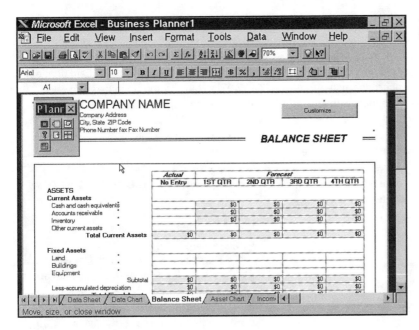

FIG. 2.4

Excel spreadsheet tracking portfolio.

The Modem

The modem connects your computer, through a telephone line, to the online world. Most computers sold today include modems as standard equipment.

If you have a notebook PC, or a machine purchased before 1995, you may have to purchase a modem. Virtually all desktop computers sold since then have a modem included as part of the standard equipment. The standard transmission rate for pre-packaged modems is still 28,800 baud, or 28.8 kilobits per second, for lower-priced computers. A 33.6-kilobit modem comes standard in some premium computer packages. (*Baud* describes the data speed of the modem. Loosely translated, it means bits of data per second—although purists will dispute that definition. Nod and smile when they do; a more technically precise definition won't change how quickly, or slowly, your modem functions.)

For World Wide Web access, don't consider anything slower than a 14.4-kilobit modem. As a general rule: The higher the speed, the better. Speeds of 33.6 and 56 kilobits per second are also readily available.

Another consideration is whether to buy an internal or external modem.

An internal modem is the simpler of the two. It consists of a printed circuit board that you plug into an expansion slot in your computer. A telephone cable plugs into a standard jack on the end of the board. If you're reluctant to open your computer, most retailers will be happy to do it for you—for a modest fee.

Slightly more expensive, an external modem has its own power supply, plastic casing, and blinking lights to tell you when it's communicating. It also has extra cables for connecting to your computer, usually through the serial port. The phone line plugs into a connector on the modem. The advantages of the external modem are that it is easily portable—meaning it can be used on more then one personal computer; that you have a visual indicator of the modem status, and that when your connection hangs up, you can shut down the modem without shutting down the entire computer.

If you're ready to invest in a modem of your own, we recommend spending the extra money on speed rather than the external box. Reduce the clutter in your work area, and buy a 33.6K internal modem.

Notebook computer users have other concerns. You could use an external modem, or you could use a PC Card internal modem. The PC Card is a credit-card-sized unit designed to plug into a PC Card (formerly *PCMCIA*) slot. Most laptop computers sold since 1995 have at least one of these slots. Costs vary, but can easily run double that of a standard modem. We recommend the fastest speed you can afford.

THE CABLE CONNECTION

Watch for the newest connection technology: cable modems. Provided by your cable TV company, these super-fast connections will allow you to transfer data at 350 times the speed of 28.8-kilobit modems. You'll find a review and comparison of cable modems at the *PC World* **(http://www.pcworld.com/hardware/communications/articles/feb97/1502p062a.html)** Web site.

◆

Communications Software

This is the software that dials your modem. The communication software you use will be determined by the type of Internet or online service you choose.

Commercial online service providers such as America Online and CompuServe provide free copies of their software. Chapter 3 explains how to contact commercial service providers.

If you opt for an Internet service provider, you'll receive with your start-up kit a good basic communications package that operates from the dial-up software included in Windows. To streamline your connection, consider purchasing better communications software. The leading contender is Quarterdeck's Procomm Plus (**http://www.datastorm.com/qdeck/products/procomm95/**).

Alternatively, visit your local software distributor for a packaged "Internet in a box" front end. If you're already online, you can learn more about these front ends at the *Byte Magazine* (**http://byte.com/art/9507/sec9/art5.htm**) Web site.

■ **NOTE**

See the appendix at the end of this book for further information on the Investor's Toolkit.

Internet Tools

The communications software got you online. These Internet tools let you do something after you get there.

■ **NOTE**

If you're using a commercial online service, these tools are already integrated into your access software.

Web Browser

You've heard about the great war between Netscape Navigator and Internet Explorer. Start with the package you receive from your Internet service provider. Then download the other from either the Navigator (**http://www.netscape.com**) or the Explorer (**http://www.microsoft.com/ie/default.asp**) Web sites to make your own comparison.

Electronic Mail Reader

Your Web browser has built-in e-mail capabilities, but there are better choices. Your Internet service provider will supply you with an e-mail reader to get you started. After you're online, try a couple of different readers to see which best suits your needs. All readers can read, create, and send mail. The better ones give you advanced features and improved screens. We recommend Eudora (**http://www.eudora.com/**) and Pronto 96 (**http://www.commtouch. com/**). Commercial online services such as AOL and CompuServe have built-in e-mail readers.

Newsreader

Both Navigator and Explorer contain built-in newsgroup readers. (Accessing and using newsgroups is explained in Chapter 10, "Use the Rest of the Internet as a Research Tool.") We prefer the features of Forté Free Agent (**http://www.forteinc.com**). Free Agent has the capability to work offline, saving you toll charges if you're being metered.

Chat Software

In Chapter 10 you learn about an Internet feature called *Internet Relay Chat*. If your service provider doesn't include chat software in your startup package, you'll want to pick up a package of your own. mIRC is our recommendation.

 ON THE WEB

The latest version of mIRC requires that after you try it, you register and pay a fee. Older versions are completely free of charge. A fast, clean front end for IRC, with useful options and tools. Download is free.

http://www.mirc.co.uk/get.html

3

Get Online

"Getting online is a simple

three-step process. The

difficult part is choosing

from among the large

number of options."

Getting online can be tremendously simple. It boils down to this: Get an Internet account, fire up the browser, and go.

If you've yet to do any one of those things, read on.

Step One: Get an Internet Account

To get to the Internet and World Wide Web sites, you need an account through a commercial online service, such as America Online or CompuServe, or through a dial-up Internet service provider, called an *ISP*.

Commercial Online Services

The major commercial services provide excellent Internet access and have adjusted their prices to be competitive with the ISPs. In addition, the commercial services offer something that the ISPs do not—content. Each service provides discussion forums, databases, and other features that are available only to its members.

Even if you already have an ISP, a commercial online service may be a worthwhile investment. Besides the additional content, commercial online services organize and categorize the most useful functions of the Internet into easily navigated menus and icons. The amount of time you save searching for data may be enough to offset the extra cost. In addition, commercial services are portable—you can access them toll-free from most large towns and cities around the world.

Connection software is provided by the commercial services free of charge. Get your software by calling the toll-free number listed in the following sections, or from the disks that fall out of any number of computer magazines and junk mailings. In addition, most personal computers sold today include the connection software for at least one of the commercial online services.

America Online and CompuServe are the two most popular services available today. Together they boast a user base of more than 10 million subscribers. (The World Wide Web addresses, called *URLs* [Uniform

Resource Locators], are explained later in this chapter.)

America Online

America Online (see Figure 3.1) features an easy-to-use graphically oriented interface. Its reputation as a fun, family-oriented service shouldn't detract from its substantial offerings in the financial arena. Some of the services include the Dow Jones Business Center, Stock Quotes, a Banking Center, a Brokerage Center, and a Mutual Fund Center. A company research center will allow you to download information on user-selected company stock reports, financial statements, earnings and estimates, and EDGAR filings from the Securities and Exchange Commission. Contact AOL at (800) 827-6364, **http:// www.aol.com**.

FIG. 3.1

CompuServe offers a full range of investor services and forums.

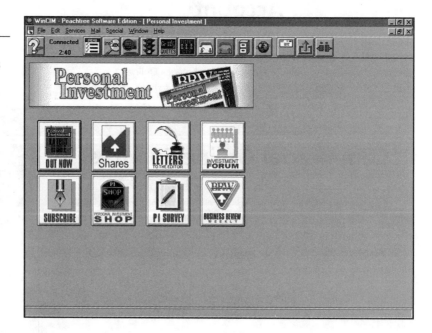

CompuServe

CompuServe was a pioneer in providing online services and is equal to the task when it comes to offering financial resources. CompuServe still maintains a more professional, business-oriented image than AOL. Its thousand-plus, business-oriented resources help to maintain that image. On the downside, CompuServe's charging policies tend to be on the pricey side. Contact CompuServe at (800) 848-8199, **http://www.compuserve.com**.

Other Commercial Services

The definition of what a commercial service is and how it is accessed is constantly changing. Competition has caused some services to readjust their focus. The following services exist in a new, not-yet-fully-explored area between a simple ISP and a full-service commercial online service:

◆ *Delphi*

(800) 695-4005

http://www.delphi.com

◆ *GEnie*

(800) 638-9636

http://www.genie.com

◆ *The Microsoft Network*

(800) 386-5550

http://www.msn.com

◆ *Prodigy*

(800) 776-3449

http://www.prodigy.com

Internet Service Providers

Cheaper (usually), more flexible (sometimes), faster (at least, potentially), and more accessible (unless you travel), *Internet service providers* are gradually putting the commercial services out of business. ISPs differ from commercial online services in lots of little ways. They tend to be local—except when, like AT&T WorldNet, they're huge. ISPs tend to be less expensive because they do not provide the additional information resources found on commercial online services.

What an ISP *does* give you is a direct gateway to the Internet.

At a minimum, your ISP should furnish:

◆ Toll-free or local telephone access

◆ Rate discounts for long-term service contracts

◆ Unlimited access

◆ Free telephone support

◆ A high ratio of access lines to users. You don't want to reach a busy signal when you call in. Seek a provider that offers about one line for every 10 users.

◆ A software bundle customized for your computer operating system. The bundle should include communications protocols, a Web browser, an e-mail reader, a newsreader, and FTP software. Better bundles will also include a Web-page builder, and Gopher, Archie, and Telnet software, none of which you need to worry a great deal about at this point.

To find a provider, check the local yellow pages under Internet Services or Computers—Internet. Read a few local newspapers, watch a few TV ads, make a few phone calls. Every ISP charges about twenty dollars a month for access, and the smaller providers may be willing to negotiate.

The CD-ROM included with this book contains the tools to connect to one ISP: EarthLink Network. See the appendix at the end of this book for instructions on using the Investor's Toolkit CD-ROM to get online.

The major Internet service providers include:

◆ *AT&T WorldNet*

(800) 967-5363

http://www.att.com/worldnet/wis

◆ *EarthLink Network*

(800) 395-8425

http://www.earthlink.net

◆ *IBM Internet Connection*

(800) 455-5056

http://www.ibm.net

◆ *MCI Internet Dial Access*

(800) 550-0927

http://www.mci.com/resources/forhome

◆ *Sprint Internet Passport*

(800) 359-3900

http://www.sprint.com/sip

Having trouble getting started with your new software? Harass your new ISP morning, noon, and night until you're online, trouble-free. Make him earn his twenty-dollar access fee.

Step Two: Start Browsing

Among the pieces of software included with your start-up software will be a thing called a *Web browser*. It's very likely that your Web browser will be called either *Netscape Navigator* or *Microsoft Internet Explorer*.

Your first act as an online investor will be to browse (you've heard it called *surf*) investment sites. Install the browser as your provider directs, open it, and in the Address or Location box—the only space on the page where you're allowed to type something—type this:

http://www.etrade.com

Press the Enter key, and you'll be transported to the home page for E*TRADE Securities (see Figure 3.2).

You'll notice that a home page, also called a *Web site* or simply a *page*, looks something like a magazine cover. The line you typed is called an *address* or an *URL*—pronounced Earl and short for Uniform Resource Locator. URLs are keys to finding every page on the World Wide Web.

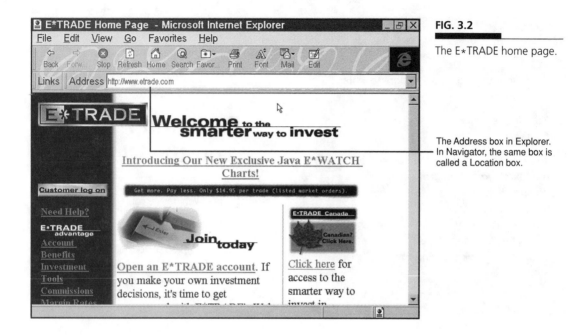

FIG. 3.2

The E*TRADE home page.

The Address box in Explorer. In Navigator, the same box is called a Location box.

Surfin' Safari— Entering URLs

Entering URLs looks a little tricky, but it's actually quite simple. Ninety-five percent of the Internet addresses you run across in your life will begin with the designation http://. Another 4.5 percent will begin with ftp://. If you run across the other half percent, you'll probably be looking at things so obscure they don't really bear a closer look.

As a rule of thumb, the HTTP designations indicate an address for a graphically enhanced, magazine-cover-like World Wide Web page. The FTP designations, on the other hand, indicate ugly, nongraphical, nonviewable files that you nearly always download to your own computer—at which point they might get installed and become quite pretty after all. FTP is the method by which you will do virtually all of your Net file transfers. When you need a file or a piece of software, chances are good that you will use FTP to get it.

A Faster Surf: Hyperlinks

As you slide your mouse pointer around the E*TRADE home page, you'll notice that it sometimes changes shape. When it points at certain elements on the page, called *hyperlinks*, it turns into a pointing finger (see Figure 3.3).

A hyperlink is a quicker way to get to another page. Click a hyperlink, and it will automatically enter the URL for you, saving you the trouble of typing. Most hyperlinks appear as underlined text, but as you'll see on the E*TRADE page, they can also take the form of pictures, clickable buttons, logos, and menu bars.

To see a menu of other things you can do with a hyperlink, position your mouse cursor over the hyperlink and click the right mouse button.

Back and Forth on the Web

To navigate your Web pages, you have three tools:

◆ *Toolbar buttons*. The toolbar buttons appear in a row across the top of your browser (see Figure 3.4). The left and right arrow keys move you back and forth through pages you've already viewed. The Stop button prevents a page from loading. The Refresh option reloads a page.

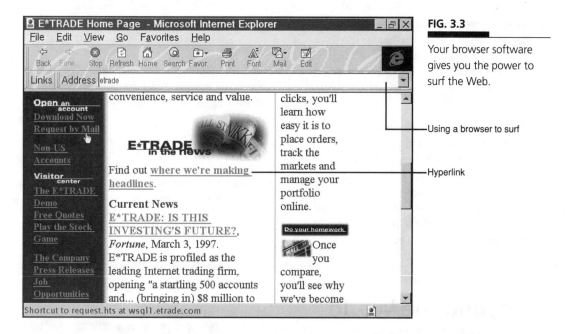

FIG. 3.3

Your browser software gives you the power to surf the Web.

— Using a browser to surf

— Hyperlink

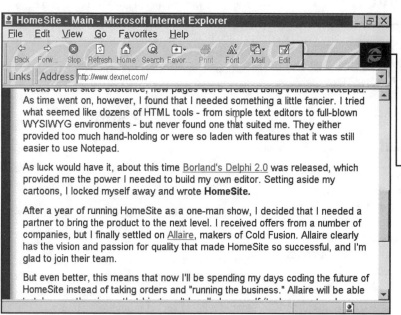

FIG. 3.4

The Toolbar buttons help you move through Web documents, go to your home page, search the Web, and more.

— Toolbar buttons

◆ *Pull-down menus*. Select recently used addresses from the pull-down Address box (Location box in Navigator) list (see Figure 3.5). Click the down arrow at the right of the box. Alternatively, go to the Go menu and select a different recently viewed page.

◆ *Scroll bars*. Pages larger than your screen can be navigated horizontally and vertically from the scroll bars across the bottom and along the right side of your screen (see Figure 3.6). If pages are consistently wider than your screen, consider decreasing your display size. (Go to the Control Panel, select the Display tool, then the Settings tab. Change the Desktop Area.)

Beyond the World Wide Web

Once you're comfortable with the whole Internet thing—or at least the World Wide Web portion of it—you're ready to graduate to something more complicated.

E-Mail

The most basic of services provided by ISPs and commercial online services is e-mail. *E-mail* is simply electronic mail sent and received over the Internet. Until recently, e-mail was strictly text based. Now it's possible to format e-mail and attach audio, graphics, and additional files. The final section of Chapter 2, "Assemble the Tools," explains where to find a good e-mail reader.

Mailing Lists

These are discussions and information exchanges conducted via e-mail. Discussions are limited to a particular subject, carried on among a group of subscribers. Subscribers e-mail their responses to the mailing list, and the list is then automatically mailed to all subscribers. Some mailing lists are *read-only*, meaning that the discussion is more of a lecture. Chapter 10, "Use the Rest of the Internet as a Research Tool," describes investment-oriented lists, and explains how to subscribe.

UseNet Newsgroups

UseNet newsgroups are open forums for public discussion. Newsgroups can be an effective way to engage a wide variety of people in on-going correspondence concerning virtually any subject. The last section of Chapter 2 describes the software you need, and Chapter 10 explains how to locate and participate in investment-oriented newsgroups.

FTP Sites

Files—data, graphics, audio and software—can be transmitted over the Internet. The method used to *upload*, or send, and *download*, or receive, files is called *FTP*, short for *File Transfer Protocol*. When we direct you to an FTP site, you'll be downloading a file. Files are stored on a remote site. When you want the file, you enter the URL, which begins with the designation ftp://, in the Address or Location box of your browser. Your browser will automatically download the file to your computer.

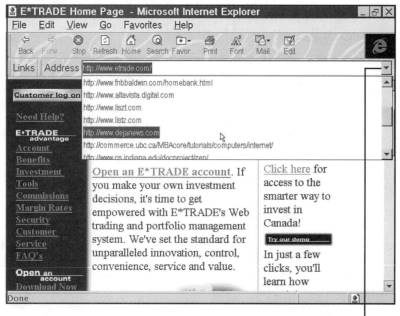

FIG. 3.5

Drop the pull down menu
to access alternate menu
options.

Click the arrow to drop
a pull-down menu

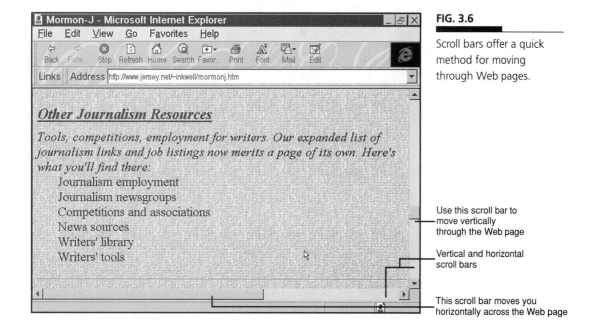

FIG. 3.6

Scroll bars offer a quick
method for moving
through Web pages.

Use this scroll bar to
move vertically
through the Web page

Vertical and horizontal
scroll bars

This scroll bar moves you
horizontally across the Web page

4

Educate Yourself About Investing

"Before leaping into the market, be sure you're familiar with basic investment principles."

Investing is more of a process than an event. The process starts with making sure your finances are in order. In the first section of this chapter, we cover some basic financial planning principles, look at your net worth, and determine how much you have to invest.

The second section provides a quick survey of investment principles that should guide you in all your financial decisions.

In the final section, we introduce securities and explain how to read the financial pages of your newspaper.

Financial Planning Fundamentals

For many people, "financial planning" is synonymous with one of two equally terrifying subjects: budgeting and life insurance. In this section, it means neither. Instead, we'll give you some quick tips on getting into financial condition to invest your money, and then we'll show you how to force yourself to do it. First, though, some Internet background on the financial planning process and getting organized—along with a smidgen of budgeting advice you're free to ignore, if you like.

These Web sites will give you some background information on starting the financial planning process:

◆ *Getting Organized.* Sections on where to find your records, where your money goes, net worth—what you own versus what you owe—and your household budget. From the Investor Learning Center (Merrill Lynch, Pierce, Fenner & Smith)

http://www.plan.ml.com/investor/organized.html

◆ *Getting Started.* Set money aside for insurance, shelter, and cash reserves before looking to security investments. Access to this site is free, but requires registration.

Register or log in at **http://www.wsbi.com/spweb**, then click the Features icon. Click the How to Invest link, then scroll down to the Index link and click. Finally, click the link to Getting Started.

◆ *Interactive Financial Tools.* Follow the steps to build your financial profile. Each step contains a tool for determining some aspect of your financial condition (see Figure 4.1).

http://www.americanexpress.com/advisors/assess

◆ *Budget/Plan.* An introduction to budgeting as a part of financial planning.

http://ourworld.compuserve.com/homepages/Bonehead_Finance/bone4c_b.htm

◆ *Overview of the Financial Planning Process.* Considerations in financial planning. Discusses the importance of making financial planning an ongoing process, rather than a one-time event.

http://www.e-analytics.com/fp1.htm

FIG. 4.1

The American Express home page is one of many that contains tools for calculating your financial status.

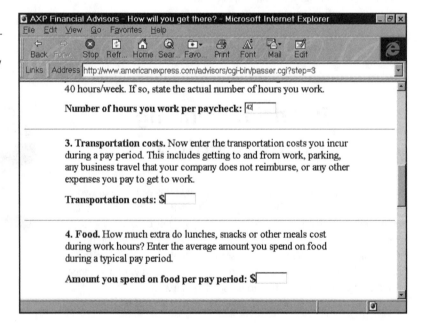

Get Your Finances in Shape

When it comes to financial planning, one important fundamental looms over all the rest: spend less than you earn. To accomplish that end, you can do several things: Earn more money, consume less, stay out of debt, and force yourself to save.

Earn More

OK, you can't just walk into the boss's office and demand a raise. Or can you? Either way, there are plenty of alternative methods for earning more money. They include:

◆ Improving your marketability with additional education

◆ Working overtime

◆ Taking a second job

◆ Keeping your résumé visible

◆ Becoming a consultant

Networking the Internet makes it all possible, giving you unlimited opportunities to improve your earnings.

Rather than printing and mailing hundreds of résumés to corporate black holes, you can use the Internet to post your resume to the world.

List your résumé with any of the Internet's dozens of resume sites:

◆ *Resumes Online*. A list of links to résumé posting sites.

http://a2z.lycos.com/Business_and_ Investing/Careers_and_Jobs Resumes_ Online

◆ *Monster Board*. A place to build and post your own résumé (see Figure 4.2).

http://www.monsterboard.com/pf/mb/ client/ui/resume/build.htm

Build your own Web page to solicit consulting or other freelance work:

◆ *Authoring*. Instructions and tools for building Web pages.

http://www.excite.com/Reviews/ Computing/Authoring/index.html?CCt

Get a college degree online:

◆ *Colleges Without Borders*. Links to schools offering distance learning programs.

http://a2z.lycos.com/Education/ College_Home_Pages/ Colleges_without_Borders— Remote_Learning

FIG. 4.2

From the Monster Board, you can build and post your résumé on the Internet.

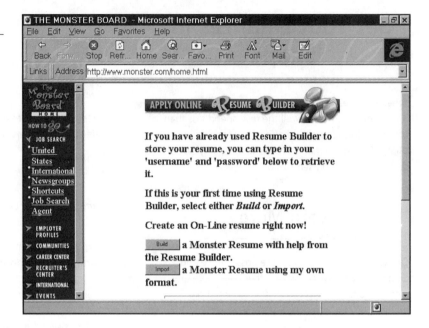

Search Internet classifieds for a better job:

◆ *Job Bank USA*. Search by key word.

http://www.jobbankusa.com/search.html

◆ *America's Job Bank*. Find employment throughout the US.

http://www.ajb.dni.us/cgi-bin/ websrch.cgi?f_mode=f_sds

◆ *Career Path*. Job listings in all the major daily newspapers (see Figure 4.3).

http://www.careerpath.com/search.html

◆ *Yahoo!'s Employment Classifieds*.

http://classifieds.yahoo.com/ employment.html

Consume Less

Learn to live simply. Cheap automobiles mean cheaper auto insurance. A smaller home is cheaper to furnish and maintain, and has lower taxes, insurance, and utilities costs. Eating meals at home saves money. Every financial decision has larger repercussions.

These Internet sites will explain what you need to know about consumption and spending:

◆ *Managing Your Money*. Articles on Where Does Your Money Go?, Stop Spending Leaks, and Developing a Spending Plan.

http://www.ag.ohio-state.edu/~ohioline/ home/money

FIG. 4.3

Using the Internet, you can review current job listings in all the major daily newspapers.

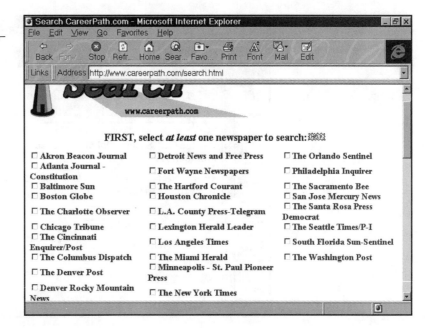

◆ *Spending Less.* Links to resources on making ends meet, stretching a dollar, and managing money.

http://idea.exnet.iastate.edu:8080/cgi/ getTitleList?Keyword=spending

Stay Out of Debt

Don't even think about investing for a *taxable* 10- or 12-percent return when you're paying 21 percent in after-tax dollars on credit cards. Pay off the credit cards first. It like getting a guaranteed 21 percent return—tax free! Here are ways to get—and stay— out of debt.

◆ *Consumer Credit Counseling Service.* Know your rights, loan calculator, tax tips, credit counseling, money management, budgeting, and general advice on consumer credit (see Figure 4.4).

http://www.powersource.com/cccs

◆ *Your Use of Consumer Credit.* Dozens of re- sources on proper use and repair of consumer credit.

http://idea.exnet.iastate.edu:8080/cgi/ getTitleList/CREDIT

◆ *Budget Counseling.* Services available in Florida. Most US locations have similarly titled services.

http://www.iandr.org/key165.htm

FIG. 4.4

A loan calculator like the one at Powersource tells how much you're really spending.

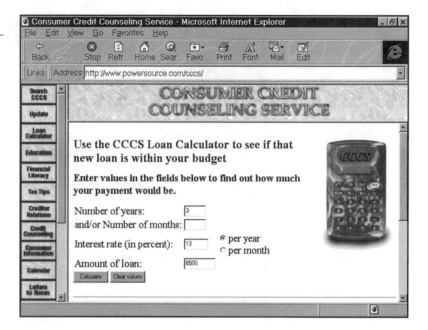

Force Yourself to Save

Pay yourself first, and all other bills will take care of themselves. If self-control is a problem, set up a separate, difficult-to-use account as a temporary, short-term holding place for your savings. Talk to your bank and your investment firm about establishing an automatic transfer to your investment account. Once you pay off a loan, continue paying the same amount into your investment account. Make arrangements to have government payments and paychecks direct deposited. If you receive a pay raise or a bonus, put the "found" money straight into the investment account. Gift money, dividends, refunds, whatever—send all of it directly to your account.

The Internet has a number of sites where you can find more information on saving:

◆ *Financial Planning.* Sections on retirement planning and saving for other goals. From AAII.

http://www.aaii.org/finplann/finplanindex.html

◆ *Fewer Boomers Save for Retirement.* An article from *USAToday.*

http://www.usatoday.com/money/wealth/saving/msw024.htm

◆ *Women Need to Save More Than Men Do for Retirement.* Another good resource from *USAToday.*

http://www.usatoday.com/money/wealth/saving/msw022.htm

Calculate Your Net Worth

Once a year you sit down to the arduous task of calculating your tax status. This year, do something a little more interesting. Determine what you're worth.

Simply put, finding your *net worth* involves adding up the value of everything you own (your assets), and subtracting everything you owe (your liabilities). The difference is your worth—at least, so far as your creditors are concerned.

If the bottom line—ignoring, for the moment, your mortgage debt—is a negative number, you are, quite bluntly, in some financial trouble and need to take care of your debts first and foremost. If the number is positive, pat yourself on the back—it's time to start an investment program.

If you add your mortgage back in, and find that the asset and liability totals are similar, you're in great condition to be investing. If you're in the fortunate crowd whose assets exceed their liabilities, you've probably been investing for a long time—and you've been doing so rather successfully.

A caveat, however. There's another number you need to consider: Cash flow—your monthly income, minus your monthly expenses. There are people in this world—primarily small business operators and self-employed professionals—who have a tremendously high net worth, and yet who have trouble buying groceries each month. If you're in this situation, stop taking comfort in your high net worth, and start working on your receivables. The money isn't a real asset until it's in your hand.

Financial planning packages such as Quicken and Microsoft Money (see Chapter 2) will accurately calculate your net worth. Alternatively, use the financial statement template included in newer spreadsheet packages, or make use of a worksheet tool from the Internet:

◆ *Your Financial Profile (Net Worth and Cash Flow).* The first step in financial planning is to figure out your net worth. Links to Net Worth worksheet and Cash Flow worksheet (see Figure 4.5).

   http://www.e-analytics.com/fp2.htm

Determine What You Can Invest

We promised not to lecture you about budgeting. Besides, if you've started using one of the financial planning packages we described in Chapter 2, "Assemble the Tools," you're already there. In any case, we will strongly advise that rather than wait until the end of each month to decide what you can invest, you become a proactive owner of your financial condition, and pick a number up front. Choose the highest number you can realistically live with. If your income is steady, pick a dollar figure. If your income fluctuates, pick a percentage. In Chapter 5, "Develop a Portfolio Strategy," we'll discuss how to allocate that number among various investments.

FIG. 4.5

Use a worksheet to determine your net worth.

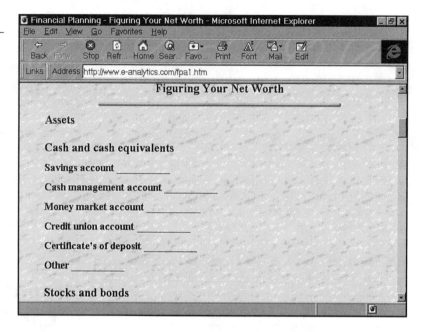

Investment Principles

No, we're not to the stock and bond material quite yet. That appears in the next section. Here, we'll show you some time-honored principles that apply to every investment you make—even your passbook savings account.

The First Rule of Interest

Confused about what your real rate of return is? You're not alone. Bankers and accountants have tried to simplify the issue of interest by agreeing to a standard way of discussing interest. From here on out, unless the information you're looking at specifically tells you otherwise, interest figures—indeed, all investment returns—are shown at an annual rate. In other words, a $100 investment that returns $5 in

six months gives you a 10 percent return, not a 5 percent return. If after two years you get $10 from your $100 investment, you're getting a 5 percent return, not 10 percent. (Of course, the principle of compounding makes all those numbers marginally inaccurate. We'll cover compounding later in this section.)

The Difference Between Yield and Total Return

Interest is just one element of total return. If you also receive dividends or *capital appreciation* from your investment—in other words, if your investment can be sold for more than you paid—your total return is the sum of all those factors. Total return is usually described as a percentage, and it's calculated like this: Your total profit, divided by your investment. If your only profit comes from interest payments, then yield and total return are identical. To learn more about calculating return, visit this site on the Internet:

◆ *A Portfolio Maintenance Program for the Long-Term Investor*. Contains a section on calculating your return. From the American Association of Individual Investors.

http://www.aaii.org/portfolo/ pfmaintn.html

Time Value of Money

Money lives in a funny place on the time-space continuum. It's a thing that looks quantifiable, but is, in reality, very amorphous. A hundred dollars kept under your mattress is, in a year, no longer the same hundred dollars. Given inflation, and lost opportunity costs, and the cost of the new door locks you buy to protect the money, it's probably only twenty dollars. (Or maybe the entire social-economic system collapses during the year, and your rare hundred dollar bill gets you 500 loaves of bread. But that's not very likely.)

As an investor, you must always be aware that any investment is a trade-off between what you're doing with the money, and what you *could* be doing with the money. Even if you do nothing, you're still doing something. Putting your money in a 2-percent passbook savings account is a conscious decision to forego other opportunities.

These Web sites discuss the importance of, ahem, making hay while the sun shines:

◆ *A Penny Saved*. Explains how money today compares to the value of money tomorrow.

http://membrane.com/invest/crond.html

◆ *Future Value of a Lump Sum*. How to calculate the value in the future of a lump sum of money you own today.

http://www.clarion.edu/cob_web1/ calculat/basicrev.htm

◆ *Mathematics of Individual Finance*. "Most of us would rather have a dollar today than a dollar a year from today, and must be given something extra to get us to defer gratification." Includes tools for calculating other financial returns (annuities, cash flow, and more).

http://www.busadm.mu.edu/mandell/ tvm.html

◆ *A Crash Course On Discounted Paper (Part II)*. The difference between interest and yield, and the effect of the time value of money.

http://www.investorama.com/features/ vaughan4.shtml

Dollar-Cost Averaging

It's a subject that fascinates most investment advisors, but it is, in reality, just common sense. It's the fact that the phenomenon called *dollar-cost averaging* works so well, so consistently, that makes it a subject for endless discussion.

Here's how it works: Each period—say, once a week—you invest the same amount of money—say, that same $100. Over time, say the financiers who track such things, you will make more money with this method than if you try to time your investments to correspond with market highs and lows.

The principle works for a couple of reasons. First, for the real-life reason that if you're a regular investor, you're not waffling endlessly over every investment decision, leaving your money collecting dust in pass-book savings. The other reason it works is the theoretical one: that $100 worth of cheap securities is a good deal, and $100 of expensive securities is a bad deal. When the market drops, you get more of a good deal; when it rises, you buy less of a bad deal—all with the same $100.

There are lots of Internet sites describing both dollar-cost averaging and some of the alternative theories of timing investments.

◆ *Traditional Formula Plans for Buying and Selling Stocks*. Traditional methods to help determine when to purchase stocks.

http://www.e-analytics.com/fp16e.htm

◆ *Dollar-Cost Averaging*. Strategically, dollar-cost averaging forces investors to be in the market when prices are depressed, but it also forces you to buy when prices are high.

http://www.prusec.com/dlravg.htm

◆ *Dollar-Cost Averaging*. Take advantage of down-swings in the market.

http://www.ml.com/investor/dolcost.html

◆ *Dollar-Cost Averaging*. As a long-term approach, one of the simplest and most practical stock investment systems is dollar-cost averaging. Access to this site is free, but requires registration.

Register or log in at **http://www.wsbi.com/ spweb**, then click the Features icon. Click the How to Invest link, then scroll down to the Index link and click. Finally, click the section 4 link to Dollar Cost Averaging.

The Power of Compounding

Compounding is real financial magic. Because of compounding, extending your investment period by 10 years means your required monthly investment to reach a goal can decline by at least half, and in some cases by a factor of 10.

The chart in Figure 4.6 shows how much you'll need to invest each month to achieve a goal. Interpretation is easy. Assume, for example, an annual return of 12 percent and a goal of a million dollars at retirement. If you're now 30 years old, you'll need to invest $155 a month until age 65 to achieve your goal. If your return is only 2 points lower (10 percent), you'll invest roughly the same amount each month ($132) and get only half a million at retirement.

	File	Edit	View	Insert	Format	Tools	Data	Window	Help		_ 🖻 🗙

	A	B	C	D	E	F	G	
1	Monthly Investment Required to Reach a Goal							
2	Ending Balance	$ 250,000						
3	Retirement Age	65						
4	Annual Yield	8%						
5	Present Age		20	30	40	50	60	
6	Monthly Investment		$47	$109	$263	$722	$3,402	
7	Ending Balance	$ 500,000						
8	Retirement	65						
9	Annual Yield	10%						
10	Present Age		20	30	40	50	60	
11	Monthly Investment		$48	$132	$377	$1,206	$6,457	
12	Ending Balance	$1,000,000						
13	Retirement	65						
14	Annual Yield	12%						
15	Present Age		20	30	40	50	60	
16	Monthly Investment		$47	$155	$532	$2,002	$12,244	
17	Ending Balance	$5,000,000						
18	Retirement	65						
19	Annual Yield	16%						
20	Present Age		20	30	40	50	60	
21	Monthly Investment		$52	$257	$1,278	$6,768	$54,924	

Sheet1 / Sheet2 / Sheet3 / Sheet4 / Sheet5 / Sheet6 / Sheet7 / She

FIG. 4.6

Compound yield has a dramatic effect on the bottom line.

Note also the spectacular effect of various interest rates. When you double the rate, your return doesn't merely double. Depending on the time period, the rate of increase is in the thousands.

Here's where you can go on the Internet to find more information about compound yield:

◆ *The Power of Compounding*. The benefits of saving early in life are greatly magnified by compounding.

Register or log in at **http://www.wsbi.com/ spweb**, then click the Features icon. Click the How to Invest link, then scroll down to the Index link and click. Finally, click the section 1 link to The Power of Compounding. Also worth visiting: the section 4 link to Dividend Reinvestment Plans.

Here's where to find sections on the importance of starting early, deferring taxes:

http://www.ml.com/investor/ compounding.html

Tax Deferral

Your goal in investing should be to maximize your return right now. Every penny you keep can work for you, increasing your returns. And every penny you give to the tax man is gone forever. The principle of tax deferral is this: If you can defer your taxes until (a) you're wealthy, and can afford to pay the taxes, or until (b) you're retired, and living in a lower tax bracket, you're ahead of the game.

Qualified retirement plans (such as the 401(k) plan you might have through your employer, or your own individual retirement account) give you a vehicle for deferring taxes. The money stays in your retirement account, compounding and earning and generally working for you, tax free—until you retire.

Certain other investments—municipal bonds, primarily—are tax-free right off the top. Of course, the lower yields reflect the tax-free status. The principle is called *taxable equivalent yield*. When corporate bonds are yielding, say, 10 percent, a municipal bond might yield only 7.5 percent. Consequently, these vehicles are of value only to people in the highest tax brackets, who can benefit from the fractional difference between 7.5-percent tax free, and 10-percent taxable income.

The following sites address the subject of tax-free investing.

◆ *Tax-Deferred and Tax-Free Investing.* Sections on retirement options and municipal bonds.

   http://www.ml.com/investor/defer.html

◆ *Easing the Tax Burden*. How to soften the impact of income taxes, with subsequent sections on IRAs and 401(k) plans, tax-deferred insurance options, and other tax considerations for investors.

   Register or log in at **http://www.wsbi.com/ spweb**, then click the Features icon. Click the How to Invest link, then scroll down to the Index link and click. Finally, click the section 3 link to Easing the Tax Burden.

Investment Basics

Every dime you earn goes to one of three places—investments, consumables, or the cookie jar.

Not everything you spend is a consumable. You invest all the time: In the home that might appreciate in value, in the automobile that gets you to work, in the food that keeps you alive to work. If it gives you the wherewithal to increase your net worth, it's an investment.

In the remainder of this book we focus on a specific kind of investment called *securities*.

The Least You Need to Know About Securities

Simply put, securities are investments that are secured. If you're an appliance dealer or an underworld-type, you can secure your loans by threat of repossession—or worse. If you're anyone else, you secure your investments by means of contractual agreements.

Securities fall basically into two categories: debt and equity.

Equities represent ownership—either partial or outright—of an enterprise. When you buy shares of stock, you're buying partial ownership.

Debt-based securities arise when you lend money—most frequently through a vehicle called a *bond*. The issuer of a bond promises to repay you the principle at the end of a specified period of time, and to make periodic interest payments over the course of that time period.

However, there is also a third kind of animal, a form of investment called a *mutual fund*. Mutual funds are pools of money, managed, for a fee, by a professional. The pooled money is invested in either bonds or stocks—or sometimes other vehicles such as money markets.

Chapter 6 describes all the variations of investment vehicles and lists Internet sites that provide additional resources. For now, here are some sites that can give you a good foundation for understanding the three major vehicles of stocks, bonds, and mutual funds.

◆ *Description of Asset Classes.* General description of various kinds of assets.

http://www.leggmason.com/Invest/ AssetAlloc/assetclass.html

◆ *Physical & Financial Assets.* Kinds of investments—physical vs. financial.

Register or log in at **http://www.wsbi.com/ spweb**, then click the Features icon. Click the How to Invest link, then scroll down to the Index link and click. Finally, click the section 2 link to Physical and Financial Assets.

◆ *Stock as an Investment.* Through 1993, stock prices, as measured by the S&P 500 (an index based on 500 large companies), rose in 16 of the previous 20 years. The annual performance ranged from a 32 percent rise in 1975 to a 30 percent decline the year before.

Register or log in at **http://www.wsbi.com/ spweb**, then click the Features icon. Click the How to Invest link, then scroll down to the Index link and click. Finally, click the section 4 link to Stocks.

◆ *Bonds as an Investment.* As with stocks, there are essentially two ways to make money from bonds: capital gains, which are achieved by selling a bond for more than it cost to buy; and the receipt of periodic interest payments. With subsequent sections on Corporate Bonds, US Government Securities, Municipals, Credit ratings, other factors affecting bond prices, and calls, convertibles, and zero coupons.

Register or log in at **http://www.wsbi.com/ spweb**, then click the Features icon. Click the How to Invest link, then scroll down to the Index link and click. Finally, click the section 5 link to Fixed-Income Investments.

◆ *Mutual Funds as Investments.* Investors who lack the capital, inclination, or time to establish and maintain adequately diversified stock or bond portfolios often buy shares in investment pools known as mutual funds. Subsequent sections on closed versus open funds, and fees.

Register or log in at **http://www.wsbi.com/ spweb**, then click the Features icon. Click the How to Invest link, then scroll down to the Index link and click. Finally, click the section 6 link to Mutual Funds.

Vocabulary

To be a savvy investor, it helps to know the lingua franca of investing. As we use new words throughout this text, we italicize them and try to explain them in context. For a more complete listing of important investment terminology, take a look at these Internet sites.

◆ *101 Investment Terms You Should Know.* Worth the visit. Easy-to-understand explanations of common financial terminology.

http://www.kiplinger.com/faq/faq101.html

◆ *Glossary of Investment Terms.* From the Securities and Exchange Commission.

   http://www.sec.gov/consumer/weisk/weisk9.htm

◆ *Glossary.* Extensive glossary, from the American Association of Individual Investors.

   http://www.aaii.org/glossary.html

◆ *Investing Glossaries On The Web.* Links to many lists of investment terms, and their definitions.

   http://www.investorama.com/glossary.shtml

Reading the Financials

The tutorial is almost complete. The last thing you need to know, before launching into investing, is how to read the financial section of your newspaper. (In Chapter 8, "Investigate the Markets," you learn how to find current stock quotes online, but for now, we'll stick with something simple.)

Major metropolitan dailies list closing prices for the stock, bond, and mutual fund markets.

Market listings follow a fairly consistent format from newspaper to newspaper, although listings vary for different exchanges. At a minimum, you'll find the name of the company, sales volume, closing price, and change from the previous day. Prices are listed with numbers like 3 5/8 or 5 9/16, which are equivalent to $3.63 and $5.56 per share, respectively. Sales volume is significant to you as an investor when it rises dramatically—an indication that other investors have taken a sudden interest in your stock, either for the good or the bad.

Most listings will also include *dividends*—payments to shareholders out of profits—declared for the last period (usually shown as an annual cash payment based on the size of the last payment), 12-month highs and lows, yield (annual dividend as a percentage of the closing price), and the *price-to-earnings ratio*, called a P/E throughout this book, meaning the share price divided by the company's annual earnings per share. Highs and lows are significant to you as an investor because they describe the *volatility* of the stock. A stock whose price rises slowly and steadily is less volatile, and hence, less risky, than one whose price sways wildly with every market wind.

Visit these Web sites for more information on reading a stock quote:

◆ *Reading a Stock Listing.* How to read a stock listing (see Figure 4.7).

   http://tqd.advanced.org/3298/doc/sbreadstock.html

◆ *Reading a Mutual Fund Listing.* You can get most of the immediate information needed to evaluate your fund's recent activity from these columns.

   http://www.mcmoney.com/paper.html

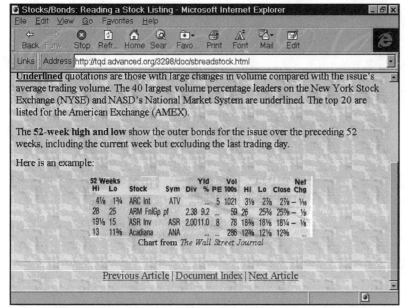

Underlined quotations are those with large changes in volume compared with the issue's average trading volume. The 40 largest volume percentage leaders on the New York Stock Exchange (NYSE) and NASD's National Market System are underlined. The top 20 are listed for the American Exchange (AMEX).

The **52-week high and low** show the outer bonds for the issue over the preceding 52 weeks, including the current week but excluding the last trading day.

Here is an example:

| 52 Weeks | | | | | Yld | | Vol | | | | Net |
Hi	Lo	Stock	Sym	Div	%	PE	100s	Hi	Lo	Close	Chg
4⅛	1¾	ARC Int	ATV	...		5	1021	3⅛	2⅞	2⅞	– ¹⁄₁₆
28	25	ARM FnlGp pf		2.38	9.2	...	59	26	25¾	25⅞	– ⅛
19⅛	15	ASR Inv	ASR	2.00	11.0	8	78	18⅜	18⅛	18¼	– ⅛
13	11⅜	Acadiana	ANA	...	...		286	12⅜	12⅛	12⅜	...

Chart from *The Wall Street Journal*

Previous Article | Document Index | Next Article

FIG. 4.7

Stock listings are less complicated than they appear.

PART II

Work Out Your Game Plan

5   Develop a Portfolio Strategy   57

6   Consider Investment Vehicles   77

7   Use Expert Research Resources   95

8   Investigate the Markets   109

9   Talk to Smart Investors   123

10 Use the Rest of the Internet as a Research Tool   133

11 Search the Internet   145

5

Develop a Portfolio Strategy

Maximize your return by planning before you invest.

Novice investors make a common mistake: They hear a "hot" investment tip, rush out to make the purchase, and after two months of nail biting (and watching the value of the security bounce around), sell out.

Seasoned investors approach the whole game differently. For these wise money managers, investing is a careful, methodical, and well thought-out process—one where the hot tip may be credible, but only because they know their own minds, and because it fits in with their overall strategy.

This chapter walks you through the goal-setting process, identifies the factors that influence your personal approach to investing, and presents a strategy for allocating your funds.

Setting Goals

The first step in creating a portfolio strategy is deciding what it is you're investing for. Unless you've got the Midas urge to simply own money, there's certainly something you're hoping to do with those assets.

Your investment goals can be short term—a down payment for a house, for example, or next year's college tuition, or an overseas vacation two years down the road.

Perhaps your goals are intermediate term. College tuition might be eight or nine years away. Retirement might be 10 years in the future. You could hope to turn your hobby into a full-time business.

Or it may be that your goals are very long term. You're 20 years from retirement. You want to leave an inheritance for your grandchildren. You want to be free to travel in your golden years.

Your first task as an investor is to decide what exactly you hope to achieve in your investment program.

The goal-setting process is simple:

1. *List your top three or four investment goals.* Think short, intermediate, and long term. Make time to discuss this critical issue with your spouse.

2. *Create a timeline for achieving your goals.* It needn't be tremendously precise, but it should reflect your basic expectations about the direction and tone of your life. No investor, no matter how savvy, can predict with accuracy interest, inflation, taxes, or most of the other factors that influence the future value of your investments— so recognize the need for some flexibility in your timeline.

3. *Calculate the return you'll require to meet those goals.* If you're working with one of the financial planning packages described in Chapter 2, it'll be worthwhile to play with the tools for calculating investment returns, as well as the tools that assist in planning for retirement needs. If you're in a hurry, though, rough manual calculations will suffice for this exercise.

The following Internet sites provide additional helpful information about setting goals. Once you've decided what you want to accomplish, you're ready to decide what you're willing to do to get there.

◆ *Retire Right.* A tool for calculating your retirement needs. It's Canadian, so substitute your expected Social Security income for the Canadian equivalent. (For information about your earnings or future Social Security benefits, call the Social Security Administration at 1-800-772-1213.)

http://www.fcfunds.bomil.ca/e/er/era.html

◆ *Determining Your Investment Goal.* Creating an investment program is very much like taking a long trip.

http://www.vanguard.com/educ/module2/ m2_3_1.html

◆ *Personal Finance Center.* Financial challenges for each age group—and how to set goals to meet them.

http://www.ml.com/personal/index.html

◆ *Do's & Don't's.* This site contains some general guidelines for stock investors from Standard & Poor's. Worth the read. This site, which is home to many of the references in this chapter, requires you to register (it's free), and then click through hyperlinks to find the page. After logon, click Features, How to Invest. Page down and click Index, then page down and under the Stocks heading, click Some Do's & Don't's.

http://www.wsbi.com/spweb

◆ *Identify Goals and Objectives.* Identifying your goals and objectives is the most important step in financial planning, and actually launches the remainder of the process.

http://www.leggmason.com/Invest/ Process/goals.html

◆ *Setting Your Goals and Objectives.* Write down what you want in life.

http://www.e-analytics.com/fp3.htm

Investment Considerations: Risk vs. Reward

You've set your goals, you know what you want. There are several issues to consider, though, in choosing the path you'll take to get there. In this section, we talk about investment risk, diversification, timing, and ethics.

It seems easy enough. Take all your money, and buy the investment that provides the highest return. Right?

Hardly. If you actually believed that theory, you'd be "investing" in lottery tickets. When your gamble pays off, there's no better return on investment.

Fortunately, you're smarter than that. You recognize that the higher the potential reward, the higher the risk. Risk and reward parallel one another so closely, in fact, that there's actually a mathematical correlation.

When investors first contemplate the idea of risk—the possibility of actually losing money in an investment—there's a natural inclination to do the opposite of gambling. To some investors, the idea of losing even a nickel in an investment is intolerable. They try to avoid all risk by making 100 percent "safe" investments—guaranteed returns, risk-free vehicles.

As you'll see later in this section, those investors may be fooling themselves. While they're safe from the risk of losing their principal, they're not at all safe from other risks—namely, inflation.

The following Web sites provide more background on the relationship between risk and return.

◆ *The Efficient Frontier*. This chart shows the mathematical correlation between historic rates of return and level of risk.

   http://www.leggmason.com/Invest/ AssetAlloc/effront.html

◆ *About Risk and Reward*. Do you understand the relationship between risk and reward?

   http://www.manulife.com/usa/wwusdpen/ 210e.htm

◆ *Investing 101*. Risk and Reward: A Course in the Basics, from Niké Securities L.P.

   http://www.nikesec.com/inves101.html

◆ *The Difference Between Investing and Gambling*. Thoughts on attaining safety of principal and a reasonable return.

   http://www.investorama.com/features/ delano2.shtml

Test Yourself

The first factor in the risk/reward consideration is how much risk you're personally able to tolerate.

Investors in adaptable periods of their lives are better able to tolerate risk than those who are in less flexible situations. Your tolerance for risk is also affected by your personality and beliefs about risk-taking. There is, of course, no "best" way to feel about risk. You are who you are, and will find the highest level of financial satisfaction in being true to your beliefs and circumstances.

This is the way the self-test breaks out:

Factors Affecting Your Capacity for Investment Risk	Lower Risk Tolerance	Higher Risk Tolerance
Age	Older	Younger
Diversification*	Narrow	Wide
Earning Capacity	Low	High
Family Status	Dependents	No dependents
Investing Goals	Critical	Discretionary
Investing Timeline*	Short term	Long Term
Net Worth	Low	High
Personality	Fiscal conservative	Fiscal maverick

* Covered later in this chapter

Still not sure? Visit these Internet sites for other ways to measure your personal tolerance for risk.

◆ *Find Your Risk Tolerance*. The Investor Learning Center. Find what kind of investor you are based on your investment goals.

http://www.ml.com/investor/risktol.html

◆ *Prudential Securities*. Investment Personality Quiz helps you determine what kind of investor you are.

http://www.prusec.com/quiz.htm

◆ *Assessing Your Risk Tolerance*. Your emotional make-up plays a significant role in how you create your investment mix.

http://www.vanguard.com/educ/module2/ m2_3_3.html

Risk Assessment

All investments carry risk. Whether you put your money into off-shore oil wells, or just put it into a hole in your mattress, you're taking a risk.

One way to measure risk is to consider all the possible outcomes of an investment. If it goes in your mattress, you risk not only the physical loss of the money, but also the losses that arise from both inflation risk and opportunity-cost risk—two of the investment risks we'll explain in this section. On an imaginary scale of 1 to 100, your total risk is, say, a level 2, and your potential reward measures a 1.

Put your money into an offshore drilling venture—if you can even find such a thing—and you risk losing it all when your partners fail to strike oil. You also risk loss because of a thing called *liquidity*. What happens if you change your mind and want to sell out?

The secondary market for offshore oil well partnerships is pretty limited. Perhaps you think it's still worth doing, though, because you stand to gain, say, a 1,000 percent return, in the unlikely event your partners strike oil the first time out. Your total risk in this case is perhaps a level 80. At the same time, your potential reward could be, say, a level 90.

Unfortunately, those risk/reward numbers are meaningless in the real world. Economists and analysts have yet to devise a reliable system for measuring total risk—in part because there are so many risk factors, and in part because there is no guarantee that historical patterns will repeat themselves in the future.

Types of Risk

As a smart investor, you need to keep in mind a rough measure of the risks you take with each investment. Don't put a lot of energy into devising precise calculations. You have more profitable ways to use your time. At the same time, however, don't ignore risk in the naive belief that bad things can't happen to *your* special little dollars. The following sections define and discuss the major types of investment risk you must factor into your strategy.

Credit Risk

Credit risk is the probability that the borrower won't fulfill his obligations. It's also called *default risk*. Polonius got it wrong. He should have advised, "Neither a borrower nor a lender be—unless the credit rating gives security." When you lend your money, you

risk losing it if the borrower defaults. Various bond rating services—Moody's and Standard and Poor's are the best known—rate the default risk of bond issuers (see Figures 5.1 and 5.2). Those with the lowest ratings are classed together as junk bonds.

The following sites provide additional information on credit risk.

▼ TIP

To reduce the risk of credit problems, check bond ratings, and stick with those rated A- or better.

◆ *Moody's.* Provides independent credit ratings, and research and financial information to the capital markets.

http://www.moodys.com

◆ *Standard and Poor's.* Credit ratings for bonds, money market funds, preferred stock, and other securities.

http://www.ratings.standardpoor.com

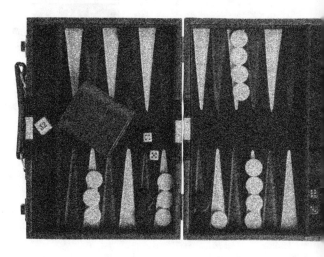

FIG. 5.1

Moody's is a leading credit rating service.

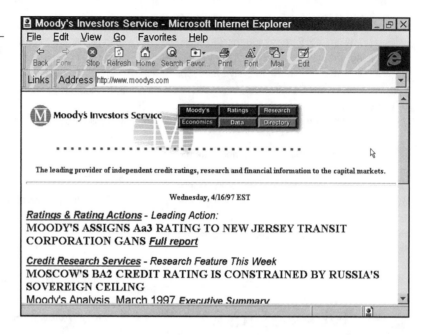

FIG. 5.2

Standard and Poor's is well-regarded for its credit ratings.

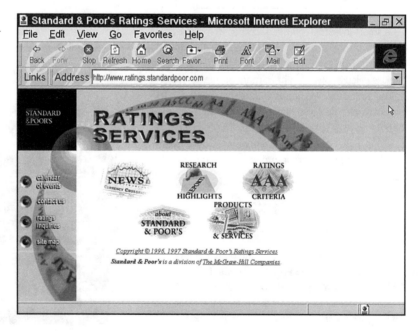

◆ *Default Risk*. Could one of your investments go bankrupt?

http://pathfinder.com/@@gDS4igcAfaqYnVfg/ money/features/falls/default.html

Cyclical Risk

Cyclical risk (also called *industry risk*) is the likelihood that the industry your security is in will go through down cycles. When the economy is roaring, sales of boxed macaroni and cheese decline. Put half the country on unemployment, and you'll see mac-n-cheese sales soar. Recognize that if one or two major, say, biotechnology companies are losing money, there's a good chance the whole industry is facing decline.

▼ TIP

To reduce the effects of cyclical fluctuations in the economy, limit yourself to the best one or two securities in a given industry, and spread the rest of your investments around other unrelated industries.

The Internet has additional information on cyclical risk:

◆ *Ways to Group Stocks*. According to Standard and Poor's, "If a stock portfolio is sufficiently diversified across various industries with different characteristics, the volatility of specific stocks will have a surprisingly small influence on how well the entire portfolio does." For details on industrial groupings and their associated cyclical risks, log on to the Standard and Poor's Web site. After logon, click Features, How to

Invest, Index, then page down to Ways to Group Stocks.

http://www.wsbi.com/spweb

Inflation Risk

Inflation risk is the possibility that inflation will outpace the return on your investment, resulting in an actual loss in buying power. (That's the reason the 2 percent you'd get in passbook savings actually costs you money!) Inflation has averaged more than 3 percent a year. If you want to reach the financial goals you've set, you have to protect the purchasing power of your capital.

▼ TIP

In times of high inflation, the best thing you can own is a low-interest, fixed-rate, tax-deductible mortgage. Don't pay off low-interest loans early; focus instead on beating inflation with growth stocks and growth funds.

The following sites provide additional information on inflation risk.

◆ *Inflation Risk*. Inflation can have an adverse effect on your real return.

http://www.vanguard.com/educ/module2/ m2_2_7.html

◆ *More on Inflation Risk*. If your investment goal is more than five years away, inflation risk can be a serious danger to your savings. Number three in a list of five kinds of risk.

http://www2.strong-funds.com/strong/ LearningCenter/5risks.htm

◆ *The Battle Against Inflation*. Standard and Poor's says that "Although every investment carries some risk, it may be even more hazardous not to invest." For more information on fighting inflation, log on to the Standard and Poor's Web site. After logon, click Features, How to Invest, Index, then page down to Battle Inflation.

http://www.wsbi.com/spweb

Interest Rate Risk

Interest rate risk is the possibility that interest rates may rise and decrease the value of an investment. It's a particular concern for bond investors, who see the value of their portfolios fall when interest rates rise. A bond paying 7 percent isn't worth much when prevailing rates are 12 percent.

▼ **T I P**

When interest rates are low, keep your portfolio focused on equities. When rates are high, look to bonds as a way to maintain your level of return.

You'll learn more about the risks associated with interest rates at these sites:

◆ *Interest-Rate Risk*. Would your investments be hurt by rising rates?

http://pathfinder.com/ @@HggrlQcAcKqYnVfg/money/features/ falls/interest.html

◆ *More on Interest-Rate Risk*. Interest rate risk is concerned with the danger that your investment will lose value because it has a fixed rate of return that will not change as interest rates

rise. Includes commentary on liquidity risk and reducing risk.

http://www2.strong-funds.com/strong/ html/LearningCenter/5risks2.htm

◆ *Credit and Interest Rate Risk*. Standard and Poor's advises that "Credit risk and interest-rate risk are the primary concerns with bonds and other fixed-income securities." To obtain additional information on these risks, log on to the Standard and Poor's Web site. After logon, click Features, How to Invest, Index, then page down to Credit Risk.

http://www.wsbi.com/spweb

Liquidity Risk

Liquidity risk accounts for the possibility that you can't escape your investment. For publicly traded stocks and bonds, there's no risk; the secondary market is endless. But for a limited partnership in a time-share condominium, you could spend years finding a buyer at any price.

▼ **T I P**

Avoid "thinly traded" securities—the penny stocks and junk bonds that are tough to unload quickly. Similarly, avoid investments in limited partnerships, real estate projects, and other vehicles that require finding a willing buyer.

Visit these sites for more background on liquidity risk:

◆ *Liquidity Risk*. Could you get a fair price for your investment if you had to sell it now?

http://pathfinder.com/@@HggrlQcAcKqYnVfg/ money/features/falls/liquidity.html

◆ *Liquidity*. While most financial assets can be bought or sold at a moment's notice, it's harder to sell physical assets. For more tips on avoiding low-liquidity investments, log on to the Standard and Poor's Web site. After logon, click Features, How to Invest. Page down and click Index, then page down to the section on Liquidity.

http://www.wsbi.com/spweb

Market Risk

When investing, there is also a *market risk*—in other words, the risk of a decrease in the general level of market prices. The numbers to watch are the indexes reported every night on the evening news—the Dow Jones Industrial Averages, the S&P 500, and all the rest. These numbers are heavily influenced by political, social, and economic changes.

■ **N O T E**

Chapters 6 through 11 of this book tell you how to research the factors affecting market prices.

The market can be erratic and unpredictable. However, there are ways to combat its changes with sound investments.

Ironically, market risk is often the inverse of inflation risk. Reduce your exposure by taking the opposite tack. When the market is in decline, you're better off in debt securities: bonds, T-bills, and money-market funds. When the market begins to rise, you want to be there with equities. The obvious problem, of course, is knowing which way the market is headed.

Avoid stocks with high price/earnings ratios. P/Es are calculated by comparing the price to the annual earnings. These numbers are often found in the stock quotes published in the daily paper. (See Chapter 8 for places to find current quotes online.)

■ **N O T E**

P/Es are explained in Chapter 17. For now, all you really need to know is that P/Es larger than 20 are risky, unless the security is growing at a similar rate.

You'll find more on market risk at these Web sites:

◆ *Basic Investment Principles of Risk and Return*. Major sources of uncertainty, or risk, that could produce unexpected returns include business and industry risk, inflation risk, market risk, and liquidity risk.

http://www.aaii.org/basics/riskretn.html

◆ *Market Risk and Time*. While the stock and bond markets can be risky in the short run, time has a moderating effect on market risk.

http://www.vanguard.com/educ/module2/m2_2_6.html

◆ *Currency Risk*. Shifts in exchange rates—the risk that comes with investing in overseas markets.

http://pathfinder.com/@@HggrIQcAcKqYnVfg/money/features/falls/currency.html

Opportunity Costs

When you park your money in investments that aren't paying well, you're missing out on the chance to earn more. Tie your money into long-term contracts, and that risk rises proportionately. You don't, for example, want to lock into long-term bank certificates of deposit just before rates rise. Nor do you want to make the mistake that some small business owners make of believing that *any* profit makes the business venture worthwhile. The problem is this: If you have half a million dollars poured into a business, and 10 years later you're seeing profits of only a few thousand dollars, you're actually losing. Always be aware, in your investing, of what you *could* be doing with your money.

▼ TIP

Keep your money invested in something, anything, rather than simply parking it. When markets are unusually volatile, keep your investments in short-term vehicles such as money market funds, so that you're ready to take advantage the moment the market hits a low.

To learn more about opportunity cost risk, investigate these sites on the Internet:

◆ *Opportunity Cost Risk*. Are you passing up better investments?

http://pathfinder.com/@@HggrlQcAcKqYnVfg/money/features/falls/opportunity.html

◆ *Opportunity Costs*. Your time is worth money, and you don't achieve financial security by working cheap. Whatever you do should be worth money to you.

http://www.we.com/hbw/advice/invest.html

◆ *The PitBull Investor*. For high-risk investors, learn methods for aggressive growth stock investment, options trading, and stock shorting systems.

http://com.primenet.com/pitbull

Price Volatility Risk

Price volatility risk is the likelihood that the value of your investment will experience dramatic shifts. Stable securities—stocks, for example—have prices that stay in line with those of the rest of the market. As the stock market rises, a stable stock will increase in value at approximately the same rate. Of course, it falls at the same rate as well. In stocks and a few other securities, a measurement called *beta* describes the historic volatility of every offering (see Figure 5.3). You'll often find betas listed alongside the stock quote or company information. (You'll learn more about locating and reading quotes in Chapter 8.)

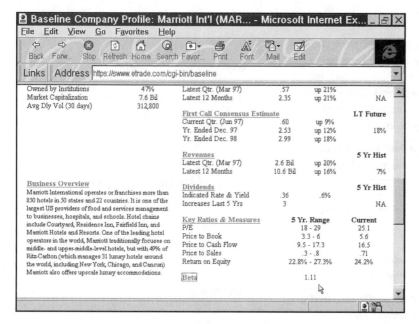

FIG. 5.3

You'll find beta measurements at E*TRADE's baseline company reports. Here, a beta of 1.11 indicates a security that's just a little more volatile than the market as a whole.

▼ **TIP**

Look for securities with a beta close to 1.0, meaning they're exactly as volatile as the market. Numbers less than 1 are less volatile and don't take advantage of natural market growth; numbers greater than 1 are more volatile, and tend to drop (or rise) much faster.

You'll learn more about volatility risk from these Web sites:

◆ *Volatility Risk*. How much do your stocks rise and fall day to day?

http://pathfinder.com/ @@bjfY7gcAfqqYnVfg/money/features/ falls/volatility.html

◆ *Volatility*. One measure of risk is price volatility. Log on to the Standard an Poor's Web site. After logon, click Features, How to Invest. Page down and click Index, then page down to the section on Volatility.

http://www.wsbi.com/spweb

Reinvestment Rate Risk

Reinvestment risk involves the possibility that you won't be able to reinvest the earnings and/or principal at the same rate of return the initial investment earned. Here's an example of how the reinvestment risk arises: Your 14 percent bond matures, and you suddenly find yourself with cash on hand and no place to reinvest it at better than, say, 8 percent.

To maximize your reinvestments, time your investments so that maturities are staggered. When markets are in a down cycle, your existing investments continue to work at the higher original rates. Look for investments that automatically and regularly reinvest earnings.

Consider investments that don't pay out in cash. Growth stocks and zero-coupon bonds qualify.

Stop by these Web sites for more information on reinvestment risk:

◆ *Reinvestment Risk*. Have you ever been unable to reinvest money at an attractive rate?

http://pathfinder.com/@@HggrlQcAcKqYnVfg/ money/features/falls/reinvest.html

◆ *Reinvestment Rate Risk*. Standard and Poor's says that "An investor may not be able to reinvest cash returns from an investment at the same level of return with the same amount of risk." Log on to the Standard and Poor's Web site. After logon, click Features, How to Invest, Index, then page down to Reinvestment Risk.

http://www.wsbi.com/spweb

Mitigating Risk

If you understand inflation risk and opportunity cost risk, you know that merely avoiding all high-risk investments doesn't solve your risk problems. The more conservative your investments, the lower the potential return—and the higher your risk of not meeting your investment goals.

In addition to the risk reduction tips listed previously, there are two ways to decrease the risks associated with investing, neither of which requires you to be conservative in your investments.

In this section, we address the two most significant risk reduction strategies: diversification and long-term investing.

Diversification

You heard the story in your childhood—the one about dropping the basket of eggs and smashing them all.

The parable is just as valid when you're an adult. The better you diversify, the lower your risk of losing it all in one big market shift.

This chart (see Figure 5.4) demonstrates how diversification can soften the risk of volatile prices.

When you graph out the numbers (see Figure 5.5), the principle becomes even more apparent.

Diversity requires you to spread the eggs out in lots of different kinds of baskets. Detailed in the following sections are several strategies for diversification.

Industries

If the tobacco industry is facing massive lawsuits, it doesn't help you at all to own a basket full of different tobacco stocks; they're all facing the same problem. Instead, diversify your holdings over a variety of unrelated industries, so that when one gets slapped with the unexpected new regulation, heavy competition, or development that obsoletes a product line, you're still protected by the health of your other industries.

| File | Edit | View | Insert | Format | Tools | Data | Window | Help | _ | 🗗 | × |

	A	B	C	D	E
2	Period	Stock A	Stock B	Stock C	Yearly Average
3	a	18.0	7.0	12.0	12.3
4	b	12.0	16.0	18.0	15.3
5	c	4.0	18.0	12.0	11.3
6	d	8.0	2.0	4.0	4.7
7	e	3.0	12.0	4.0	6.3
8	f	12.0	3.0	12.0	9.0
9	Total Average Return	9.5	9.7	10.3	9.8
10					

◄ ◄ ► ►◄ Sheet1 / Sheet2 / Sheet3 / Sheet4 / Sheet5 / Sheet6 / ◄

FIG. 5.4

In this sample portfolio, diversification softens the risk of volatile prices. The diversified average beats the returns of two stocks, and compensates for low returns on the best stock in its worst periods.

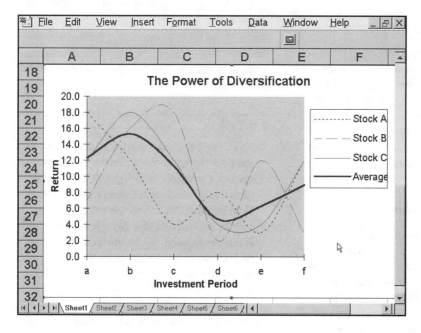

| File | Edit | View | Insert | Format | Tools | Data | Window | Help | _ | 🗗 | × |

The Power of Diversification

Return

Investment Period

-------- Stock A
— — Stock B
——— Stock C
—— Average

◄ ◄ ► ►◄ Sheet1 / Sheet2 / Sheet3 / Sheet4 / Sheet5 / Sheet6 / ◄

FIG. 5.5

A graphic demonstration of how diversification evens out volatile returns. The heavy line shows the average return of a diversified portfolio in each period of time.

Maturities

Big on bonds? The last thing you want is to have them all come due at once. Stagger maturities on certificates of deposit, bonds, treasuries, and any other income producing asset, so that you can continue taking advantage of market lows, and avoid being hurt by overpriced securities during market highs.

Economies

Hooray for patriotism and all that, but when it comes to your portfolio, think globally. The U.S. economy is as likely as any other developed market to take a dive. If you have part of your assets in European and Canadian markets, and another part in growing Asian-Pacific and Latin American economies, you're less likely to feel the pain of a domestic hit. Newer economies are coming of age, too; for the well-diversified investor, they're worth a look.

Vehicles

Mix it up. A pure bond portfolio is going to move up or down in unison as interest rates change. A little diversity helps you avoid the hits. Spread the risk over a variety of stock groups—small cap, growth, high yield, and others—and toss in an appropriate mix of other kinds of vehicles for the times when the entire stock market is in decline. Chapter 6 describes various investment vehicles available to the individual investor.

Philosophies/Advisors

Generally, it's wise to follow a couple of different philosophies in your investing for a few reasons. Computerized trading has lead to a condition where many large investors have designed software to automatically and immediately act on certain market conditions—well in advance of when you, the individual investor, get to digest and act on those factors. If the market has already acted on your single favorite theory when you're ready to make your trade, you're too late.

■ **NOTE**

Chapter 18 describes various theories and philosophies about how markets perform.

Likewise, if you're a mutual fund investor, the portfolio manager at your fund has a few pet philosophies. That's great, when they work. But if they fail, you want to have some backup in a fund managed by an entirely different manager.

Diversification is, in fact, the major attraction of mutual funds. Their structure means that for a very small investment, you can diversify in every direction. A mutual fund is diversified because it invests in dozens, sometimes hundreds, of different securities, spread across several industries, sectors, and businesses. While larger investors have the assets to do their own diversification, the smallest investors sleep better at nights knowing their assets are completely diversified.

▼ **TIP**

If you want to get a measure of *how much* you should diversify, the magic number is eight. Work toward a portfolio large enough that you can spread your investments among eight vehicles in eight industries. Your goal is eight different maturities, eight funds, and eight economies. The investments need not be divided equally, of course. Invest more heavily in the places your research finds more attractive.

The Internet is a good place to learn more about the subject of diversification.

◆ *Benefits of Diversification.* By diversifying, your portfolio will not be subject to the volatility of one asset and can offer a more consistent pattern of results.

http://www.leggmason.com/Invest/ AssetAlloc/diverse.html

◆ *Diversification.* Diversifying minimizes the risk and maximizes the rate of return in your overall portfolio.

http://www.manulife.com/usa/wwusdpen/ 2182.htm

◆ *The Importance of Diversification.* Diversification of investment holdings is the most important shield against risk. For additional pointers on diversifying your investments, log on to the Standard and Poor's Web page. After logon, click Features, How to Invest, Index, then page down to Diversification.

http://www.wsbi.com/spweb

Term of Investment

The law: Given enough time (and a degree of diversity), you *will* make money in the stock market. Nothing short of total global economic collapse can stop it.

Are we stating our case too strongly? Don't think so. The key, you see, is time.

By keeping a long-term perspective—and by long term we mean 10 years or more—you allow time to overcome the short-term whims of the market. The key here is to decide in advance to have the discipline to ride through volatile markets, to avoid making emotional decisions about market timing.

Here are some other basic truths about markets:

◆ *Go with stocks.* Over time, stocks and stock funds perform better than bonds or other fixed-income vehicles.

◆ *Give it time.* Time compensates for the volatility of the stock market.

◆ *Have faith.* The stock market always rises, given sufficient time. In fact, it is more profitable to buy stocks and stock funds when the market is at its worst. Figure 5.6 demonstrates the wisdom of buying heavily when the market is at its worst.

◆ *Take a risk.* Time mitigates most risk. (See Figure 5.6.) In other words, riskier investments—small capitalization stocks, for example—are safer over time. (Of course, no amount of time can compensate for downright foolish levels of risk. So don't start licking stamps for the Internet pyramid scheme du jour.)

There are several Internet sites for learning more about investing for the long term.

◆ *Considering Your Investment Horizon.* The amount of time you have to reach your destination often helps to determine the most effective mode of transportation.

http://www.vanguard.com/educ/module2/ m2_3_2.html

◆ *Individuals Should Focus on the Long-Term.* A long-term fundamental approach to stock selection is best.

http://www.investorama.com/features/ longterm.shtml

FIG. 5.6

Over time, the market compensates for its declines. The rolling average line shows the average level of the market over the illustrated time period. Like the overall market, it's always on the rise.

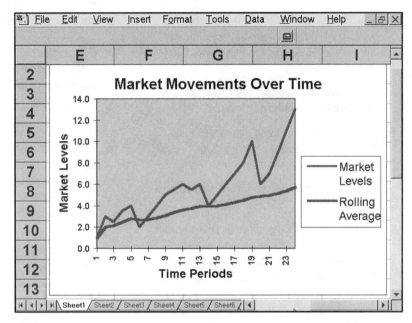

◆ *A Portfolio Maintenance Program for the Long-Term Investor.* Guidelines for setting up a portfolio maintenance program

http://www.aaii.org/portfolo/ pfmaintn.html

Other Considerations in Creating a Strategy

There are two other considerations that will enter into your overall portfolio strategy: tax-free investing and ethical investing. This section addresses both the mercenary and the charitable.

Tax-free Investing

Tax-free investments sound tempting. Who isn't lured by the notion of beating Uncle Sam—and staying out of jail? Unfortunately for lower-income taxpayers, tax-free investments aren't necessarily a good idea.

Tax-free investing means purchasing certain kinds of federal debt instruments or municipal securities, or bonds issued by the authority of a state or local government. Municipal bonds are generally issued to fund public projects—new schools, roads, or public transportation. Sometimes they're even issued to benefit private industries that a government body wants to attract to its area. These debt instruments are tax-free because the state is willing to forego tax revenue to gain a price advantage in the bond market. They're tax-free on the federal level because the

U.S. government has decided it's better to allow states to raise capital at an advantageous cost.

Because investors aren't losing part of their income to taxes, they're willing to accept lower yields.

It's these lower yields that make tax-frees a questionable investment for investors in the lower tax brackets.

There's a simple formula, though, for deciding whether or not you're a candidate for tax-free investments.

◆ *Determine your tax bracket.* Your tax bracket is not the average tax you pay on all your income. It is the amount of tax you'd pay on your *next* dollar of income. The current tax brackets are 15, 28, 31, 36, and (effectively) 39.6 percent. If your next dollar of income is greater than the following amounts, it's taxed at 36 percent:

- Married filing jointly: $147,700

- Single: $121,300

- Head of household: $134,500

- Married filing separately: $73,800

Income in excess of $263,750 (or $131,875 if you're married filing separately) is taxed at the higher 39.6 percent rate, computed by adding the new 10 percent "surcharge" to the 36 percent rate.

For this example, we'll use a rate of 36 percent.

◆ *Determine the return on the tax free investment.* For this example, say it's 9 percent.

◆ *Determine the effective rate of return.* To determine rate of return, use this formula: tax-free return divided by (1 minus the tax bracket). In this example, the formula is .09 / (1 - .36), equaling .1406, or 14.1 percent.

◆ *Compare the effective rate to the market rate for taxable securities.* In this example, if you can earn 14.2 percent or better in similarly rated taxable bonds, you're better off paying the tax.

Visit this Internet site for other educational information on tax-free investing:

◆ *The Benefits of Tax-free Investing.* Most municipal investments are designed to be exempt from federal and, in many cases, state and local income taxes. Includes section on calculating tax-equivalent yields.

   http://personal.fidelity.com/decisions/ benefits.html

Ethical Investing

For many investors, all potential investments have to work their way through one more "screen": Social responsibility.

These investors are looking for investment vehicles that further their social agenda. Their concerns range from environmental issues—they refuse to lend financial support to polluters or strip miners—to political matters to social problems.

Socially responsible investors will find a great deal of support for their concerns on the Internet. The following Web sites are highly recommended; each provides a wealth of thinking and practical guidance on the social issues that motivate responsible investment decisions.

◆ *Ethical Investing—"Green" Money.* A member of an "ethical" investment club shares his thoughts on socially-responsible investing.

   http://www.investorama.com/features/ oswald1.shtml

◆ *A Guide to Social Investing*. Most adherents to the "social investment" concept generally agree on broad principles underlying their social screens. In other words, they share a similar ethical platform. What does this platform look like?

http://www.aaii.org/portfolo/socialin.html

◆ *Getting Started as a Socially Responsible Investor*. Some simple steps and strategies.

http://www.zacks.com/magazine/ good.html

Allocating Assets

In Chapter 4, you calculated how often—and how much—you can afford to invest.

Now that you've worked your way through to this point in this chapter, you also have a pretty good notion of what your investment goals are, what levels of return you need to achieve those goals, and what level of risk you're willing to accept.

Additionally, you've learned how to reduce your exposure to various investment risks, and you've determined how much diversification you need to minimize your risk. Finally, you've decided what your investment horizon is, whether you're a candidate for tax-free investments, and what role social responsibility will play in your investment decisions. The only task remaining is deciding how, exactly, you'll allocate your investments.

The process is fairly straightforward. Create a tentative portfolio mix based on the decisions you've made. Investment advisors argue over precise asset

mix recommendations, but for the most part, your portfolio should look something like the asset mix in Figure 5.7.

More specific recommendations on portfolio mixes can be found at any number of Internet sites. Be careful when reading recommendations from brokers or other people who make a nice commission when you shift your portfolio toward the products they're selling. These sites are worth visiting because they tend to be fairly neutral in their recommendations:

◆ *The Right Investment Mix*. Sample portfolios based on different goals, time horizon, risk tolerance, and financial resources.

http://www.vanguard.com/educ/module2/ m2_4_0.html

◆ *Asset Allocation*. Some generalizations can be made about what kind of financial assets are appropriate for people at different stages of their lives. For insight into asset allocation, log on to the Standard and Poor's Web site. After logon, click <u>Features</u>, <u>How to Invest</u>, <u>Index</u>, then page down to <u>Allocating Assets</u>.

http://www.wsbi.com/spweb

◆ *Investment Goals*. Growth investing, with subsequent section on investing for value. Registration is free, but access takes some time. For tips on setting investment goals, log on to the Standard and Poor's Web site. After logon, click <u>Features</u>, <u>How to Invest</u>, then page down and click <u>Index</u>; then page down and under the Stocks heading, click <u>Growth Investing</u>.

http://www.wsbi.com/spweb

◆ *Sample Investment Portfolios*. Recommended mixes based on Conservative, Balanced, Growth, and Aggressive strategies.

http://www.leggmason.com/Invest/ AssetAlloc/portfolios.html

	A	B	C
3	**Investment Horizon**	**Risk Profile**	**Asset Mix**
4	**0 to 2 years**	Low	100% income
5		High	50% growth, 50% income
6	**3 to 9 years**	Low	60% income, 40% growth
7		High	30% income, 70% growth
8	**10 years or more**	Low	20% income, 80% growth
9		High	100% growth

FIG. 5.7

Recommended asset mix. Income investments are those that throw off high dividends, interest payments, or other income—bonds, utility stocks, money markets. Growth investments are those that appreciate in value without generating much—or any—income.

◆ *A Look at Historical Investment Returns*. Which investment class has performed best over time?

http://www.vanguard.com/educ/module2/m2_2_2.html

◆ *The Importance of a Mix of Assets*. The way in which funds are allocated among various asset categories is the most important long-run determinant of the return on investment. For advice on mixing assets, log on to the Standard and Poor's site. After logon, click Features, How to Invest, then page down and click Index. Page down to the Asset Mix link.

http://www.wsbi.com/spweb

◆ *Investment Rules*. Consider risk tolerance, life circumstances, diversification, research, and sticking with the plan.

http://www.ml.com/investor/rules.html

◆ *Life Cycle Investing: Your Personal Investment Profile*. There are four basic aspects that compose an investor's personal investment profile: your personal tolerance for risk, return needs and whether current income or future growth needs to be emphasized, time horizon, and tax exposure.

http://www.aaii.org/basics/lifecycl.html

◆ *Determine Your Investment Strategy*. Studies have shown that the asset allocation decision is the most important investment decision you can make.

http://www.leggmason.com/Invest/strategy.html

◆ *Allocation Adjustment: How to Transform Your Portfolio*. Changing asset allocation strategies means that you will be making major changes to your portfolio. How do you make the transition?

http://www.aaii.org/portfolo/allocadj.html

◆ *Asset Allocation.* Different strategies based on several factors, and differing in how they balance risk and reward. The Investor Learning Center.

http://www.ml.com/investor/assetal.html

◆ *What to Do with Different Levels of Investable Money.*

First $1k

http://pathfinder.com/ @@jA*WxwYAlZXDFkHe/money/features/ plunge_0695/plunge1K.html

First $10k

http://pathfinder.com/ @@jA*WxwYAlZXDFkHe/money/features/ plunge_0695/plunge$10K.html

Second $25k

http://pathfinder.com/ @@jA*WxwYAlZXDFkHe/money/features/ plunge_0695/plunge25K.html

6

Consider Investment Vehicles

Sit up straight. It's time to study up on investment options. No, we won't jump straight into warrants, puts and calls...although we'll cover those in a later section.

In this chapter, you'll find brief descriptions of investment vehicles available to private investors, along with a listing of Internet sites that provide tutorials, price comparisons, analyses, and anything else you might want to know about any given investment.

The Basics

All investments fall basically into two groups: debt and equity. *Debt investments*, such as bonds, are promises to repay borrowed money with interest. When you park your money in a passbook savings account, you're making a fairly unprofitable debt investment.

Equity investments, on the other hand, convey some degree of ownership. *Stock* is the best-known form of equity investing. With equities, you make a profit when the value of the investment goes up, or when it pays a dividend to the owners. You're also making an equity investment when

you store a first-edition Marvel comic book in your attic, hoping its increase in value will make up for the cost of the storage unit you rent for your other excess goodies.

Investigate these Internet sites for more information on investment basics:

◆ *Types of Investments.* A rundown from the U.S. Securities and Exchange Commission.

http://www.sec.gov/consumer/weisk/ weisk3.htm

◆ *Basic Types of Investments.* Sections on stocks, bonds, and mutual funds from the Investor Learning Center (Merrill Lynch, Pierce, Fenner & Smith).

http://www.ml.com/investor/basic.html

◆ *misc.invest FAQ.* These Frequently Asked Questions include a wealth of material about investing.

http://www.cis.ohio-state.edu/hypertext/ faq/bngusenet/misc/invest/top.html

Stocks

Certainly the most familiar form of investment is stocks. When you purchase shares of stock, you become a part owner of the company. So long as that company performs well, the value of your stock will—in theory, at least—rise. Your profits come from periodic dividend payments from the company, and from an increase in the market price of the actual stock (see Figure 6.1).

As a part owner, you have the right to vote on certain matters. If the company performs badly enough to go into bankruptcy, however, you, as an owner, stand at the end of the line of creditors. Generally, shares of stock are sold as either common or preferred stock. The preferred owners normally don't vote, but they do have a slightly higher claim to assets in the event of a liquidation.

When you purchase stock on most exchanges, your goal is to buy in *round lots*, multiples of 100 shares. Smaller purchases, called *odd lots*, cost slightly more. Some discount brokers—E*TRADE, for example— charge no premium for odd-lot market orders.

The following list contains some helpful Internet sites for learning more about stocks:

◆ *Why Invest in Equities?* Site author says historically, investments in common stocks have been superior contributors to building and protecting wealth over the long term. Includes articles on Different Kinds of Stocks and Nine Common Mistakes to Avoid When Investing in Equities.

http://www.prusec.com/whyeq.htm

◆ *Equities Are Performers.* Over the long term, stocks build wealth better than any other investment vehicle. From the Investor Learning Center (Merrill Lynch, Pierce, Fenner & Smith).

http://www.ml.com/investor/ equitperf.html

◆ *Stocks & Commodities.* Trading methods, techniques, and products.

http://www.traders.com

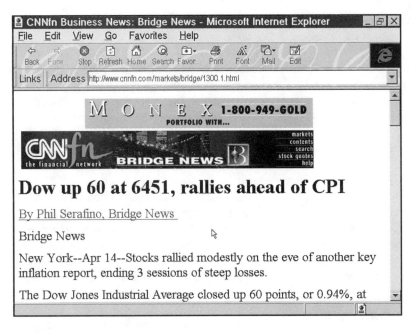

◆ *The Advantage Newsletter.* Sample newsletter from Advantage, an evaluator of emerging or undervalued small-capitalization stocks. Newsletter costs $120 per year.

members.aol.com/schase3367/advantag/ index.htm

◆ *U.S. Stocks.* Analysis, today's closing prices.

http://cnnfn.com/markets/bridge/ 1300.1.html

Bonds

Bonds, no matter who the seller is, are promissory notes. When you "purchase" a bond, the issuer is, in effect, borrowing your money. The bond represents the issuer's agreement to pay you interest over a specified period of time, and return your principal at the end of that period. Some bonds—U.S. Government EE Savings Bonds and zero coupon bonds—do not pay periodic interest.

Bonds are issued by governments and corporations, and as with most investments, bonds carry risk. A few firms, most prominently Moody's Investors Service and Standard & Poor's, offer credit ratings for municipal and corporate bonds.

The greatest risk associated with bonds is inflation and expected interest rate increases. Both factors have a tremendous impact on the resale value of the bond.

Another risk comes with bonds that retain a *call* option, one that gives the issuer the right to buy back the bonds. When that happens, the 20-year high-interest bond you'd been counting on for retirement is withdrawn before maturity, resulting in an unexpected change in the net worth of your investment.

For more information on bonds see the following sections on Corporate Bonds, Municipal Bonds, Government Securities, and Zero Coupon Bonds.

Following are some general bond-related Internet sites of interest:

◆ *Why Invest in Fixed-Income Securities?* Tutorial on bond investing. Includes sections on What a Bond Is, Maturity Dates, Types of Bonds, Why Invest in Bonds?, Advantages of Investing in Fixed-Income Securities, Why Do Bond Prices Change?, and Disadvantages of Investing in Fixed-Income Securities.

   http://www.prusec.com/whyfi.htm

◆ *Bond Market Tutorial.* Another online educational page.

   http://www.danainvestment.com/tutnofrm.html

◆ *Building a Bond Ladder. Portfolio laddering* is a technique to help boost fixed income returns and control risk. It simply means systematically staggering maturities within your portfolio. From the Investor Learning Center (Merrill Lynch, Pierce, Fenner & Smith).

   http://www.ml.com/investor/bondladder.html

Corporate Bonds

Corporate bonds are similar, in most ways, to U.S. government and municipal bonds, except that they don't have the government backing. Last time we

checked, corporations had not been given the power to tax to pay off their debts.

Bondholders have no ownership in the company, and so don't receive dividends or voting rights. The upside is that their investment doesn't depend on the success of the company. Bondholders receive a guaranteed rate of interest, plus the return of their original investment at the end of the specified time period.

There are basically two types of corporate bonds: secured bonds and debentures. *Secured*, as the name implies, are backed by real assets. *Debentures* are secured by the good will of the issuing corporation. A more reliable barometer of the security of a particular bond is the ratings given by Moody's (see Figure 6.2) and Standard & Poor's.

Here are some Internet corporate bond sites of interest:

◆ *Moody's Investors Service.* Independent source of credit ratings, research, and financial information.

   http://www.moodys.com

◆ *Standard & Poor's.* Major rating service for credit and market risk. Provides corporate ratings, financial institutions ratings, insurance ratings, international ratings, public finance ratings, and structured finance ratings.

   http://www.ratings.standardpoor.com
   http://www.bluelist.com/

◆ *Corporate Bonds.* An educational slide show on bonds by a professor at the University of Rochester's Simon School of Business.

   http://www.ssb.rochester.edu/about/fac/schwert/e481bond7.htm

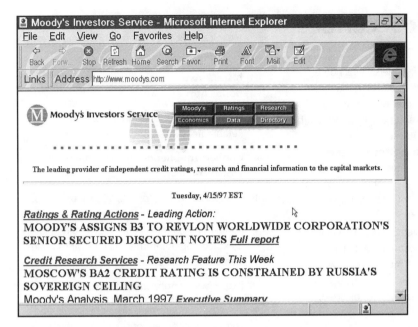

FIG. 6.2

Moody's Investors Service rates bonds.

◆ *The ABCs of Bonds.* Part of an educational series from Vanguard Marketing.

http://www.vanguard.com/educ/module1/ m1_3_2.html

◆ *The Bond Professor's Glossary.* A directory of bond-related terminology.

http://www.bonds-online.com/bpgloss.htm

Municipal Bonds

Municipal bonds are debt certificates issued by local cities and states, usually for the purpose of funding a local government project. Their primary appeal is their tax-free status. Be aware that "tax-free" refers only to federal income taxes; some state and local taxes may still apply. Additionally, should you sell the bonds before maturity, and at a profit, you'll be liable for the capital gains tax.

Following are some Internet municipal bond sites of interest:

◆ *Municipal Bonds.* If you're interested in tax-advantaged investments, municipal bonds may be right for you. Includes articles on What Are Municipal Bonds?, Why Municipal Bonds Make Sense As an Investment, Selecting the Bond That Is Right for You, Types of Municipal Bonds, and Alternative Minimum Tax (AMT).

http://www.prusec.com/muni.htm

◆ *Current Municipal Bond Yields.* Today's municipal bond prices, sponsored by Bloomberg Personal.

http://www.bloomberg.com/markets/ psamuni.html

Government Securities

Government debt securities include savings bonds, treasury bills (known as *T-bills* and having maturities of up to one year), treasury notes (with maturities between one and 10 years), and treasury bonds (with maturities between 10 and 30 years). Other U.S. government agencies issue bonds, notes, debentures, and participation certificates. Modest rates of return are offset by the highest possible form of security: the financial backing of Uncle Sam.

EE savings bonds are convenient, and can be purchased through payroll deductions. The minimum investment is small, and unlike most bonds—which pay out interest in installments—EE savings bonds accrue interest. No payment is received, or taxed, until the bond is cashed in.

Government debt instruments are very liquid. Treasuries can be easily sold on the open market. Savings bonds can be cashed out after six months at 50 percent of their face value, plus whatever interest has accrued. The interest rate credited on a bond cashed prematurely is less than if the bond had been held to maturity. Ironically, the biggest advantage and disadvantage is the same: The unpredictable effects that inflation can have on a long-term instrument.

Here are some Internet sites of interest for U.S. treasuries:

◆ *Current US Treasury Yields.* Compiled by Bloomberg Personal.

http://www.bloomberg.com/markets/ C13.html

◆ *U.S. Treasury Bonds.* Commentary, analysis, technical indicators, charts. By Optima Investment Research.

http://www.oir.com/sample/bonds/ bonds.htm

◆ *Department of the Treasury.* The basics of marketable Treasury securities.

gopher://gopher.gsa.gov/00/staff/pa/cic/ money/t-bills.txt

Internet sites of interest for U.S. EE savings bonds:

◆ *Bureau of the Public Debt.* Bet you didn't know it existed! Great information on savings bonds, Treasury securities and the public debt.

http://www.publicdebt.treas.gov

◆ *Savings Bond Informer.* Hot tip, tax trap, and common misconceptions. Includes other helpful links.

http://www.bondinformer.com/ p0000246.htm

Mutual Funds

In a category by itself is *mutual funds.* Because of the diversified risk, low cost of entry, and ease of management, mutual funds serve small investors well.

A mutual fund is an investment group that uses large sums of investor money to achieve specific goals. It begins as a vision: A fund could be created to invest in the environment, developing economies, or small companies. After the legal work is completed, the fund is ready to accept money from investors. The collected money is invested by a money manager in any of the other investments described in this chapter, in a form consistent with the stated purpose of the fund. Some are aggressive growth funds; they take greater risk. Some are conservative, with little or no risk. Several funds can be found whose investment policies are guided by religious or political principles.

Mutual funds come in two flavors: *load* and *no-load*. All funds charge an administrative fee—it's the way they get paid. The load funds also charge a sort of "admission" fee when you first sign on. Many impartial fund watchers say there's no evidence that the load funds perform any better than their no-load counterparts. Be wary of no-load mutual funds that charge an annual marketing fee, called a 12(b)1. Over a period of years the 12(b)1 could easily exceed any up-front commission.

Additionally, funds come in closed-end and open-end varieties. *Close-ended funds* set a limit on the number of investors they'll admit, on the theory that

economies of scale stop being economical when funds get so big that they can't move without shifting the entire market, creating instability. As might be expected, the creators of open-end funds discount the theory.

The Internet provides a wealth of mutual fund-related information (see Figure 6.3). Here are some Internet sites of interest to mutual fund investors:

◆ *Mutual Funds Online. Mutual Funds* magazine is a leading resource on mutual fund investing. Reports and newsletters are free of charge. Other features require a subscription.

   http://204.242.72.2

◆ *Building Toward an Investment Plan Starting from Scratch.* What kinds of funds can serve as starter funds? Here are two approaches.

   http://www.aaii.org/portfolo/invplan.html

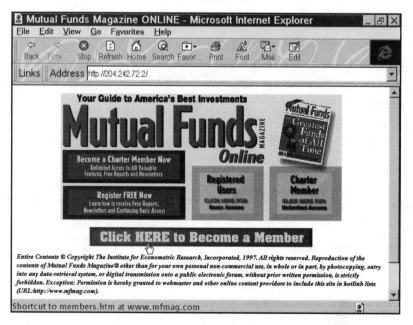

FIG. 6.3

Mutual Funds Online: Use the Internet to research mutual funds.

◆ *The Advantage of No-Load Mutual Funds.* How a mutual fund's fees can reduce your investment return.

**http://www.investorama.com/features/
piazza1.shtml**

◆ *misc.invest.funds FAQ.* Frequently Asked Questions about mutual fund investing.

**http://www.moneypages.com/syndicate/
faq/index.html**

◆ *Morningstar On Demand.* Top mutual fund rating service. Unabridged reports on mutual funds. Search funds by ratings, return, objective, or other factors. Requires downloading free Adobe Acrobat to read files.

**http://www.investools.com/cgi-bin/Library/
msmf.pl**

◆ *A Brief Guide to Closed-End Funds.* Lots of links to well-written educational articles on closed-end funds.

http://www.icefi.com/tutorial

◆ *Funds 101.* Mutual Funds for the New Investor. Brill Editorial Services' Mutual Funds Home Page.

http://www.brill.com/newbie.html

◆ *Getting Started: Investing with Mutual Funds.* The basics of mutual funds, from T. Rowe Price.

**http://www.troweprice.com/mutual/
basics.html**

◆ *Mutual Funds.* Educational site that includes checklist for making a mutual fund decision.

http://www.ml.com/investor/mutual.html

◆ *Investor Education Center Vanguard Mutual Funds.*

**http://www.vanguard.com/educ/
inveduc.html**

◆ *Top U.S. Mutual Funds.* A current ratings list, from Bloomberg Personal.

**http://www.bloomberg.com/markets/
mutual.html**

Index Funds

Index funds seek—quite successfully—to mirror the results of major stock market indexes. The theory is that market indexes have always risen, given enough time, and that following the index is bound to bring continuing rises in the future. Index funds have a low cost of administration because there's no thinking involved. The fund manager simply buys all the stocks included in, say, the Dow Jones Industrial Averages market index, and sits back to watch them move. You could, of course, seek to create your own index portfolio, but most individual investors find it more economical to let a mutual fund do the diversification on their behalf.

Some good Internet sites on index investing include:

◆ *Index Investing versus Active Investing.* Investors need a more disciplined approach to traditional and alternative investments.

**http://www.investorama.com/features/
woodrif1.shtml**

◆ *U.S. Index Movers.* Bloomberg Personal.

**http://www.bloomberg.com/markets/
mover.html**

Alternative Investments

Investments in this category are less celebrated than stocks, bonds, and mutual funds, but they each have advantages—and disadvantages— not found any-where else.

Annuities

An *annuity* is a contract you make with an insurance company or other financial institution, to make regular payments now in exchange for a guaranteed return in the future.

Annuities can be immediate or deferred. With an *immediate annuity*, payment of the agreed-upon return begins immediately after the last payment has been made by you into the annuity. A *deferred annuity* will hold off making payment to you until a predetermined date, such as upon retirement.

Payment can generally be received in one of two ways: a lump sum payment, or in lifelong or limited-period installments.

Some Internet sites of interest for annuities buyers include:

◆ *A Basic Look at Variable Annuity Contracts.* Because of the higher costs associated with annuities, you should first invest as much as you can in regular retirement plans, such as the 401(k), IRA, and Keogh. If you still have money to put away on a tax-sheltered basis, then you can start thinking about a variable annuity.

http://www.aaii.org/insuranc/ varannty.html

◆ *Frequently Asked Questions about Annuities.* CornerStone Financial Products, Inc.

http://www.annuity.com/tsafaq.html

◆ *A Bibliography on Life Insurance and Annuities.* NAIC Research Library. Operated by the National Association of Insurance Commissioners.

http://www.naic.org/products/libr/ sub39.htm

◆ *Why Annuities?* Oval Financial Services.

http://www.groupweb.com/oval/ anuities.htm

◆ *A List of Annuities.* Includes a toll-free number for questions.

http://www.unitedheritage.com/va.htm

Certificates of Deposits

Certificates of deposit are FDIC-insured time depos-its, available from most banks and savings and loans. They're purchased in denominations commonly ranging from as low as $500 to as much as $100,000. The purchase terms for CDs can range from six months to five years.

CDs are a relatively safe way to invest your money. That safety does extract penalties, however. The rate of return for CDs is generally lower than for other investment vehicles. Once your money goes into a CD, it is, for all intents and purposes, locked up for the life of the CD. Interest rates may rise, or fall, while your money is tied up in a CD. While there is the comfort of a guaranteed rate of return with a CD, there's no calculation for missed investment opportunities while your money is tied up in a CD. Early redemption of CDs, while often possible, incurs penalties and significant loss of interest.

Sites of interest for CD investors:

- *Brokered CDs: The Whys and Hows.* About buying CDs through an agent, rather than a bank.

  http://205.129.194.50/bankrate/publ/ tip6a.htm

- *Want to Make More $$$??? Invest in a CD!* Tri County Area Federal Credit Union.

  http://www.tcafcu.org/whatis.html

- *Savings Rates by State.* Current CD and other rates, compiled by Bank Rate Monitor Inc.

  http://205.129.194.50/bankrate/ locdeps.htm

- *CD Rate Sheet.* Wilber National Bank. Compare your locally obtained rates against someone else's rate sheet.

  http://www.wilberbank.com/ratedep.htm

Collectibles

It's possible you could hit pay dirt with grandpa's autographed baseball glove—the one stashed in the garage for decades and last seen on the way to the Salvation Army—but don't count on it. The best and only reason to collect "collectibles" is to enjoy them. There's history and a lot of reminiscing to be found in a deck of baseball cards. The Web is a great hunting ground for sharing information on collectibles (see Figure 6.4). Just don't expect to find your retirement hiding between Willie Mays and Mickey Mantle.

Some Internet sites of interest for collectors include:

- *Dan's Hobby Shop* . Trading Cards plus.

  http://www.fred.net/sports

- *The Art of Collecting Animation Art.* Vintage production art is highly collectible because so little of it exists. An educational site.

  http://www.artmiller.com/animation/ info.htm

- *Dave's Appreciation Of Numismatics.* Graphical Gallery of American Coinage.

  http://www.thewebcorp.com/~daveti/ coins.htm

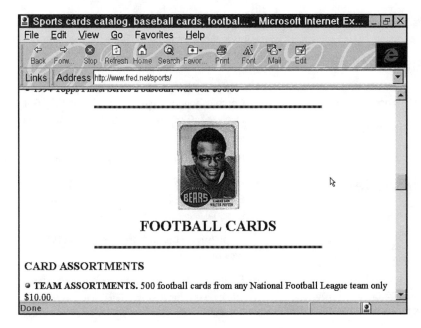

FIG. 6.4

Collectibles are finding a secondary market on the Internet.

Commodities/Futures

If it's useful to somebody, it's a commodity. Oil, corn, wheat, oats, and gold are commodities. The futures market is where commodities are bought and sold, sort of.

Purchasing a commodities future doesn't involve a real exchange of commodities—you won't have to store those barrels of oil in your basement. A *commodity future* is only an agreement to pay for a commodity at a specified time and at a specified price. The commodity future's contract expiration date is dictated by the commodity purchased, harvest time, and so on. Your job, as an investor, is to purchase the commodities future, hope the market price of the commodity rises above what you paid before the contract expires, and sell your commodity future. It's a high-risk game.

Some Internet sites of interest concerning commodities include:

◆ *Answers to Frequently Asked Questions About Trading Commodities.* Easy to read, good background information.

   http://www.lloyd.com/~babcock/q&a.html

◆ *Futures, Options, and Commodities Trading Tutorial.* Wharton Student Network.

   http://journal.wharton.upenn.edu/careers/ibanking/futures.html

◆ *Become a Real-time Commodity Futures Trader.* Excerpts from the acclaimed guide to trading for beginners and experienced investors.

   http://www.investorama.com/features/krieger1.shtml

◆ *Active Futures Contracts.* Prices from Bloomberg Personal.

http://www.bloomberg.com/markets/ future.html

◆ *NY Precious Metals.* Analysis and closing prices.

http://cnnfn.com/markets/bridge/ 2333.1.html

Foreign Currencies

Foreign currencies are a high-risk game for trying to beat the fluctuations in currencies. To play it well requires intimate knowledge of indicators and expectations and events both at home and abroad. Of course, currency investing is a necessary evil if you receive income from offshore business or investments.

You'll get plenty of foreign currency information on the Internet (see Figure 6.5). Some Internet sites of interest to foreign currency buyers include:

◆ *Foreign Exchange Markets: A Brief Tutorial.* Contains foreign exchange articles on Why Get Involved?, Glossary, and Fundamental or Technical Analysis?.

http://all-biz.com/trendway/tutor.htm

◆ *Foreign Currency Exchange Rates.* See how your Eurodollars are faring. Sponsored by Bloomberg Personal.

http://www.bloomberg.com/markets/ wcv.html

◆ *Right on Japan, Wrong on the Yen.* Keep the odds in your favor when making investment decisions.

http://www.investorama.com/features/ delano5.shtml

FIG. 6.5

Research current foreign exchange prices on the Net.

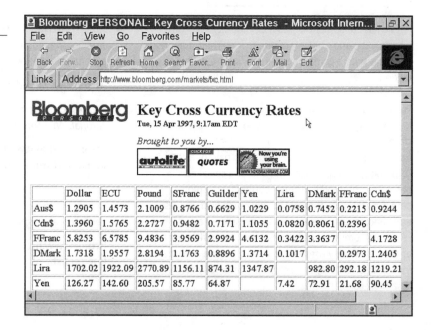

	Dollar	ECU	Pound	SFranc	Guilder	Yen	Lira	DMark	FFranc	Cdn$
Aus$	1.2905	1.4573	2.1009	0.8766	0.6629	1.0229	0.0758	0.7452	0.2215	0.9244
Cdn$	1.3960	1.5765	2.2727	0.9482	0.7171	1.1055	0.0820	0.8061	0.2396	
FFranc	5.8253	6.5785	9.4836	3.9569	2.9924	4.6132	0.3422	3.3637		4.1728
DMark	1.7318	1.9557	2.8194	1.1763	0.8896	1.3714	0.1017		0.2973	1.2405
Lira	1702.02	1922.09	2770.89	1156.11	874.31	1347.87		982.80	292.18	1219.21
Yen	126.27	142.60	205.57	85.77	64.87		7.42	72.91	21.68	90.45

◆ *International Exchange Data.* From Market Broadcasting Corporation.

http://www.fixedincome.com

International Investments

International investing features all the thrills and chills of domestic investing, plus the added risks of fluctuating currency exchange rates and political and economic instabilities. Other risks? A lack of reliable public information, and reduced liquidity.

There is an upside, though. By diversifying across countries, you compensate for the risks of fluctuating economic cycles in the United States.

Foreign corporations wanting to sell securities in the United States must register with the Securities and Exchange Commission (SEC).

Use the Internet to research your offshore investments (see Figure 6.6). Some Internet sites of interest concerning international investments:

◆ *International Equities.* To be truly diversified, you should consider international equity investments.

http://www.prusec.com/intleq.htm

◆ *A Guide to the International Marketplace.* Individual investors are not only following international financial markets, but they are also investing abroad, seeking higher returns and diversification.

http://www.aaii.org/portfolo/intlindx.html

◆ *Global Investing.* Divide up the markets in which you're invested.

http://www.ml.com/investor/global.html

FIG. 6.6

The Internet is a good resource for information on offshore investing.

◆ *International.* Investing outside the borders of the U.S. can be accomplished in several different ways. International investing articles from the American Association of Individual Investors.

http://www.aaii.org/internat

◆ *International Equity.* Foreign investments involve greater risks than U.S. investments. A list of risks, plus a listing of international funds available from Fidelity.

http://personal.fidelity.com/funds/ funds_net/INE.html

◆ *Traps for the Unwary in Foreign Investing.* Good reasons for dealing with a reputable broker when considering overseas investments.

http://www.haledorr.com/publications/ invmgr/1995_08_InvMgrTraps.html

◆ *Micropal.* Offshore Performance tracking.

http://www.iii.co.uk/micropal/index.htm

◆ *Morgan Stanley.* Daily international market updates, news, world stock market performance data for developed-market countries and emerging markets, along with historical graphs going back two years.

http://www.ms.com/mscidata

◆ *T. Rowe Price.* Week-end international market summary, with tutorial section on the basics of international investing.

http://www.troweprice.com/interspot

◆ *World Equity Indices.* Current levels for international stock markets.

http://www.bloomberg.com/markets/ wei.html

Junk Bonds

Why do you think they call it *junk*? Clichés aside, junk bonds, or *high-yield bonds* for the politically correct, offer very high yields in exchange for very high risk.

Following are some Internet sites of interest concerning junk bonds:

◆ *Junk Bonds—They're Baaack.* Surprise! High yield bond funds are back on top.

http://www.investorama.com/features/ tompkin1.html

◆ *Birds in the Hand—Once Again, Junk Has Its Uses.* Feature article from Barron's Online.

http://www.barrons.com/bie/articles/ 19970228/mutual_funds_2.htm

Initial Public Offerings

Much hyped, and highly volatile, *initial public offerings* (IPOs) of new stock have a recent history of shooting sky high at the time of offering, and then dropping hard before leveling out. The phenomenon has been particularly true with technology and Internet-related IPOs. Large investors—and some funds—attempt to take advantage of the bounce.

Here are some IPO Internet sites worth watching:

◆ *IPO Center.* The IPO analysis diary, and IPO resources.

http://nestegg.iddis.com/ipo/

◆ *IPO Central.* Latest SEC information on companies that have filed to go public. No charge.

http://www.ipocentral.com/

Life Insurance

While the names may change and the variations may be many, there are basically two types of life insurance: *term* and *permanent*. Term insurance is the simplest, and generally the cheapest form of insurance. You insure your life for the term of the policy, usually one to 10 years.

Permanent, or whole life, insurance is a combination of term and an investment vehicle. Most legitimate financial planners are vehemently opposed to using insurance as an investment. Not only are returns low, but if you die before the policy terminates, your family loses all the money in the investment portion of your whole life policy, and receives only the face value of the policy. Insurance agents will madly chart and graph and pull rabbits from hats to convince you otherwise, but in virtually every case, a term policy and a completely separate investing program provide superior returns to a whole life policy.

Some educational life insurance sites of interest include:

◆ *Insurance.* An educational site from American Association of Individual Investors. Includes articles on replacing cash value policies, what to look for in a disability income policy, the ABCs of GICs, the use of life insurance for estate, and a life insurance primer.

http://www.aaii.org/insuranc/ insurancindex.html

◆ *How to Avoid Estate Taxes on Life Insurance.* Assuring that proceeds from your life insurance are free from estate taxes.

http://www.investorama.com/features/ frucht2.shtml

Money Markets

Money market funds are generally considered good places to hold your money while trying to decide where to invest. They're basically mutual funds that invest in safer, short-term vehicles such as U.S. Treasury bills and CDs.

There are some potential risks with money market funds. For one thing, they're not insured. If security of principal is a concern, minimize risk with a money market fund that deals in nothing but U.S. Treasury or government securities. There are also the twin risks of inflation and falling interest.

Some Internet money market fund sites of interest:

◆ *Money Market Funds: Advantages, Risks, and Costs.* Includes articles on Describing Money Market Funds and Types of Money Market Funds.

http://www.vanguard.com/educ/module1/ m1_2_2.html

◆ *Money Market Data.* Collected by Market Broadcasting Corporation.

http://www.fixedincome.com

Collateralized Mortgage Obligations (CMOs)

Ginnie and Fannie Maes, and Freddy Macs are a series of mortgage-backed bonds, called *pass-throughs*, and are backed by the federal government.

The pass-throughs are issued by the Government National Mortgage Association, the Federal National Mortgage Association, and the Federal Home Loan Mortgage Corporation, respectively. These are federal agencies, and though technically not a part of the U.S. government, they're secure.

Interestingly, though, these obligations carry a bizarre risk—the risk that homeowners will behave irrationally and pay off their mortgages early, without regard for prevailing interest rates.

To compensate for this risk, the *collateralized mortgage obligation* was invented. Collateralized mortgage obligations are at the safer end of a whole variety of packaged securities known as *derivatives*. These complex securities are collected, divided, reassembled, and split like a deck of cards by brokers who search for common sellable elements among the stacks of mortgages. At this point, of course, CMOs lose their safety, because they become corporate obligations, and stop being government obligations. The risk can be high. Orange County, California, went broke speculating in similarly styled, highly leveraged, derivatives.

Mutual funds are the primary mechanism for individual investors who want to get involved in these securities.

Some Internet sites of interest concerning Ginnie and Fannie Mae, and Freddy Macs, collateralized mortgages, and derivatives in general:

◆ *Who Wins from Derivatives Losses?* To understand who is on the other side of the trade, first you have to understand a little about derivatives.

http://www.turtletrader.com/newspr.html

◆ *Mortgage-Backed Securities.* Contains answers to these questions: What Are Mortgage-Backed Securities? Who Issues Mortgage-Backed Securities? How Safe Are Investments in Mortgage-Backed Securities? What Market Risks Are Involved in Mortgage-Backed Securities?

http://www.prusec.com/mbs.htm

◆ *Collateralized Mortgage Obligations.* History, explanation of how CMOs work.

http://www.barra.com/ResearchPub/ BarraPub/cmo-n.html

◆ *CMOs.* Definitions, characteristics, yields, models, the problem with prepayments.

http://www.firstinstitutional.com/about/ cmo/index.htm

◆ *Experts' Corner.* What happened in Orange County, and why you need to be careful with derivatives.

http://nestegg.iddis.com/nestegg/may95/ expert.html

Options

When buying options, you're not really purchasing stocks or bonds, and you're not placing money in an account to grow interest. You're not making a commitment to buy in the future. What you are doing with an option is buying the *right* to buy or sell a specified stock, at a specified price, within a specified time frame. Should you decide not to buy or sell within the option's lifetime—for instance if you guessed wrong about the direction of the particular stock's value—then the option simply expires and is of no value. Money paid for the option is lost.

On the other hand, if you guess correctly you own the right to buy (or *call*) expensive stock at a very cheap price, or dump your losing stock (*put*) at a high price. Options are traded on many stock exchanges, and on the Chicago Board Options Exchange.

Some Internet sites of interest to options buyers are as follows:

◆ *Barron's Online—March 10, 1997*. Options perk up on talk of takeover. Register first. It's free.

http://www.barrons.com/bie/articles/ 19970307/the_striking_price.htm

◆ *The Chicago Board Options Exchange*. Full of educational materials, from beginner to expert.

http://www.cboe.com/intro/whatis.html

◆ *Minneapolis Grain Exchange*. What options are, and how they function.

http://www.mgex.com/why/ shrimpcost2.html

Real Estate Investment Trusts

Set up like mutual funds, *real estate investment trusts* (REIT) buy and manage real estate and finance real estate construction projects.

Some Internet sites of interest concerning real estate investment trusts:

◆ *REIT Fever Cools as Analysts' Ardor Fades*. Barron's Online. Requires no-cost registration.

http://www.barrons.com/bie/articles/ 19970110/in_the_know.htm

◆ *What is a REIT?* Definition and legal requirements.

http://www.frk.com/properties/ prop028.html

Zero Coupon Bonds

Zero coupon bonds are an invention of the '80s. A different way to issue standard treasury, corporate, U.S. agency, and municipal bonds, zeros are basically bonds without the periodic interest payments. The name derives from the practice of ripping off a coupon from traditional bonds to redeem the periodic interest.

In exchange for foregoing the interest, you get to buy at a deep discount. At the end of the period, you receive the entire face value of the bond, generally $1,000. When you purchase zero-coupon bonds, you know on the day you buy them exactly what your investment will be worth at maturity.

Following are some Internet sites of interest for zero coupon bonds:

◆ *Zero Coupon Bonds.* The inherent predictability of zero coupon bonds makes them an excellent vehicle to use when saving for a college education or retirement planning.

http://www.prusec.com/zero.htm

◆ *Cash Flo.* Zero coupon bonds are ideal for funding a specific goal, such as a child's college education, your own graduate school tuition, or buying a house. A Q&A on zeros from Women's Wire.

http://www.women.com/wwire/archives/ html/qacash/951206.qa.cas.html

◆ *Making the Most of Zeros.* Zeros are simple, but their tax treatment isn't. From Deloitte & Touche OnLine.

http://www.dtonline.com/pfa/zeros.htm

7

Use Expert Research Resources

"Knowledge is power.

Spend time every day at a

few of these research sites

for financial news."

What do the experts think? How has a particular company, bond, or mutual fund performed in the last year, two years, or five years? While a book can't tell you what to buy, or when to buy it, we can tell you where to find this information on the Internet. In this chapter, we'll concentrate in areas where most of the compilation of data has been done for you.

Online Business and Finance Publications

Traditional newsstand publications have joined the World Wide Web in a big way. Almost all of them feature impressive graphics, grabber headlines, and a variety of information tools unavailable in a print media.

The content—and purpose—of the feature publications' Web pages vary. Some are complete online versions of the newsstand issue. Others present selected feature articles and a regular column or two. Most offer some sort of database search, allowing you to access previously published articles.

Look for other services as well. Many sites offer 15-minute delayed stock quotes, newsletters, and even public bulletin boards.

The most exciting aspect of online publications is probably their ability to publish news stories as they develop. This is the media that has been dreamed of for years: the immediacy of television combined with the kind of in-depth reporting available, previously, only from a newspaper. It's an Internet-only reality.

The paradox of writing about online publications in a traditional (print) medium is that they can, and will, change. To attempt a critical rating of dynamic Internet publications from a static (although we prefer to think of it as *stable*) format is futile and a bit unfair. If there's something we don't like, the chances are pretty good that somebody else won't like it either. And in an environment such as the Internet, where rapid change is not only a possibility but a necessity, site features—especially those proving unpopular—will change.

What this chapter does do is tell you where the sites are located, and highlight the features being offered now. In addition, we'll further break down the online business and finance publications into four categories: feature publications, news publications, newsletters, and electronic-only publication sites.

As you explore online resources, be sure to look for the features described in the following sections.

Online Archive Searches

One of the most useful forms of research is the capacity to look back and examine the history of a particular situation. All of the major financially oriented online publications offer some form of archival searching. The amount of data available, and the extent to which it goes back in time, varies from publication to publication.

Online Stock Quotes

Several online publications offer delayed stock quotes. Delays average 15 minutes. Many offer this service free to registered users.

Reports

Most of the financial Web sites provide reports. Updates can range from monthly to weekly, daily, or even continuously. Most common are the performance reports for stocks, bonds, mutual funds, and other investment vehicles.

Feature Publications

In this section, feature publications are defined as those that made their reputation on the magazine stand.

Different publications have approached this move to the Web in different ways. They range from offering just a few highlights to creating an entire publication with interactive and real-time features never before possible.

Some of the familiar faces you'll find on the Web include:

◆ *Barron's Online*. Flash with substance. *Barron's* Online (see Figure 7.1) offers editorial perspective along with an impressive list of user services. Delayed stock quotes, company performance reports, daily performance reports on stocks, bonds, interest, and exchange rates.

There's a searchable archive of previous editions of *Barron's* Online.

http://www.barrons.com

◆ *Business Week*. On the surface, *Business Week* appears to be just like its magazine rack twin. Underneath, however, it's loaded with the sort of online features just not available to print. Regular features include a late-breaking news column, 15-minute delayed quotes, and two archive areas. One features stories compiled in logical groupings by the editor; the other incorporates a search tool looking back 20-plus months.

http://www.businessweek.com

◆ *The Economist*. *The Economist* is a British publication known for cutting right to the bone of an issue with a definite point of view. Non-committal objectivity is just not *The Economist's* style. The magazine was just beginning to get

its feet wet on the Web as this text was being written. The site currently consists of selected articles from the latest edition. There is a searchable archive of past articles. Expanded offerings are promised for the future.

http://www.economist.com

◆ *Financial World*. America's oldest financial magazine cuts a new figure on the Web. Regular features include The Corporate News, Investment Advisor, Bank Rankings, and a 15-minute delay stock quote page. The archive includes recent cover stories (four issues back when we looked) as well as regular features "At The Close" and "From the Editor."

http://www.financialworld.com/home.htm ✓

◆ *Forbes*. Unlike the *Forbes* purchased at your favorite newsstand, Forbes online comes with a cyberspace twist: Its news stories are updated

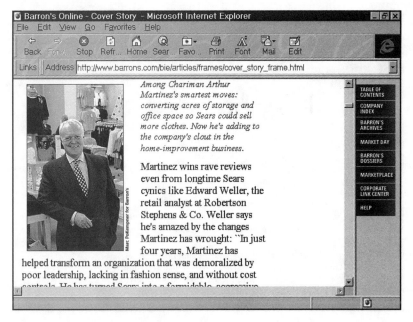

FIG. 7.1

Barron's Online: A premier site for company analysis.

daily. Regular features include the Gilder Tech Report, Fact and Comments, and Forbes FYI. Back issues of Forbes are available dating back to the first online publication. Don't forget to mark your place in Forbes' List of the 400 Richest People in America.

http://www.forbes.com

◆ *Fortune.* Next on the list is *Fortune* magazine. Online-only extras include *Fortune's* featured columnist, business reports, and, of course, the Fortune 500 database. Fortune Forum provides a public forum for posting comments or questions. A search engine allows readers to search by topic for information. The search can be limited to Fortune only or can be expanded to include other Web sites.

http://www.pathfinder.com/fortune

◆ *Kiplinger Online.* From the people who bring you the *Kiplinger Letter* comes Kiplinger Online

(see Figure 7.2). This is an easy-to-use no-nonsense page. Regular sections include News of the Day, Stock Quotes, Top Funds, Retirement Advice, and Business Forecast. Samples of the *Kiplinger Letter* are available. Also buried in the main menu is *Kiplinger's Personal Finance Magazine,* featuring the current month's cover stories. An article archive search is available.

http://www.kiplinger.com

◆ *Money Online.* Money Online may be brought to you by the folks from *Money* magazine, but it looks and feels like it was made for the Internet. Regular items include stock quotes, portfolio news, Money Daily, and Money Business Reports. Money Goals has six subheadings: Investing, Saving/Borrowing, Retirement, Home, College, and Taxes. Each subheading features targeted articles and subject-relevant operator interaction features.

http://www.pathfinder.com/money

FIG. 7.2

Kiplinger's personal finance section is packed with useful information.

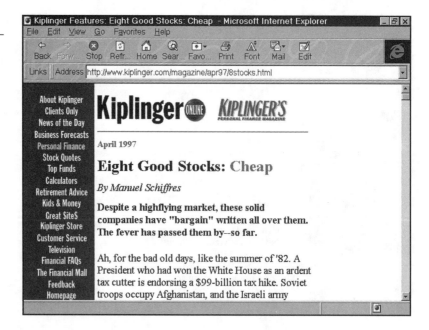

◆ *Mutual Funds Online.* Mutual funds, and nothing but mutual funds. That is the best way to describe *Mutual Fund* magazine and the best way to describe this site. It's about achieving your financial goals through mutual funds. It's about finding the safest mutual fund, the best performing mutual fund, and pretty much everything else concerning mutual funds. An archive of past issues, going back two-plus years, is available. Full access requires a $5 monthly subscription fee.

http://www.mfmag.com

◆ *Electronic Publishing.* Academic journals containing information of interest to economists and anyone who needs to be smart about the economy. There's even a section on Jokes About Economists.

**http://www.finweb.com/
finweb.html#Publish**

News Publications

News publications, formerly known as newspapers, were once famed for their text-based format, fish-wrapping capacity, and lack of gloss appeal. Not anymore. The business pages from the world's leading papers are now available to anyone on the planet.

◆ *Financial Times.* This London paper has long been unavailable to Just Folks. Stop by for international business, economic, and political news. Includes closing prices for shares and managed funds, discussion groups, Your Views, and Eagle Eye.

http://www.ft.com/

◆ *Investor's Business Daily.* The *Investor's Business Daily* is presented in an easy-to-read, easy-to-navigate format (see Figure 7.3). Feature stories are grouped by Inside Today, Front Page, Executive Update, Computers & Technology, The Economy, The Market, and Vital Signs.

http://www.investors.com

◆ *Los Angeles Times.* Feature stories on personal and corporate finance, with access to Hoover's Company Capsules and Quote.com.

http://www.latimes.com/home/business

◆ *New York Times.* National business stories, with search tool to locate older articles. Free, but requires registration.

**http://www.nytimes.com/yr/mo/day/
business**

◆ *San Jose Mercury News.* Leading source of business news on technology companies.

http://www.mercurynews.com/business

◆ *USA Today/USA Today Financial Marketplace.* *USA Today* online is presented in the same high gloss that you've come to expect in the print version. Accessible to online browsers is the Money section. Sub-sections worth looking at in USA Today's Money section are Moneyline, Stock Quotes, Market Indexes, Dow 30, Industry Groups, and Global Markets. The USA Today Financial Marketplace offers additional links to live quotes and other service providers.

The front page: **http://www.usatoday.com**

The Financial Marketplace: **http://
www.usatoday.com/marketpl/resource.htm**

◆ *Wall Street Journal Interactive.* Designed for the World Wide Web, *Wall Street Journal Interactive*

FIG. 7.3

A top investment newspaper goes online.

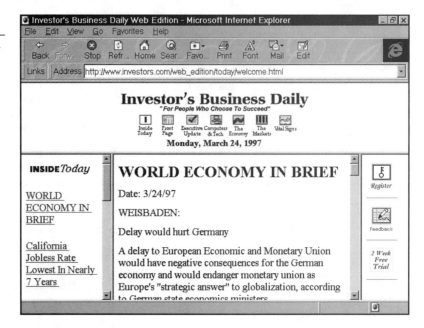

(see Figure 7.4) is a subscriber-based, business-oriented news publication. Featured departments in the interactive *Wall Street Journal* include Front Section, Marketplace, and Money and Investing. Global news stories are updated continuously. An interesting feature of this site is Personal Journal. It allows users to personalize their news and stock presentations. The annual subscription is $49.

http://www.wsj.com

◆ *All the Rest*. Listings for every known newspaper in the world, compiled by journalists at *Editor and Publisher*.

**http://www.mediainfo.com/ephome/
npaper/nphtm/online.htm**

Newsletters

Newsletters are small focused publications. In spite of their name, they tend to be oriented more toward analysis than hard-breaking news. They're included here not so much for reference features but for their educational value.

◆ *Hulbert Financial Digest*. Here's a newsletter focused on…newsletters. The *Hulbert Financial Digest* tracks the performance of the more than 170 investment newsletters and the portfolios it recommends. The cost of a one year subscription is normally $135; however, Internet subscribers can get a discount rate of $59 for the first year.

http://cybersurfing.com/hfd

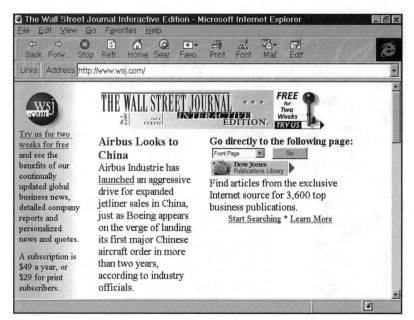

FIG. 7.4

One of the few profitable sites on the Internet, the *Wall Street Journal Interactive* attracts paying subscribers.

◆ *INVESTools*. The INVESTools mission is to provide high quality independent financial research materials. INVESTools covers the editorial content of over 400 newsletters with research reports covering more than 10,000 securities. Cost for INVESTool newsletters range from $49 to $249 per year.

http://www.investools.com

◆ *Investors Newsletter Digest*. Similar to INVESTools, the *Digest* compiles investment news and advice from other publications, and lists recommendations. Twelve issues cost $100, but free samples are available online.

http://www.investorsnews.com

◆ *Money Talks*. Financial journalists produce regular columns, feature articles on investment topics (see Figure 7.5). Free access.

http://www.talks.com

◆ *Stock Manager's Investment Report*. Low-risk philosophy: A belief in the creation of personal wealth based upon long-term investing in relatively low-risk stocks and dramatically reducing transaction fees. Lots of free information on the site, but the newsletter itself costs $25 per year.

http://www.lbfinc.com

◆ *Zacks On-line Magazine*. Financial matters for the novice investor. Good educational materials cover the fundamentals of investing.

http://www.zacks.com/magazine/ index.html

FIG. 7.5

Quality editorial, and free access, make Money Talks a prime newsletter site.

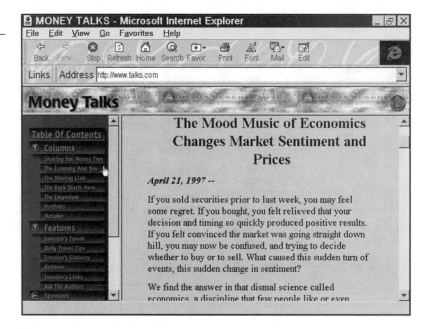

Electronic-Only Collections

These sites are an eclectic mixture of databases, editorial material, educational information, and advice. They have no print counterpart.

◆ *Bloomberg Personal.* A very large site focusing on all aspects of financial planning (see Figure 7.6). Includes news, financial analysis, sports, weather—even a lottery scoreboard. You can listen to Bloomberg News Radio as you work.

http://www.bloomberg.com

◆ *CNNfn Financial Network.* Regularly updated business and financial news from CNN—yes, the same folks who brought you the Gulf War.

You'll find it just as timely in your personal financial war.

http://www.cnnfn.com

◆ *Dun and Bradstreet.* What don't these guys know about business? Get profiles on millions of companies for $20 apiece.

http://www.dnb.com

◆ *EDGAR Online.* Surprisingly nice, for a government site. Uncover corporate reports filed with the Securities and Exchange Commission.

http://www.sec.gov/edgarhp.htm

◆ *E*TRADE's Web Resources List.* Well-organized extensive list of additional investment resources on the Web, but it's available only to E*TRADE account holders (see Figure 7.7).

http://swww.etrade.com/cgi-bin/cgitrade/webresources

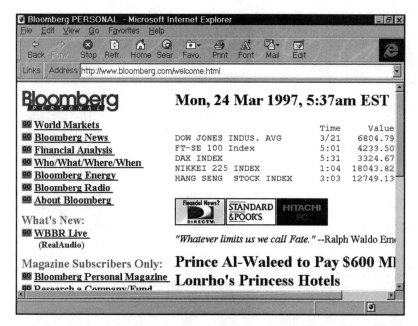

FIG. 7.6

Bloomberg's Web page is packed with investment advice.

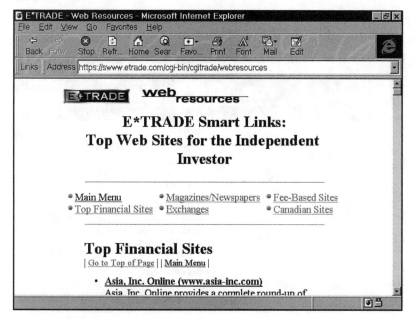

FIG. 7.7

E*TRADE's resource list is extensive.

◆ *Hoover's Online*. Hoovers is a subscription site, but there's plenty of good, free, information worth viewing. Company reports, quotes, charts, IPO Central, and corporate Web sites are all accessible through Hoovers.

http://www.hoovers.com

◆ *Microsoft Investor*. Contests, investment advice, daily market summaries, along with the usual lineup of quotes, portfolio management, and charts (see Figure 7.8).

http://investor.msn.com/contents.asp

◆ *Motley Fool*. Calling themselves fools doesn't make it so. These investors have a strategy. The trendy Motley Fool investment site has some very solid investment advice, and don't miss the 13 Steps to Investing Foolishly.

http://www.fool.com

◆ *MSNBC*. You heard about it on television; now it's right there on the Web. MSNBC brings you up-to-the-minute news from around the globe.

http://www.msnbc.com

◆ *Pawws Financial Network*. Large site with plenty of in-depth information. Features include News & Commentary, Market Analysis, and Advisory Services. Registration is free.

http://www.pawws.com

◆ *The Pristine Day Trader*. Stock picks for day traders and other frequent investors. Includes educational materials, other links, quotes, and graphs. Two-week free trial, but after that, subscriptions are expensive.

http://www.pristine.com

FIG. 7.8

Microsoft's popular investor area provides valuable news analysis, among its other features.

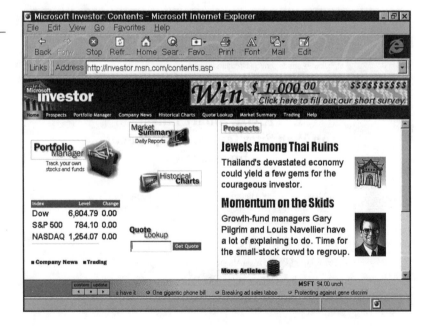

◆ *Quote.com*. Best online financial news source. Pulls stories from top financial publications. Search by headline, by topic, or by source.

http://www.quote.com/news/index.html

◆ *Reuters Money Network*. Features breaking news stories from around the world (see Figure 7.9). Also includes quotes, company news, business news, and indices.

http://www.moneynet.com

◆ *Smart Money*. The Wall Street Journal Magazine of Personal Business doesn't have a lot of material online, yet, but they're planning a consumer site for fall.

http://www.dowjones.com/smart

◆ *Stock Research Group*. Top stories, humor, Hot Companies list, and an Analyst Corner for undervalued high growth stocks.

http://www.stockgroup.com

◆ *Thompson MarketEdge*. Investment tools, analysis, commentary, market monitor, bulletin boards, and question-and-answer sessions. Subscriptions are $7.95 a month.

http://www.marketedge.com

◆ *Zacks Investment Research*. This huge financial site provides everything, even an online bookstore (see Figure 7.10).

http://www.zacks.com

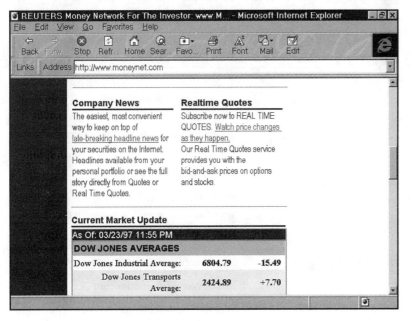

FIG. 7.9

Good statistical and analytical material is available from Reuters.

FIG. 7.10

Zacks: Everything you're looking for.

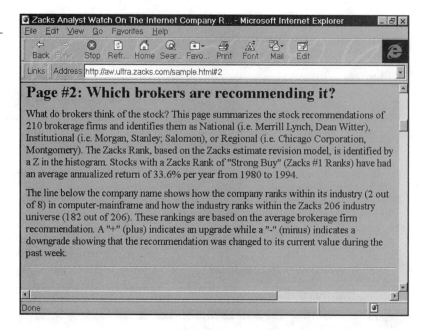

Page #2: Which brokers are recommending it?

What do brokers think of the stock? This page summarizes the stock recommendations of 210 brokerage firms and identifies them as National (i.e. Merrill Lynch, Dean Witter), Institutional (i.e. Morgan, Stanley; Salomon), or Regional (i.e. Chicago Corporation, Montgomery). The Zacks Rank, based on the Zacks estimate revision model, is identified by a Z in the histogram. Stocks with a Zacks Rank of "Strong Buy" (Zacks #1 Ranks) have had an average annualized return of 33.6% per year from 1980 to 1994.

The line below the company name shows how the company ranks within its industry (2 out of 8) in computer-mainframe and how the industry ranks within the Zacks 206 industry universe (182 out of 206). These rankings are based on the average brokerage firm recommendation. A "+" (plus) indicates an upgrade while a "-" (minus) indicates a downgrade showing that the recommendation was changed to its current value during the past week.

Push the News

Is all this Web surfing just too much trouble? If you'd rather skip the surf and get your news delivered directly to your desk, take a look at the newest Internet invention, Push Technology. Push involves downloading a piece of (free, usually) software that intermittently calls up your Internet provider, downloads the news, and displays it on your screen—all without any help at all from you. Each push technology site uses its own software client, the screen that displays the news. Like TV, you'll be able to pick from various "channels" to get the news you're interested in. Like cable, some of the news is free, and some of it comes from subscription-based "premium" channels.

Here are some of the best Push Technology providers.

◆ *BackWeb*. An offering of 40 some channels—including finance, items of local interest, computing, software, general news, and technology news.

http://www.backweb.com

◆ *FreeLoader*. Personalized news from about 600 information sources. The premium channels feature MSNBC, Pathfinder, ZD Net, SportsLine, and Quicken Financial Network. Also includes FreeLoader Daily, an inside look at Web culture.

http://www.freeloader.com

◆ *Intermind Communicator*. A growing list of some 200 channels categorized into arts and entertainment; business, computers, and Internet; health and science; news and politics;

retail and shopping; society and culture; and sports, travel, and leisure.

http://www.intermind.com

◆ *PointCast*. Operates on the commercial network model, with commercial advertisers footing the bill. PointCast provides free news, stock information, industry updates, weather, and sports from CNN, CNNfn, *Time*, *People*, and *Money* Magazines, Reuters, PR Newswire, BusinessWire, Sportsticker, and Accuweather.

http://pioneer.pointcast.com ✓ ✓

8

Investigate the Markets

> "All the stock market news, analysis, and summary you need is located on the Internet."

One approach to making investment decisions is to hang out at the water cooler and ask the people at work what they think of various stocks. The better approach, of course, is to conduct a little research.

That doesn't necessarily mean running down to the county library to make armfuls of photocopies. You'll find a wealth of research information, much of it free, on the Internet.

In this chapter, we describe places to find all the background information you'll need to do a thorough analysis of the securities that interest you. In Chapter 16 and subsequent chapters, we show you how to compile and analyze the data you find here.

This chapter covers three levels of research: individual companies, whole industries, and the entire economy, including individual securities markets.

Individual Companies

A few years back your dentist would've pulled an eyetooth—yours no doubt—to get data you can find on the Internet today for free. All you need is a functioning computer, Internet access, and a place to put your feet up. It's time to do some research. We start by looking at information on individual companies.

Quotes Online

Stock and securities quotes come in two varieties: the *delayed quote*, usually available 15 or 20 minutes late, and the *real-time quote*. The first comes free; the second will cost you.

The Delayed Quote

As white bread and pasteurized milk have become staples in the American kitchen, the free, slightly delayed online stock quote has become a fixture of the Internet. Virtually every commercial site on the Web now offers some sort of stock quote service—even, we're told, *Playboy* magazine. Not that either of the authors of this book has ever looked, mind you.

So what's to distinguish any of the services? Well, they're not all exactly the same. Some sites offer far more features than others.

All the sites we'll list offer, at a minimum, a 20-minute delayed stock quote service and the ability to search for stock symbols by company name. Here, we concentrate our focus on Web sites that are financially oriented, and leave the **www.playboy.com** offering for someone else to, er, cover. (For a quick refresher on reading stock quotes, see Chapter 4, "Educate Yourself About Investing.")

◆ *Check Free Investment Services.* From Check Free Investment Services, formerly Security APL. Stock quotes are delayed 15 minutes. Links to subscriber-only resources, along with Market Watch, a running report of the day's market activity, and a few slow-loading financial calculators. Features: symbol lookup, 5 quotes/request, hyperlinked glossary (click any term in the quote for an explanation), 18 elements per quote. Notable feature: lists the number of

trades, an indication of how widely traded a stock is. Rating: A-

http://qs.secapl.com/cgi-bin/qs

◆ *DBC Online.* Data Broadcasting Corporation (see Figure 8.1). Stock quotes are delayed 15 minutes. This site also features links to news and commentary. Free registration allows users access to an investors online live-talk area called *Stock Chat*. Features: symbol lookup, hyperlinked glossary, 23 elements per quote, plus dozens of additional data items in other views. Notable features: Tick (indicating most recent direction of trading), links to corporate home page, dividend dates. Rating: A.

http://www.dbc.com

◆ *E*TRADE.* Stock quotes are delayed 20 minutes. The site offers free quotes for visitors and a demonstartion of the E*TRADE online trading process. In addition there is the The E*TRADE Game, the ultimate what-if game for market players. E*TRADE customers can view quotes for six companies at a time and link directly to late-breaking news, charts, and research. Features: symbol lookup, 18 elements per quote. Notable feature: high/low dates. Rating: A.

**http://www.etrade.com/visitor/
quotes.shtml**

◆ *PC Quote.* Stock quotes are delayed 20 minutes. The information provided with the quotes is extensive. It includes 52-week highs and lows, a volatility rating, dividend information, P/E ratio, yield, and the number of outstanding shares. Additional subscriber-only services are available. Quote display is badly designed, but it provides a lot of data. Features: symbol lookup, 23 elements per quote, plus dozens of additional data

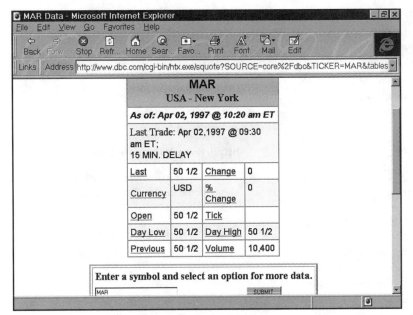

FIG. 8.1

Delayed quotes provide near-immediate feedback.

items in other views. Notable features: Size of last trade, hyperlink to recent company news, charting tools. Rating: A-.

http://www.pcquote.com

◆ *Quicken Financial Network.* Stock quotes are delayed 15 minutes. A graph option displays how a selected stock has performed over the last 30 days. Other areas include Mutual Fund Market Manager and the Equities Center. Mildly confusing initial interface. Features: symbol lookup, charts, hyperlinked glossary, 16 elements per quote (some combined). Notable feature: Option to link quote to a portfolio manager. (See Chapter 16, "Track Your Portfolio," for more on portfolio management.) Rating: A-.

http://quotes.galt.com

◆ *Quote.Com.* Stock quotes are delayed at least 15 minutes. Quotes for bonds, futures and options, and mutual funds are available to registered users. Portfolio, news, and research sites are available for a 30-day free trial. Unattractive, unhelpful opening page. Features: symbol lookup, multiple quotes, 12 elements per quote, hyperlink to company news (by subscription). Notable feature: Retrieve a variety of charts. Rating: B-.

http://www.quote.com

◆ *StockMaster.* Quotes are delayed 20 minutes. Features: Top stocks, symbol lookup. Notable feature: Mutual fund quotes, historical price charts.

http://www.stockmaster.com

◆ *Yahoo!* Yahoo!, yes, Yahoo! of Web search fame, is also an excellent source for stock quotes. Quotes are delayed 20 minutes. Features: Symbol lookup, 16 elements per quote, automatic chart display, limited company news links. Notable features: Company profile, SEC filings, and research on buy/sell recommendations. Rating: A.

http://quote.yahoo.com

The Here-and-Now Quote

For some people, a 15-minute delay in stock quotes is just too slow. If you're an active trader, buying and selling throughout the day in hopes of making small but instant profits, you need your quotes immediately. You're in luck. Many of the sites previously listed also offer real-time quotes—for a fee, of course. One of the most popular is *PCQuote*, with an annual subscription fee ranging as high as $2,500, or even more, for very specialized services.

The following sites provide real-time quotes.

◆ *MarketSmart*. Real-time quote service. PCQuote provides the service for free, but the exchanges charge a small subscription fee. Subscribe to combined U.S. equities (AMEX, NASDAQ, and NYSE) and options for $13.50 a month. Fees for other exchanges are as high as $88 a month.

http://www.pcquote.com/ ms/msrates.html

◆ *Market Watch*. DBC's real-time quote source. Monthly $29.95 fee includes NYSE, AMEX, and NASDAQ quotes, portfolio manager, real-time financial news, sports scores, and more.

http://mw.dbc.com

◆ *InterQuote*. Streaming tick-by-tick quotes at an annual fee of $629.95.

http://www.interquote.com

◆ *TeleQuote Web*. Canadian-based service with international quotes. Real-time quotes at $19.25 a month.

http://www.telequote.com

The Quote's in the Mail

There are alternatives to going online and clicking buttons. There's the daily paper, of course—but perhaps you really want something a little more focused. After all, very few people own a piece of all the hundreds of securities listed there, and many news stories are irrelevant when it comes to your portfolio.

Naturally, there's an Internet answer. Newsletter publishers can tailor an e-mail newsletter to your exact specifications. Receive only the news you're interested in. Quote delivery services, which also provide their services via e-mail, limit their offerings to e-mail quotes.

◆ *Closing Bell*. Closing Bell is a free e-mailing service from Mercury Mail (see Figure 8.2). Receive news stories and closing prices for the market indices, mutual funds, and securities you select. E-mailed stories are edited for brevity. Hyperlinking within the e-mail document lets you link to the full story area on the Mercury Mail Web site.

http://www.merc.com/main/cgi/
main_merc.cgi

◆ *End of Day*. InterQuote provides end-of-day quotes by e-mail, at an annual fee of $45.

http://www.interquote.com/packages.html

Company Reports

Company Reports provide background information on the stock prices, history, yields, and other data for individual corporations. Look to these reports for background information before investing in a particular stock.

◆ *E*TRADE's Company Profiles from BASELINE*. Available at no cost to E*TRADE subscribers (see Figure 8.3). Enter the stock symbol (and there's a tool to find the symbols if you don't already know) for any of about 7,000 publicly traded companies, and view a profile that includes Closing Price, Price Changes, Dividend Yield, Price/earnings Ratios, Investor Relations Contact Information, One-year Chart of Price Actions, Capitalization (LT Debt to Total Cap, Owned by Institutions, Market Capitalization, Average Daily Volume) Earnings, Revenues, Dividends, Key Ratios and Measures (P/E, Price to Book, Price to Cash Flow, Price to Sales, and Return on Equity), Beta and a Business Overview.

https://swww.etrade.com/cgi-bin/cgitrade/baseline

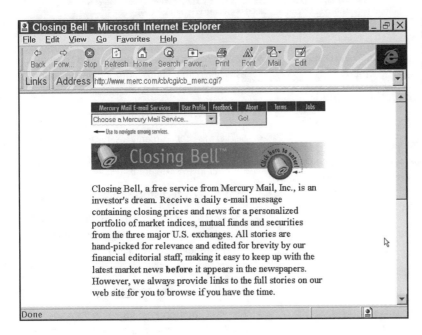

FIG. 8.2

Sign up with an e-mail service to have custom quotes delivered.

FIG. 8.3

Company reports give good background information.

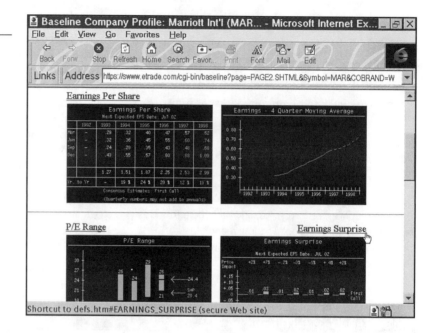

- ◆ *E*TRADE's Dividend & Split Data.* Review Dividend Announcements by Stock Symbol.

  https://swww.etrade.com/cgi-bin/cgitrade/dividend

- ◆ *Hoover's Online.* Short company profiles on more than 10,000 companies, both public and private. The site includes Web links, wherever available, to listed companies. Two thousand extended profiles are available for a fee.

  http://www.hoovers.com

- ◆ *Money Magazine.* Features the Hoover 100, taken from the Hoover 2,000. These are profiles of the 100 largest companies in the United States.

  http://www.pathfinder.com/@@0fJBvwQA1sA*Z07E/money/hoovers/corpdirectory/pf_ml.html

- ◆ *Research: Magazine.* Features free S&P reports, as well as other sources of fundamental information. Free registration is required.

  http://www.researchmag.com

- ◆ *Silicon Investor.* Primarily a service for investors interested in technology stock, but includes links to other investor-related sites.

  http://www.techstocks.com

- ◆ *The Wall Street Research Net.* A directory of information. Look up a company by name or ticker symbol. Provides online links to related information sources.

  http://www.wsrn.com

- ◆ *The Wall Street Journal's Briefing Books.* A graphics-oriented source of corporate overviews of companies.

  http://interactive.wsj.com

◆ *Thomson MarketEdge*. For a fee, although the first month is free, you can access fundamental information including comprehensive company reports.

http://www.marketedge.com

◆ *Zack's EPS Surprises*. Complimentary Earnings Per Share Surprise Service. The top positive surprises and the bottom negative surprises for today.

http://www.ultra.zacks.com/cgi-bin/AW/ EPS/Extreme

◆ *FDIC*. Information on the banking industry and specific institutions.

http://www.fdic.gov

◆ *PR Newswire*. Breaking stories and immediate news from industries and individual corporations worldwide.

http://www.prnewswire.com

◆ *Industry Briefing*. Each day Reuters focuses on breaking news from a different industry.

http://www.reuters.com/briefing

Industry News and Analysis

Another factor in your buy/sell decisions should be the overall health of the industry you're buying into. Prices for industries as a whole respond to reports of new regulation, lawsuits, inventions, and other factors. For example, concerns over potential lawsuits caused tobacco-industry stocks to drop. At about the same time, prices for biotechnology stocks rose on interest in genetic cloning.

Industry News

Don't be sheepish. Double your store of information with the breaking industry news found on these Web sites. No cloning around.

◆ *Yahoo! on the Money*. Two weeks' worth of financial news, categorized by industry (see Figure 8.4).

http://biz.yahoo.com/industry

FIG. 8.4

Read industry news to anticipate market movements.

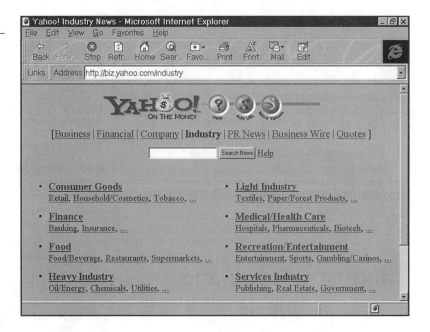

Industry Analysis

The following sites offer commentary on industry-wide issues. Rather then letting someone convince you that "plastics" is the future, do some checking on your own. Many investors in eight-track tape players and 50-pound portable computers will tell you they wish someone had shown them the hand-writing on the wall.

◆ *E*TRADE's Sector Ratings.* Analysis of various industries, available only to E*TRADE customers. Includes Household Products, Aerospace, Precious Metals, Health Care, Oilfield Equipment, Steel, and Securities—Brokerage, Pharmaceutical, and Computer Networking (see Figure 8.5).

https://swww.etrade.com/cgi-bin/cgitrade/bcomsectorframe

◆ *Where to Invest.* Analysis, stock picks, and libraries sorted by industry. Streetnet also features links to Black & Company, a bank and securities brokerage firm in the Pacific Northwest, and Van Kasper, a California brokerage firm. Both firms offer analysis and their current list of top stock picks.

Feature stories: **http://www.streetnet.com/features/home.html**

Research site: **http://www.streetnet.com/research/home.html**

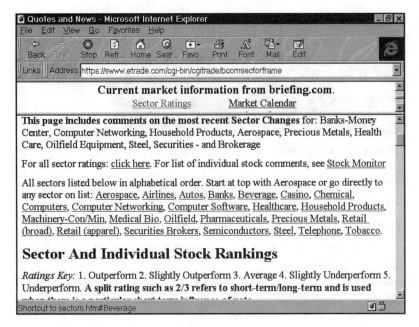

FIG. 8.5

Analysis services do the work for you.

Economic and Market Trends

Tracking current trend indicators and revisiting past trends and indicators is the best way to project where the market is heading—tea leaves and crystal balls excepted.

◆ *AAII - Economic Indicators.* An educational site from the American Association of Independent Investors on the importance of tracking leading indicators, monetary indicators, and the Federal Reserve's movements.

http://www.aaii.org/refer/econindc.html

Economic News and Indicators

All those leading economic indicators—unemployment figures, consumer price index, factory orders, and all the rest—actually come from someplace. If you're an active investor, track the announcements on a daily basis.

◆ *What the Markets Will Watch, and Why.* If you read nothing else on the entire Internet each day, you must read this. Late at night or early in the morning, don't miss a day. Bookmark it, watch it, and stay current on the day's economic news *before* it happens. A service of CNNfn (see Figure 8.6).

http://cnnfn.com/markets/bridge/66.1.html

FIG. 8.6

Keep an eye on today's
market movers.

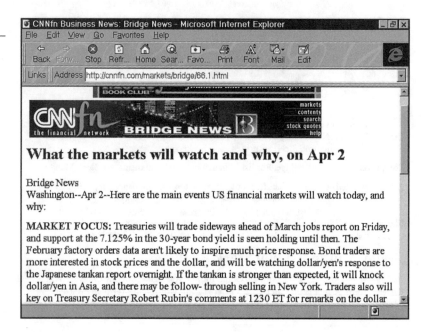

The Economy. Investor's Business Daily provides
regular economic updates and forecasts.

**http://www.investors.com/web_edition/
today/vieweconomy.html**

USA Today's Economic Indicators. Features
include information on Business inventories,
Construction, Consumer confidence, Credit,
Economic growth forecast, Employee Costs,
Factory orders, Federal Reserve, Gross Domestic
Product, Housing, Personal Income, Leading
Economic Indicators Index, Prices Indices (Con-
sumer/Producer), Productivity, Retail sales, U.S.
Trade Reports, and Unemployment.

**http://www.usatoday.com/money/
economy/econ0001.htm**

The Yahoo! List. Extensive list of sites providing
additional economic indicators.

**http://www.yahoo.com/
Business_and_Economy/
Economic_Indicators**

*Media Logic—The Economics/Markets/Invest-
ments Index.* Absolutely every economic indicator ever invented, from Aluminum Ingots & Mill
Products to Yield on new high-grade corporate
bonds. Unfortunately, some links are outdated.

http://www.mlinet.com/mle/ec_1000.htm

Business Cycle Indicators. Historical information
on 256 indicators used for tracking and predicting U.S. business activity. In most instances, the
data is complete from 1948 to 1995, and much
of it is more current than that.

http://www.globalexposure.com/bci.html

Economic Analysis

Seeking out qualified commentary on the state of the economy is another way to help yourself formulate solid buying strategies.

Here, we offer a rundown of sites specializing in the analysis of economic and market trends and indicators.

◆ *Money Magazine*. Offerings include a free daily e-mail newsletter called *Money Daily*, which arrives each evening with a short article about a financial topic or a market commentary.

http://www.pathfinder.com/money

◆ *Bos' Economic Forecasts*. Lots of opinions, backed up with links to leading economic indicators (see Figure 8.7).

http://bos.business.uab.edu/forecast/ fore.htm

◆ *US Credit Market*. Analysis plus the latest reports.

http://cnnfn.com/markets/bridge/ 310.1.html

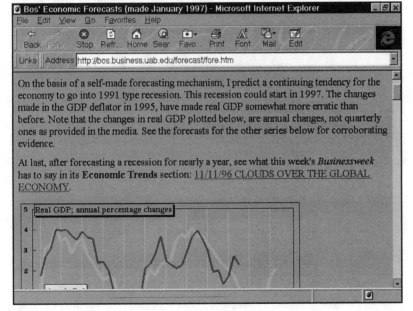

FIG. 8.7

Market analysts put their reputations on the line.

Market News and Commentary

While economic news undeniably affects the entire market, so also do other factors. Market commentaries analyze all the events that influence the day's market movement. (See Figure 8.8.) Some sites provide a running commentary as the day progresses. Others provide only an end-of-the-day analysis.

◆ *Market Commentary.* Closing commentary on today's markets from Standard and Poor's.

http://www.stockinfo.standardpoor.com/comment.htm

◆ *Yahoo! Finance.* A good quote site, but it's even more useful for its up-to-the-minute Market News. New stories appear around the clock. Contains links to Economic Calendar and Investment News Events.

http://quote.yahoo.com

◆ *Legg Mason.* This site includes the Daily Market Commentary, a summary of the current day's market activity.

http://www.leggmason.com/Stocks/stocknews.html

◆ *Merrill Lynch.* One of its more significant features, as it pertains to investors and this chapter, is the daily midday and closing market commentaries.

http://www.merrill-lynch.ml.com/financial

FIG. 8.8

Market commentaries abound on the Internet.

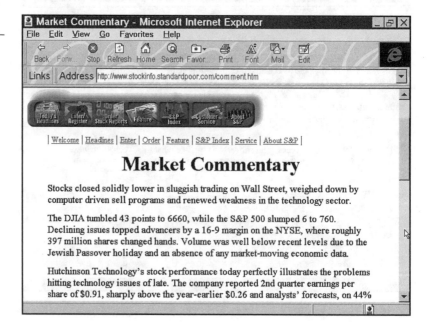

◆ *A.G. Edwards & Co.* Contains free information on several topics including short- and long-term market outlooks, plus research reports highlighting various investment opportunities.

http://www.agedwards.com

◆ *American Stock Exchange.* A daily summation of market news, in tabular form. Describes daily market volume and activity in options and equities.

**http://www.amex.com/summary/
summary.htm**

◆ *Capital Markets Commentary.* Weekly market analyses plus strong international bond coverage.

http://www.intdata.com/capital.htm

◆ *Prudential Securities.* This site offers daily and weekly market commentaries. Regular mail publications are also made available through this site.

www.prusec.com

out the day. Edited by economists, Briefing.com is incomparably the best source of stock analysis, market movement commentary, predictions, and cautions we've encountered thus far on the Web. Briefing.com contains information comparable to the services provided to professional brokers from companies such as Reuters and Telerate, but does so at a greatly reduced price.

◆ *Briefing.com.* Briefing.com is a free service for E*TRADE customers (see Figure 8.9). Others pay $6.95 per month for the stock service, and $25 per month for the professional-level service, which includes foreign exchange and bond analyses. To subscribe to Briefing.com, visit the site at

Public access: **http://www.briefing.com**

E*TRADE customer access: **http://
www.briefing.com/etrade/index.htm**

Combined Company, Industry, and Market News

The combination category is the final stop in this chapter. The discussion will be limited to one outstanding site: Briefing.com. This site fits squarely in between all of our arbitrary categories, proving once and for all that sometimes it is possible to be all things to all people. Briefing.com is a subscription service providing high-quality analysis and commentary, along with on-going market reporting through-

FIG. 8.9

Briefing.com provides a wealth of analysis in every category.

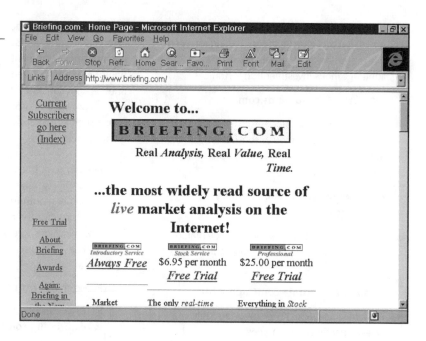

9

Talk to Smart Investors

> "Choose your friends wisely. It's good advice in real life...and critical counsel when you're seeking investment wisdom from people you don't know. "

Smart investors talk to other investors who talk to other investors—it's like a bad telephone commercial. Be careful, though. Discerning the legitimate tip from the urban legend is a formidable task, especially when both are accompanied by good intentions. Recognizing a carefully calculated ruse is even more difficult.

Words of financial "wisdom" can be found in many forms on the Internet. The professional investment advisor, the friendly huckster, the inside trader, and quite frequently, the truly helpful fellow investor who's willing to help out a newcomer.

This chapter tells you how to sort out the good from the bad.

Find a Mentor

Potential Internet gurus come in a variety of shapes and manners. Nonprofit, as well as for-profit, organizations run Web sites where the raison d'etre goes well beyond quotes and headlines.

Popular investment mentors range from the grim-faced-serious types to the room full of class clowns. Whichever point of view they take, the primary purpose of all the sites described here is still the same: to educate you about investing. In later sections we introduce you to more interactive sites, but in the mentors guide, all the information flows one way—from the advisor to you.

The American Association of Independent Investors (AAII)

The American Association of Independent Investors is a not-for-profit organization dedicated to helping individual investors become effective managers of their own funds (see Figure 9.1).

The AAII routinely sponsors seminars across the country on such subjects as stock analysis, financial planning, portfolio management, and more. Presentations by investment professionals are organized for local chapters of AAII. In addition, members receive the AAII Journal. Published 10 times every year, this journal offers information and how-to articles geared toward the individual investor. Anything else you need to know about AAII membership is covered in links from its home page, at **http://www.aaii.org**.

Even nonmembers, though, can still find a wealth of helpful information on the AAII Web site. Reports are available on Bonds, Brokers, Computers, Financial Planning, Insurance, Investing Basics, Mutual Funds, Portfolio Management, and more. This site is highly recommended.

As a mentoring site, we rate AAII a solid A.

CNBC

CNBC is the cable outlet of NBC (see Figure 9.2). The same people who bring you *The Tonight Show* also supply a quality network whose primary focus is news and business matters.

The major news portions of the CNBC home page have been moved over to MSNBC—The Microsoft/ NBC joint-venture. But a lot of useful information

FIG. 9.1

For the individual investor, AAII materials are a must read.

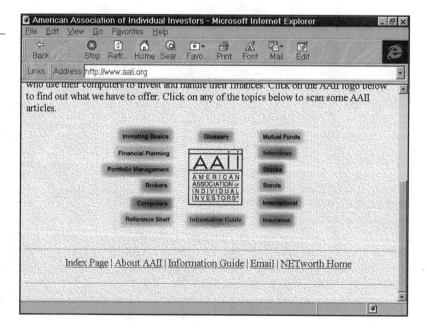

remains for the new individual investor at **http://www.cnbc.com**.

At the bottom of the page, in what looks like an inconsequential footer, are links that can be of particular benefit to new investors. There you can find a list of the NASDAQ 100 symbols and companies, definitions of the market indicators, common terminology, and commodity symbols.

The Investor Toolkit offers a menu of worksheets that can give you an understanding of where you stand today. Among the many things you can do are calculate your net worth, estimate your income tax, set up a goal planner, and calculate your true cash flow.

Another useful site feature is The MoneyClub chat, a question-and-answer session on personal finance held every weeknight at 7:30 p.m. Eastern time.

The features are useful, but the site has little sense of enthusiasm. For mentoring, we rate it a B-.

Invest-o-rama

Invest-o-rama is sponsored by Doug Gerlach, author and according to the liner notes, "Internet investing crusader." (See Figure 9.3.) This site offers many fine articles of interest. Highly recommended are the Ask Doug, Education Center, Feature Articles, and the HedgeHog Competition. The place to get started is **http://www.investorama.com.**

Other useful features of Invest-o-rama include a couple of different stock watch sections, some investment strategies worth studying, quote and company research services, and a long list of financial headlines.

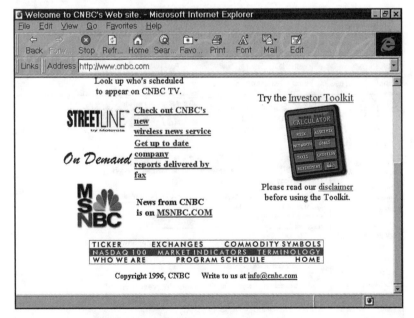

FIG. 9.2

CNBC provides links to valuable tools.

Invest-o-rama has more links than you could read in a lifetime. It makes a great bookmark site. For its mentoring capabilities, Invest-o-rama gets an A-.

Motley Fool

Motley Fool was started by a couple of brothers, David and Tom Gardner, as a place to gather and dispense information. (See Figure 9.4.) The Motley Fools make no excuses for their often unorthodox point of view; in fact they delight in it. The page is located at **http://www.fool.com**.

At this site you'll find all you need to know about investment fundamentals, presented with an attitude and a sense of humor. A few of the key educational areas are Fools School, Dow Approach, the Foolish Workshop, and Valuing Stocks. We discuss other areas in later sections of this chapter.

Nobody is more enthusiastic. If you're looking for mentors, you can't do better than the Motley Fools. The site earns a solid A+.

Reading the Fine Print

Cyberspace is a reflection of the real world. While the majority of online participants are probably honest folks, just like in the real would, the criminal element lurks not too far away. There are a few cyber-criminals and virtual con artists stalking the Net, attempting to hatch their cyber-scams under the unwary. There have been several instances of unscrupulous persons knowingly spreading false innuendo or outright lies in hopes of manipulating a stock price to their advantage.

FIG. 9.3

Invest-o-rama is required reading if you're looking for an investment education.

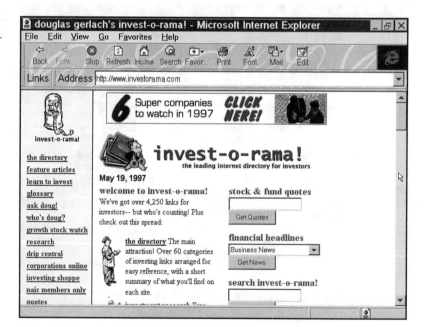

FIG. 9.4

Motley Fool: Invest for fun and profit.

It's not all bad, though. The Internet is a long way from needing a cyber-Wyatt Earp to save investors from the bad buys. There are a lot of groups that have a vested interest in assuring that the Internet maintains a high degree of integrity. Consumer groups, financial institutions, and government agencies are already on the lookout for cyber-fraud or anything that even hints at being underhanded.

Their most effective tool in assuring that the Internet doesn't turn into Dodge City is consumer information. A knowledgeable consumer is the best defense against cyber-criminals on the outskirts of town.

The following sites provide solid advice about avoiding scams. They also post alerts to keep you informed of known acts of dishonesty:

◆ *National Fraud Information Center.* The National Fraud Information Center, an undertaking of the National Consumer League, tracks and reports instances of fraud to appropriate government agencies. It also publishes relevant news articles and current fraud alerts.

http://www.fraud.org

◆ *NASD Regulation, Inc.* NASDR is an independent subsidiary of the National Association of Securities Dealers, Inc. It was created in 1938 by Congress to regulate the securities industry and the NASDAQ Stock Market. Of special interest to online investors is a page called What Investors Should Know. It's a valuable resource that covers, in depth, online securities trading issues.

Home page: **http://www.nasdr.com**

What Investors Should Know: **http://www.nasdr.com/2500.htm**

◆ *What Every Investor Should Know.* No, it's not deja vu. This time the information is coming straight from the Investor Assistance and Complaints section of the SEC—The Securities and Exchange Commission. Be sure to check the Investor Alerts page. Of particular interest will be the links to Investment Fraud and Abuse and Telecommunications Fraud.

Home page: **http://www.sec.gov/invkhome.htm**

Investment Fraud and Abuse: **http://www.sec.gov/consumer/cyberfr.htm**

Telecomms Fraud: **http://www.sec.gov/enforce/wireless.txt**

◆ *Cyber-Investors and Cyber-Fraud.* Advice on spotting fraudulent "hot" investment tips, pyramid schemes, chain letters, and "make-money-fast" scams.

http://www.investorama.com/features/fraud.shtml

◆ *The Wild, Wild Web.* A feature from Kiplinger's personal finance magazine. The author says that in the untamed frontier of online investing bulletin boards and home pages, insider tips often come from outlaws.

http://www.kiplinger.com/magazine/nov96/wildweb.html

Interactive Web Sites

Now we arrive at the most amusing, diverting part of the Internet: interactive investment sites. (See Figure 9.5.) In these pages you'll get to talk to, and play games with, real people. On some sites you'll find hot stock tips; in others you'll get to ask questions, post tips of your own, and discuss your experiences in investing.

Message Boards

Lots of thoughtful advice, debates, shouting, persuasion—all focused on various publicly traded securities. Jump right in with comments of your own. Sponsored by Motley Fool.

http://www.fool.com/Messages.htm

Silicon Investor

Stock Talk area provides a place for posting and reading technology stock tips.

http://www.techstocks.com

Socialize

A "hang-out" area for investors, courtesy of Morningstar.

http://www.morningstar.net/WebProj/Socialize/Socialize.html

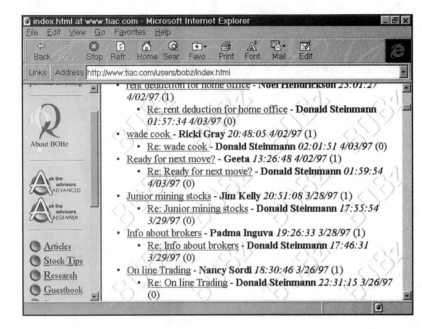

FIG. 9.5

Interactive sites let you participate in the discussion.

Participate

Participate in a monthly online discussion or interview on Wall Street Net.

**http://www.netresource.com/wsn/
interv_submit.html**

Bob'z

Post and read hot stock tips from—well, from anybody. Includes advice sections, articles, and a research tool.

**http://www.tiac.com/users/bobz/
index.html**

Join Our Discussion

Advice, investor profile, and viewer reactions to a PBS report on America and Wall Street.

**http://www.pbs.org/wgbh/pages/frontline/
shows/betting/discuss**

Michael Campbell's Money Talks

Ask financial questions, state your opinion, and collect lots of free advice.

http://mastermall.com/money/talks

Mutual Funds Online

Opened in April, these public chat rooms are limited to 30 participants at a time.

http://www.mfmag.com

Talk to Other Investors

This site contains links to roundtables, forums, user groups, and newsgroups.

http://www.wallstreetcity.com/
Talk_to_other_Investors.html

Bust the Tipster

An educational game from Motley Fool. Read the premise, guess an answer. Right or wrong, you'll get smarter about investing. There's even a prize drawing for participants held every three months.

http://www.fool.com/Tipsters/Tipsters.htm

Conference Calls

Publicly listed companies constantly churn out news. When the news is big, lots of those companies sponsor toll-free telephone conference calls to announce the news and respond to questions. Motley Fool's Conference Call page posts notices of scheduled conference calls, and the corresponding phone numbers, so that you can join the party yourself.

http://www.fool.com/Calls/Calls.htm

Investment Clubs

They've been around for a century: groups of people who pool their money and share the burden of research in a thing called an investment club. (See Figure 9.6.) Where they once met strictly in private homes and restaurant booths, now, they've gone high tech; many even have their very own Web sites.

This is how a club works: A small group of like-minded investors—usually no more than 15 or 20 people—gets together to decide how to invest. The group meets, either online or in person, about once a month to review the status of its investments, to report on research, to vote on changes to the portfolio, and to participate in some kind of educational activity. Members of investment clubs typically contribute from $20 to $50 per month toward the investment pool.

Investment clubs achieve remarkable returns, in part because when you're part of a group, there's less of a tendency to "panic" and overreact when the market moves. By sharing the research burden, there's time to do a better job of tracking the club's portfolio than you might have as an individual. And by

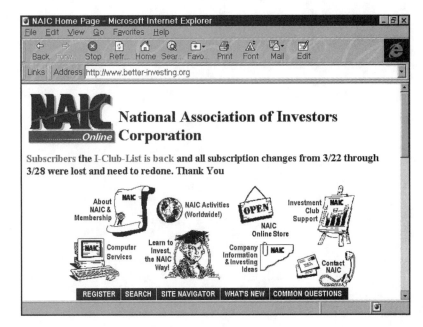

FIG. 9.6

Investment clubs provide support to small investors.

sticking with a philosophy, diversifying, and taking advantages of price breaks given to larger "round lot" buyers, you're doing all the right things to increase your bottom line.

Here are some of the best sites on the Internet for learning how to start and operate an investment club of your own:

◆ *So You Want to Start an Investment Club?* Some solid, basic information about starting an investment club.

http://www.investorama.com/features/ club.shtml

◆ *National Association of Investors Corporation.* The organizing body for the National Association of Investment Clubs. This site provides help for individual investors and investment clubs. The NAIC's focus is helping individuals to learn about investing in the stock market. Here you'll

find everything you need to know about the world of investing—including books, magazines, software, and study tools. Join NAIC and its computer group, download demonstration software, or learn how to start an investment club of your own.

http://www.better-investing.org

◆ *Investment Clubs on the Web.* Listing of organized investment clubs and their Web sites.

http://www.investorama.com/olclubs.shtml

10

Use the Rest of the Internet as a Research Tool

"The mechanics and the rules for communicating on the Internet."

Up to this point, we've looked at only one part of the Internet: The World Wide Web. Commercial Web sites like the ones we've explored in earlier chapters are great for disseminating expert advice. But because they're mostly a one-way form of communication, they're not so great when you want to get involved in discussions, or ask specific questions.

In Chapter 9 we introduced you to a handful of Web sites that carry on-line conversations. That's only the beginning. The Internet offers better options when it comes to the interactive exchange you crave. These alternative services enable you to interface with millions of people, many of whom share the same dreams and ambitions and have the same questions you have. Even now, with the Internet so firmly in the public conscience, the free exchange of ideas is a resource not being fully exploited by the people who should be there. Why permit sci-fi fans, lonely-hearts clubs, and professional organizations to have all the fun, and reap all the benefits of the less familiar parts of the Internet? As an independent investor, the back roads of the Internet can be an invaluable resource for you. You owe it to yourself to explore them all.

In this chapter we examine the three Internet services that let you get personally involved: UseNet newsgroups, mailing lists, and Internet Relay Chat. We conclude with the rules for civilized Internet usage, known as *Netiquette*.

UseNet Newsgroups

Like old-fashioned bulletin boards, and new-fashioned electronic *BBSs*—or bulletin board systems—newsgroups are the place to go when you want to post comments, questions, and announcements. *UseNet* is the name given to the collection of special-interest newsgroups that can be found on the Internet. There, any of the Internet's more than 30 million users can log in to discuss thousands of topics from "a2i.outgoing" to "z.netz.wissenschaft.mathematik". Recent estimates put the number of discussion topics at over 15,000.

Messages posted to UseNet boards are available for public viewing and comment. Depending on the interest generated by a particular subject, the membership of a newsgroup can range from ten to ten-thousand.

UseNet newsgroups are divided into a hierarchical structure according to type. For example, a "comp" at the beginning of a name indicates that the group discusses a computing topic. An "alt" or "misc" at the beginning of the name will indicate the newsgroup has an alternative or miscellaneous—read: anachronistic—topic. There you'll find subjects not easily categorized elsewhere: alt.business.multilevel.scam.scam.scam, for example. More traditional categories include "biz" for business, "news" for news about newsgroups, "rec" for recreation, "sci" for science, and "soc" for social topics.

Many newsgroups tend to have "a low signal-to-noise ratio," meaning that many of the postings have little or nothing to do with the topic. If you don't care to work through all the clutter yourself, seek out a moderated newsgroup. Moderated newsgroups have *gatekeepers*—moderators who ensure that messages don't deviate too far from the stated topic of the newsgroup.

Accessing newsgroups is usually a simple matter; the level of simplicity is entirely dependent upon the software you choose.

For users of commercial online services, accessing and subscribing to the service's proprietary newsgroups is a simple point-and-click procedure. Commercial newsgroups go by different names, depending on the service you use. On CompuServe, they're called *Forums*. On America Online, they're called *Message Boards*. Other services use other names. These groups are inaccessible to anyone who's not a member of the service.

Internet newsgroups, on the other hand, are available to all users, even those accessing via a commercial online service. Whether you're using a Web browser such as Navigator or Internet Explorer, or a stand-alone program such as Free Agent (download the free software from **http://www.forteinc.com/forte**), check with your Internet service provider for the newsgroup settings for your software. If you're using Navigator 3.01 or earlier, the built-in news reader feature is badly implemented. We strongly advise using Free Agent or another reader until you're ready to upgrade. (See Figure 10.1.)

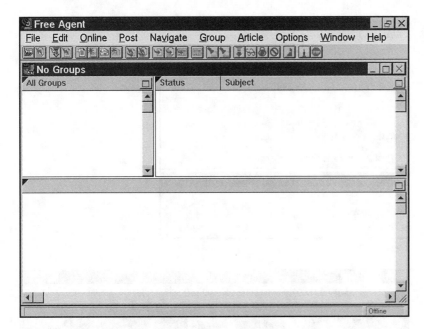

FIG. 10.1

The opening window of a newsreader.

Getting in is simple. From Internet Explorer, click the Mail icon, and choose Read News from the drop-down menu. Explorer opens an entirely separate program to access the newsgroups. From Navigator, go to the Window menu and click Netscape News.

Regardless of its name, each Internet newsreader works the same way. The first time you start it up, the software creates a database of all the newsgroups it can find. (See Figure 10.2.) In some packages the process is automatic. Others require you to issue a command. Be patient—there are a lot of newsgroups out there.

When you've got your list of newsgroups, use the search or find feature to find the name of a group that interests you. (See Figure 10.3.) We list the most popular newsgroups in the next section. But feel free to search on your own using key words and partial words such as *invest, tax, finance, money, business, stock, portfolio,* and *fund.*

Use the Subscribe command to add groups to your personal list of subscriptions. (See Figure 10.4.) Usually it's wise to visit the group before going through the trouble of subscribing.

Now you're ready to return to the main screen and start reading. (See Figure 10.5.)

Etiquette requires certain behavior from a first-time user. Before posting your first message, read a day's worth of messages to see how the group functions. Your first time out, it's considered polite to briefly introduce yourself to the group, and respond to an existing message, either with a question or a comment. Messages remain visible for approximately four days, after which they get bumped to make room for new messages.

As you respond to a particular topic, you're building a thread, a hierarchy that ties topics together with their responses.

FIG. 10.2

Building the database requires collecting or updating the newsgroups.

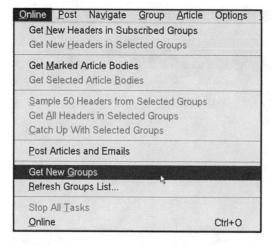

Online	Post	Navigate	Group	Article	Options

Get New Headers in Subscribed Groups
Get New Headers in Selected Groups

Get Marked Article Bodies
Get Selected Article Bodies

Sample 50 Headers from Selected Groups
Get All Headers in Selected Groups
Catch Up With Selected Groups

Post Articles and Emails

Get New Groups
Refresh Groups List...

Stop All Tasks
Online   Ctrl+O

FIG. 10.3

Use the Find or Search tool to locate newsgroups by key word.

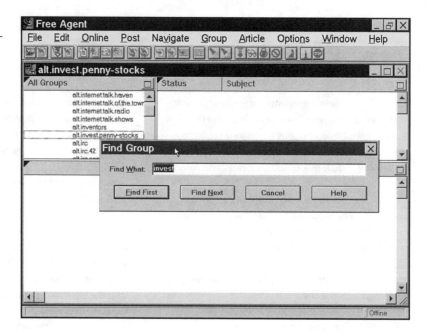

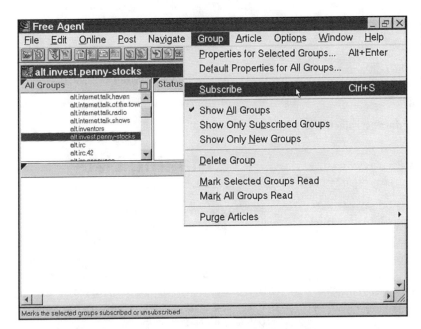

FIG. 10.4

To subscribe, just click a newsgroup and execute the Subscribe command.

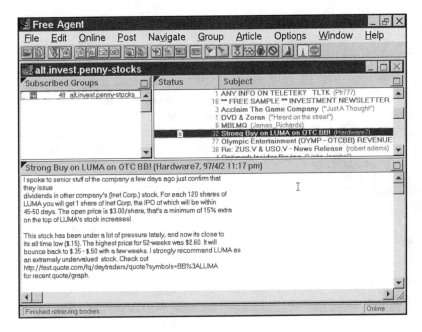

FIG. 10.5

A standard main screen for a newsreader.

Learn more about newsgroups from these Internet sites:

◆ *UseNet News.* Absolutely the best tutorial anywhere on all things UseNet. What it is, how it works, the rules for using it.

http://www.cs.indiana.edu/docproject/zen/zen-1.0_6.html#SEC31

◆ *news.newusers.questions.* Pointers for new UseNet users.

http://www.cis.ohio-state.edu/hypertext/faq/usenet/news-newusers-intro/faq.html

◆ *Newsgroups of Interest.* Chosen from among the more than 15,000 available newsgroups, here are a few that should be of special interest to independent investors. You'll find tools for searching additional newsgroups in Chapter 11. The most active investment-oriented newsgroups are:

- misc.invest
- misc.invest.stocks

- alt.invest
- misc.invest.funds

The location for frequently asked investing questions.

http://www.invest-faq.com

Mailing Lists

Ready to expand your horizons? Here's another "back road" of the Internet you'll enjoy using: Investment-related mailing lists. Mailing lists are a cross between newsgroups and private e-mail. Consider this simple analogy: E-mail is like receiving a letter from a friend—one person writes to another person, and waits for a return message. It's private, confidential…and rather lonely.

An e-mail mailing list, on the other hand, is more like an "invitation-required" cocktail party. Several people sharing similar interests discuss a single topic, and receive input from other people in the group. Mailing lists are semi-private in that nobody but other members of the group will read the discussion. The conversation tends to stay highly focused. Mailing lists act as electronic fan clubs, user groups, academic conferences, debating societies, information centers, continuing education classes, and public libraries.

Many—perhaps most—smaller mailing lists are *moderated,* meaning that messages are sent to a single person, called the *list owner*, who scans them to ensure that they're related to and appropriate for the discussion at hand. In other cases, the lists get so large that the owners turn over much of the work to automated list management software. (The three most significant kinds of list managers are called ListServ, Majordomo, and Listproc.)

Before you can start receiving mail from a mailing list, you must first "subscribe" to the list. For the most part, mailing lists tend to be open to the public, and subscribing involves nothing more than sending off a request via e-mail.

The most fundamental rule of mailing lists is this: Regardless of which list (or lists) you subscribe to, you must send administrative queries to one address, and topic discussion to a similar, but different, address. To subscribe to a Majordomo list, for example, you would send the subscribe message to **Majordomo@HOST.COM**.

The address goes in the To: line of your e-mailer. Leave the Subject: line blank. The message goes in the body of the e-mail message, with no other information (for example, if your browser is set to issue signatures, turn them off for this message). (See Figure 10.6.)

You'll receive an e-mail confirmation—probably within a minute or two—and the confirmation will tell you where to send your list comments.

When you send comments they would, of course, go to the address associated with the mailing list. For instance, **Listname@HOST.NET** might be the discussion address associated with the subscription previously illustrated.

These Web sites will be helpful to if you want to know more about using lists:

◆ *Mailing Lists.* Good background information on using mailing lists.

   http://ac.acusd.edu/html/USD/ getting_started/mailinglists.html

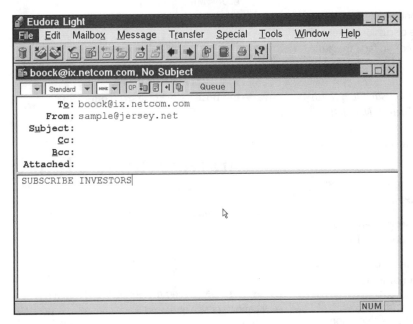

FIG. 10.6

Subscribing to a list is easy.

◆ *Tips for Newcomers.* This site explains mailing lists, and provides warnings and links to other mailing list sites.

http://www.liszt.com/intro.html

◆ *Groups.* A good list of investment-related newsgroups, maintained by the Syndicate Finance Pages.

http://www.moneypages.com/syndicate/ finance/newsgrps.html

The following sections describe some of the best investment-related mailing lists on the Internet. Chapter 11 shows you how to find others.

Mailing Lists of Interest: Participatory

Unlike the lists you'll read about in the next section, these mailing lists encourage discussion by subscribers. So feel free to get involved—in fact, that's the whole point!

◆ *Investors—Stock Market Investment in North America and Overseas Financial Newsletter.* Features edited articles and moderated discussions concerning U.S., Canadian, and overseas stock markets.

To subscribe, e-mail the message SUBSCRIBE INVESTORS to **boock@ix.netcom.com.**

◆ *Investment-Talk.* A discussion of anything, possibly of interest to the independent investor.

To subscribe, e-mail the message SUBSCRIBE INVESTMENT-TALK to **Majordomo@mission-a.com.**

◆ *Mutual Fund Discussion List.* A discussion of mutual fund-related information and goal planning.

To subscribe, e-mail the message SUBSCRIBE INVESTORS to **Majordomo@shore.net.**

Mailing Lists of Interest: Read-Only

Other lists provide information, but don't allow responses. These lists tend to have very wide distribution. They obtain their contents from commercial or authoritative sites. Some read-only lists have a separate mailing for readers who want to discuss the information on the primary list.

◆ *Economics By E-Mail Distribution List.* Here you will see a distributed list of economic statistics and indicators of the U.S. economy.

To subscribe, e-mail the message SUBSCRIBE to **econ@aimhere.com.**

◆ *Stock and Investment News Distribution List.* This is a distributed list of timely investment information.

To subscribe, e-mail the message SUBSCRIBE to **bobbose@stockresearch.com.**

Internet Relay Chats

Unlike newsgroups and mailing lists, where you must wait for responses to your comments, Internet Relay Chat, or IRC, lets you talk in real time with other investors on the Internet.

Using a broadcasting metaphor, the IRC system is channel- or station-based. Each channel is a virtual place where a topic, usually referred to in the heading, is discussed. Though users might not strictly adhere to the topic, you may assume that they are at least interested in it.

Internet chats are enjoyed by many, but focused conversations in the real cyberworld are hard to find.

Commercial online services such as America Online and CompuServe have made their fortunes by perfecting the chat concept. If you've used their chat rooms, you've seen what IRC has to offer.

If you want to try chatting, moderated conversations with prominent guests may be a far better use of time, since they are scheduled events that attract a crowd more interested in learning about the subject matter.

To connect to Internet Relay Chat, you'll need a small chat program such as mIRC. Chapter 2 explains where to find it.

Getting your IRC set up is tricky. These sites provide good step-by-step tutorials of the process. They also give tips for finding channels that will be of most interest to investors.

◆ *IRC Help.* Comprehensive site with primers, help files, server lists, and more.

http://www.irchelp.org

◆ *Internet Relay Chat FAQ.* A list of frequently asked questions—and answers—about IRC.

http://www.kei.com/irc.html

Netiquette

There are no laws against rudeness, but it's never been known to make a positive contribution to the overall quality of a conversation. In the end, rude exchanges just end up wasting everyone's time.

In the slightly off-kilter world of cyberspace, it is sometimes possible to be obnoxious without meaning to be so. It happens when you fail to express your views politely or humorously; it also happens when you break the code of conduct.

Just as in the real world, the Internet has an accepted set of etiquette rules. Violate them—knowingly or otherwise—and you risk anything from being ignored to being mail bombed. The most offensive Net users have seen their mail boxes filled with tens of thousands of messages, numbers that can stagger their Internet providers and result in being kicked off the service entirely.

In other cases, users have violated the real-world law by posting libelous or defamatory comments, or by publishing large amounts of copyrighted materials without permission. These users find themselves traveling straight out of the cyberworld into real-life courts of law.

The Internet experience needn't be bad, of course. The legal issues are simple. Limit your quotations to brief excerpts, with commentary, and you're on safe ground with the copyright law.

The libel and defamation issues are only a bit trickier. The overriding rule is: Avoid attacking other human beings. You're fairly free to post factual, verifiable information. Hold yourself to higher standards than the supermarket tabloids, however. Remember that private individuals have far more legal protection against invasions of privacy than celebrities have. Learn more about copyright and other Internet legal issues at these Web sites:

◆ *About the Net.* Discusses the accepted use of copyrighted material and other legal issues.

http://sehplib.ucsd.edu/aboutnet/cr.html

◆ *Defamation Law and Free Speech.* An explanation of the Australian law of defamation, but it parallels U.S. law almost exactly. Explains how to state your opinion without crossing the libel line. Worth a read.

http://helix.ucsd.edu/~bssimon/dissent1/ documents/ defamation.html

◆ *Defamation and Libel in Cyberspace.* A regularly updated list of articles about the current state of the debate.

http://www.gahtan.com/techlaw/ defame.htm

◆ *Computer Law: Defamation Online.* Online services have experienced a flurry of recent legal disputes regarding their liability for statements posted on their services.

http://www.brmlaw.com/doclib/ complaw71195.html

In reality, few people have to worry overmuch about violating the law. The rules you're more likely to confront in your online ventures are the standards set over the years by the Internet community itself. In the following sections we'll take a look at a few of the de facto rules of cyberspace.

Lower the Volume, Please

DON'T SCREAM!

If you correspond in capital letters, expect a sharp rebuke. In cyberspace, capital letters—other than in their grammatically proper spots)—are considered the equivalent of yelling.

The Personal Response

Posting and sending unsolicited notes is acceptable in virtually all situations, provided they're not harassing or inflammatory. Many people welcome the opportunity to correspond with fellow users. In all cases, the wishes of the recipient are paramount. If a person doesn't wish to correspond, you must respect the request.

Commercial solicitations, on the other hand, while not exactly prohibited, are considered by the vast majority of users to be a capital offense.

Worst of all offenses is a thing called *spamming,* the practice of sending out mass commercial mailings to people—and newsgroups—that have no interest at all in your product. Even the most liberal Internet user supports the death penalty for spammers.

The Public Response

Notes posted on public forums sometimes drift away from the main subject matter. It becomes difficult to keep a discussion going when the forum is clogged up with personal exchanges. In a discussion on tax-law does anybody really want to read how somebody named Jim is doing with his Rogaine treatments? Try to keep your responses on topic.

It is appropriate and helpful to quote part of the text you are responding to. Use the mark >> to set off the part you're quoting. Some software will insert the marks for you automatically. Feel free to edit down the quotation. Include only as much information as is absolutely necessary to clarify the subject.

Ownership

The author of any correspondence, even on a public forum, is the owner. Don't forward someone else's words without their permission. E-mail sent to you is considered private and should not be forwarded or copied without permission.

All the Other Rules

Those are the basics. But spend some time learning the rest. It's useful knowledge—a bit like learning to ride escalators.

◆ *User Guidelines and Netiquette*. The civilized use of limited resources.

   http://rs6000.adm.fau.edu/rinaldi/net/ index.htm

◆ *Net Abuse FAQ*. Frequently asked questions about abusive practices.

   http://www.cis.ohio-state.edu/hypertext/ faq/ usenet/net-abuse-faq/top.html

◆ *Roadmap for the Information Superhighway*. "When thou enter a city abide by its customs." More rules, and their explanations.

   http://www.hart.bbk.ac.uk/~trish/ maponline/MAP07.html

11

Search the Internet

Every time a bell rings, the Internet gets new things…or something like that. There are millions of sites out there; new locations appear every day. Few of those sites are static. The Web is continuously transformed as sponsors seek ways to attract new clients. Sites we describe in this book change their status from free to subscriber only. They disappear, they move to new locations, or they get competition from new and better sites. Whatever the case, you'll want to have the knowledge and expertise to go out and search on your own for whatever you need or desire on the Internet.

Search Engines

Simply put, a search engine is akin to a phone book for the Internet. They're free, and they're invaluable for their flexibility and their power to light the darkest corners for the information you're seeking. Use a search engine much as you'd use the index of a book or the yellow pages of a telephone directory. Bookmark them (see following sidebar) so that they're easily available.

MARK THE SPOT

A Web browser's Bookmark feature makes it easy to return to a favorite site. We recommend that once you find a great search tool, you add it to your list of bookmarks. Here's how:

Go to the page you want to bookmark. Bookmarks are most useful for pages that require you to drill down past the front page to a subpage.

In Internet Explorer: Go to the Favorites menu, and click the Add to Favorites command. Use the Organize Favorites command to set up folders for grouping your bookmarks by category.

In Netscape Navigator: Use the Ctrl+D key combination to add the command to your bookmark list. Alternatively, go to the Bookmarks menu, and click the Add to Bookmarks command. The Go To Bookmarks command lets you organize your bookmarks by category.

To return to the bookmarked page at a later time, simply click the Favorites (or Bookmarks) menu and select the site from the drop-down list.

◆

The search engines in this chapter are much grander in scope than the search vehicles you might find on other Web sites featured in this book. For the most part, on-site search engines don't reach beyond the archives of their particular site.

Search engines in this chapter index more sites—in some cases, the entire Internet—to accumulate information for vast databases. From these free tools, you'll be offered better, more varied methods of querying for data and interpreting results.

Even though many of the search engines featured may seem similar, significant differences lie just below the surface. Their primary focuses differ. Some are dedicated to business matters, some to UseNet groups. Several different types of user interfaces are featured, some extremely user friendly and some extremely powerful and better left to the seasoned user.

A Few Words About Boolean Algebra

It's the backbone of all search engines. It sounds French but isn't. And it's certainly worth knowing about before beginning what could be a lifetime of sweeping Internet searches.

Boolean algebra was developed by the English mathematician George Boole in 1847. It brings together logical concepts and mathematical representations. A special set of mathematical *operators*, each having specific characteristics, are used to define Boolean logic. The basic operators, those used in most search engines, are AND, OR, and NOT.

Here, we explain the operators; in the next section, we'll show you how to use them for searching.

The AND Function

The AND function requires that all elements within an equation be present.

The AND function in a search engine is usually represented by placing a **+** sign directly in front of a word, without a space. Some engines ask that you type the word AND in all caps. In a few engines, the AND is assumed.

The OR Function

The OR function requires only one of the elements to be present for the equation to produce a positive result.

The OR function is the presumed default function in most search engines. In other words, if you type in a list of words, the search engine will return a list of sites containing any of the words in the list.

The NOT Function

The NOT function produces a positive result only if the designated element is not present.

How to Conduct a Search

All search engines feature an input box where you can enter what are known as *keywords*. The keyword is the beginning of your search. You begin your

search when you enter your keyword, click the Search or equivalent button, and wait for the search engine to produce results.

It's not feasible to cover every method of conducting a search in the space allotted here. But it will be possible to touch on the basics, those things that are common to all search engines.

Unique Word Searches

You can begin your search by entering a single word in the keyword box and clicking the Search button. This is a wonderfully simple way to conduct a search if the keyword you're using is so unique that it is unlikely to produce too many results. Searching for the keyword **Trafalga** produces no more than a handful of results. But a less specific term, **finance** for instance, can easily produce over 10 million matches.

Don't despair. Ten million places to look isn't really as hopeless as it sounds. Search engines don't return results in a random order. Using complicated algorithms, the best search engines rank the matches and list the most relevant sites first.

Combined Word Searches: Using the AND, OR, and NOT Operators

A better method of conducting a search is to combine words. In this way, you can easily narrow the field from tens of millions of matches to a much more manageable number. Multiple word searches take advantage of the Boolean operators.

The OR operator is the default condition for most search engines. Type in the keywords without any symbols in front or in between to invoke the OR operation.

As an example, the search string

finance personal

will produce results if either, or both, of the keywords are present.

On the surface, this doubling up would seem to run counter to the previous "minimize it" advice. If one word produces tens of millions of results, shouldn't two words produce more? They should and do. However, once again, the ranking algorithms come into play.

The ranking of sites depends on several factors including, but not limited to, the number of times your word combination appears in a document, at what point—nearest to the beginning—the words appear in the document, how closely the two words appear in a document, and others. The criteria used for ranking may vary from search engine to search engine.

The more words you give the algorithm to work with, the more accurate the resulting rankings will be. Again, the highest-ranked sites are listed first.

What this means is that although you'll likely get millions upon millions of matches for multiword searches, the most relevant matches will be the relatively few that appear at the top of the list.

To further define your search, invoke the AND operator. Although the method for invoking the AND function varies among search engines, the characteristics of the function do not. Currently, the most

common way of doing searching with AND is to place a **+** sign directly in front of the keyword.

The AND function in the search string **+finance +personal** produces results only when both keywords, finance and personal, are present.

Likewise, the term **+CD1 +invest** will return lists of sites touting certificates of deposits, as well as companies seeking investors in their CD-ROM factory. It's unlikely to give you a list of songs on William Shatner's latest musical endeavor.

The NOT function provides an excellent means of eliminating items that may often be present with your keywords, but are of absolutely no interest to you. The NOT function can generally be invoked by placing a minus (**-**) sign in front of the keyword. The search **+finance +personal -sleazy** will return documents containing the keywords finance and personal, but only if those documents do not contain the word sleazy.

Grouping Words

Placing your words in groups can further narrow your search. Use this method when looking for **"personal finance"** but not **"finance personal."**

The method for placing words in groups varies among the search engines. The two most common methods are placing them within quotes (**"personal finance"**), or joining them with a colon (**personal:finance**).

Spelling Counts—Somewhat

Not sure how many p's there are in Kiplinger? Sometimes you're not sure of the exact spelling of a word. Other times, you're looking for several similar words (investing, investments, investors). In either case, a wild card character allows you to enter the part of the word you know and ignore the rest. For instance, try entering **Kip*** if you're looking for the personal finance publication. In this case, the asterisk (*****) is the wild card character that tells the search engine to look for all words beginning with the letters "Kip."

Filters

All search engines employ some sort of "search only" filtering mechanism. As the name implies, you can use a filtering mechanism to force the search engine to consider only pages in a defined category. All other pages are filtered out. Selecting the category Business, for example, restricts your search to business-oriented sites. Methods for applying filters vary among search engines, but basically they all involve selecting a primary subject category for your search.

The Search Engines

In this section, we list a few of the growing number of search engines on the Internet. With a few exceptions the home pages consist of a list of topics to choose from—to help focus your search—and an input box for your keyword.

Searches on different engines yield different results. There are reasons for this variation, including the frequency with which the search engine database is updated, the algorithms used to determine the most relevant matches, and the different restrictions the search engines place on themselves when listing sites.

The search engines are listed here alphabetically. Each offers unique features, advantages, and disadvantages. Ratings are based on our personal likes and dislikes.

AltaVista

AltaVista (see Figure 11.1) claims to be the largest Web index. The 31 million pages on 627,000 servers, plus 4 million articles from 14,000 UseNet groups, go a long way in supporting that claim. AltaVista is the primary search engine powering many of the subject-oriented search engines on the Internet.

The primary user interface consists of a simple keyword box and a Submit button. (See Figure 11.1.) Alta Vista uses Boolean searches. Detailed search instructions are available by clicking the Help or Advanced Help buttons.

Perhaps because we're old fogies who enjoy doing things manually, AltaVista is one of our favorite search engines; however, because it does not feature an intuitive user interface we can only rate it an **A-**. Visit the site at **http://altavista.digital.com**.

America Online Mailing List Directory

America Online Mailing List is an easy-to-use directory featuring over 3,000 mailing lists. The search function includes filtered keyword searches. When it locates a mailing list, it provides a synopsis and

detailed information on how to subscribe. The home page (see Figure 11.2) features links to useful items including Working with Mailing Lists, Glossary of Terms, and a weekly Top 20 list. Even though 3,000 sounds like a lot, it's still a small percentage of what the Internet has to offer.

This is a nice site, but 3,000 seems small once you're used to tens of thousands. We rate this site a **B-**. The site is located at **http://ifrit.Web.aol.com/mld/production**.

Deja News

Deja News (see Figure 11.3) is a search engine dedicated to newsgroups. It employs a Boolean-style search mechanism to weed through what it claims is the largest collection of indexed archived UseNet news available.

FIG. 11.1

Alta Vista's home page: A simple concept. Type in the keyword and click Submit. The Help, Advanced Help, and On-Site Knowledge features are only a click away from this page.

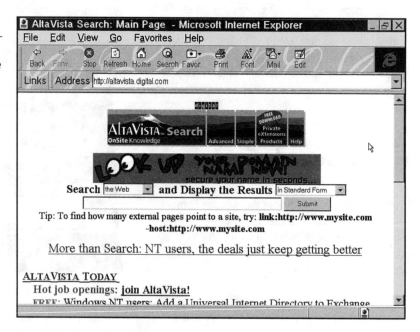

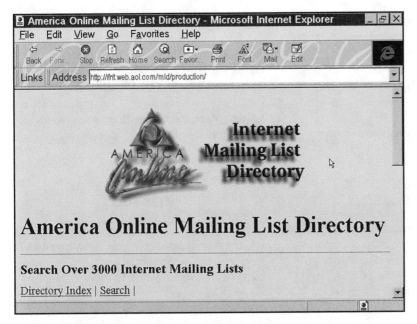

FIG. 11.2

Although some of the information on the America Online Mailing List Directory site is restricted to AOL members, there is still plenty for others to choose from.

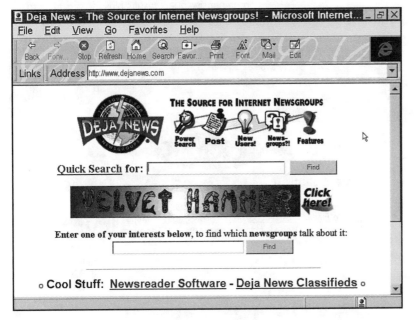

FIG. 11.3

The Deja News home page may use only a simple search mechanism, but advanced filtered searches can be accessed by clicking Power Search.

Search features include pattern matching (the use of partial words with wild cards), filtered searches, and time-sensitivity ranking.

For depth and scope, as well as ease of use, we give this site an **A** rating.

Visit Deja News at **http://www.dejanews.com**.

Excite

Excite features Boolean Web search capability. Filtering selections help to re-direct your search from the entire Web to UseNet groups, NewsTracker, or Web Reviews. The home page (see Figure 11.4) also includes links to yellow pages, e-mail directories, shareware, maps, and more.

It's worth noting that Excite's search engine has the capability to build relationships between sets of words and concepts. In other words, Excite can equate the term "peace officer" with the word "policeman" when conducting a search.

For ease of use and the usefulness of reviewed sites, we rate this site a **B+**. You'll find all this excitement at **http://www.excite.com**.

Infoseek

Infoseek is another search engine that attempts to make Web browsing easier by creating hierarchical categories and subcategories to filter searches. (See Figure 11.5.) Infoseek offers several methods of searching the Web, which the developers have dubbed Ultrasmart and Ultraseek. Ultrasmart offers comprehensive query results plus the capability to

FIG. 11.4

The Excite page features the standard keyword input box, Search button, and links to other useful locations.

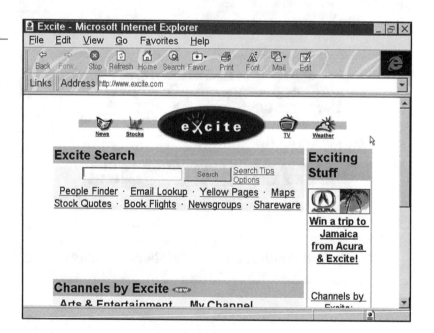

drill down within your query. Ultraseek is a stream-lined version of Ultrasmart, aimed at power users who know precisely what they're looking for.

Small problem: With our Internet Explorer content filter on, all our Infoseek searches stalled out, warning us of the presence of "obscene gestures." Whether it's someone's idea of a practical joke, or a protest against self-censorship, it's an annoyance.

It's otherwise a fairly useful engine, but because of the annoyances, we rate this site a **B**. You'll find Infoseek at **http://www.infoseek.com**.

InfoSpace

InfoSpace (see Figure 11.6) is a comprehensive directory tailored to locating people, businesses, government offices, toll-free numbers, fax numbers, e-mail addresses, road maps, and URLs. You'll be able to locate businesses by city, by near address, or by name. Get door-to-door directions, obtain local city guides, access apartment locators, and even check weather and ski conditions.

Directory information is also available for federal, state, and local government offices. Just because it appears to do everything it's advertised to do—and that's a lot—we rate this site an **A**. Make space at **http://www.infospace.com**.

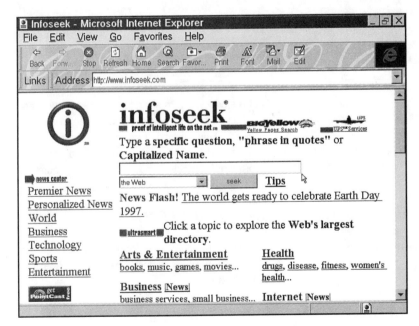

FIG. 11.5

Infoseek includes links to news, directories, and other services.

FIG. 11.6

InfoSpace locates virtually any business and draws a map to get you there.

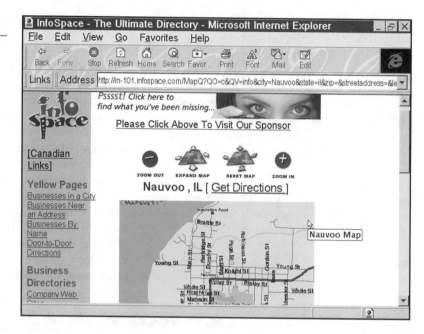

LawCrawler

LawCrawler (see Figure 11.7) is a search engine geared toward the specific needs of legal professionals. Of course, there's nothing illegal about folks interested in tax laws sneaking a peak. All searches are restricted to sites with legal information and within specified domains.

On the advice of our attorney, and by our own accord, we rate this site an **A**. Do your own legal sleuthing at **http://www.lawcrawler.com**.

Liszt

Liszt is a directory of mailing lists. Currently, there are over 70,000 entries compiled from servers around the world. Searches can be conducted using Boolean search methods, or you can choose from a smaller assortment by selecting specific topics (see Figure 11.8). Perhaps even more important is the fact the Liszt is updated each week, ensuring against wasting your time with expired mailing lists.

For ease of use, depth and scope we rate this site an **A+**. You'll find the site listed at **http://www.liszt.com**.

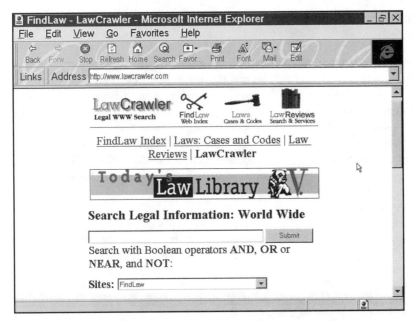

FIG. 11.7

Be like, feel like, Perry Mason. LawCrawler uses the Alta Vista Boolean search engine.

FIG. 11.7

Be like, feel like, Perry Mason. LawCrawler uses the Alta Vista Boolean search engine.

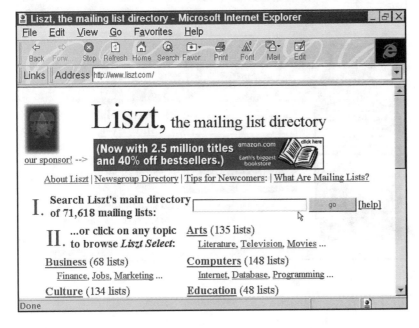

FIG. 11.8

Check out the Tips for Newcomers before signing on the Liszt site.

Lycos

Lycos (see Figure 11.9) is an especially user-friendly indexed Internet search engine. It features excellent instructional pages for its point-and-click-driven search protocol. Lycos employs a fuzzy search mechanism, finding like words and concepts. If you're looking for a lost roommate, Lycos' People Find feature is probably the best on the Internet.

For basic ease and convenience, we rate this an **A** site. Lycos lies at **http://www.lycos.com**.

Magellan Internet Guide

Magellan (see Figure 11.10) would be just another entry in the user-friendly, category-oriented search engines if not for the unique filtering options offered on the home page. Searching the entire Web is one option. Selecting Reviewed Sites Only limits your search to the 60,000 plus Web sites reviewed by Magellan's editorial staff. Select the Green Light option to avoid those sites intended for mature audiences.

Because full access is always a plus but options are good too, we rate this a **B+** site. Magellan is found at **http://www.mckinley.com**.

FIG. 11.9

Among its many features, the Lycos home page contains links to money sites, a stock locator, and a people finder.

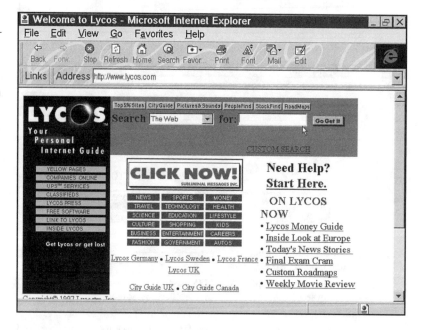

FIG. 11.10

Magellan's home page features the standard keyword box plus unique filtering options.

SEARCH.COM

CINET's tool SEARCH.COM (see Figure 11.11) is designed to be a user-friendly search vehicle. Features include links to telephone and e-mail directories. Search topics include Arts, Business, Computers, Employment, UseNet, and Web. SEARCH.COM is one of several sites powered by the Alta Vista search engine.

As another in a long list of excellent search engines, this site gets a **B** rating. Start your search at **http://www.search.com**.

Starting Point

Starting Point (see Figure 11.12) provides a standard keyword Boolean search. In addition, Choice Web Sites offers a large assortment of selected Web sites grouped in 12 categories: Business, Computing, Education, Entertainment, Investing, Magazines, News, Reference, Shopping, Sports, Travel, and Weather.

Unfortunately, Starting Point's searches require jumping through a lot of hoops. But for overall ease of use, and an ability to customize, this site gets a **B** rating. Get started at **http://www.stpt.com**.

FIG. 11.11

SEARCH.COM, through Express Search, links to other search engines from its home page.

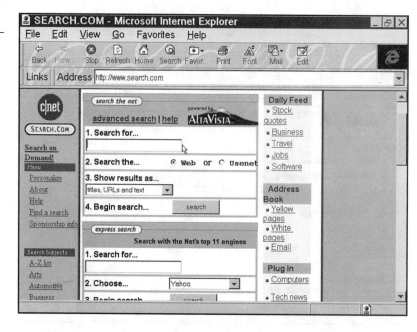

FIG. 11.12

Starting Point offers a simple-to-use, no-nonsense approach to search the Web.

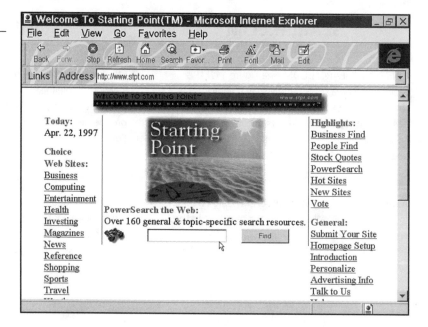

WebCrawler

WebCrawler (see Figure 11.13) features a comprehensive index of the World Wide Web. The primary user interface supports Boolean search operators. Searches can be aided by selecting one of the 18 categories listed. A help section offers detailed instructions for conducting advanced searches. Click Special to find the Top 100 list and other items of interest.

WebCrawler returned plenty of matches for virtually every word we entered. However, it seemed as though many of the listings were dated; the sites no longer exist. In spite of that, we still rate WebCrawler a **B+**. Crawl over to the site at **http://www.webcrawler.com**.

WorldPages

WorldPages is an online business telephone and fax directory. It claims to provide access to numbers in over 100 countries. At the time of writing, Hong Kong companies were listed, but Europe appeared to be on hold. For that reason, we'll rate this site a **C**. You'll find it at **http://www.worldpages.com**.

FIG. 11.13

WebCrawler has the flexibility to go from the simple, this home page, to complex searches.

Yahoo!

Yahoo! (see Figure 11.14) is an indexed search engine, capable of comprehensive searches. Yahoo! prioritizes matches and returns the highest-rated 100 matches. Searches can be better focused by choosing from e-mail listings, UseNet groups, or the seemingly endless hierarchy of categories and subcategories.

Yahoo! offers links to News, Stock Quotes, Weekly Picks, and other helpful categories. Searches can be as simple or as complicated as you choose.

Because it tries to be all things to all people, and generally succeeds, we rate this site an **A+**. Do your own whooping and hollering at Yahoo!'s Web site, at **http://www.yahoo.com**.

FIG. 11.14

Yahoo!'s home page is but the tip of the iceberg.

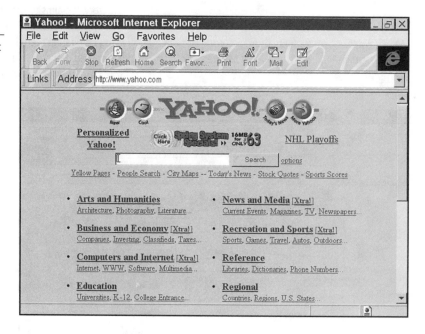

PART III

Game Day

12 Prepare to Invest Online 163

13 Make an Online Trade 171

14 Advanced Trading Techniques 183

15 Locate Other Internet Investment Tools 195

12

Prepare to Invest Online

Your final instructions before take off: All you need to know about the exchanges, the brokers...and paying for it all.

Homework's done. Megabytes of data have been downloaded to your PC. The research phase is complete, and you now have a pretty good idea of how you want your cash to work for you. You're ready to invest. Well, almost. Before proceeding, a few more formal introductions are in order.

In this chapter, we'll present a brief overview of the *exchanges*, the markets where your money will be working. A word or two will follow concerning the *brokers*, the people—or companies—that act as your conduits to the market. The final section describes cash versus margin trading, the two alternatives for actually funding your purchase.

The Exchanges

The exchanges: the sacred temples to the moneychangers. They're where the magic happens, were averages rise or fall. They command a sense of awe much greater than they deserve. In fact, exchanges are simply the marketplace, the spot where the exchange of securities is transacted. Stock exchanges, financial exchanges, commodities exchanges—anyplace where you can buy or sell stocks, bonds, commodities, funds, and options— in spite of their apparent sophistication, in concept remain similar to the old farmer's markets. The catch-of–the day can still be traded for farm fresh eggs.

Interestingly, exchanges don't actually buy or sell anything. Nor do they set the prices. Buying and selling on the floor is handled routinely by computers and sometimes by human beings, called *specialists*.

The origins of most of the major exchanges are similar. They were organized as cooperative market-places by businesses to satisfy a common need. Very often that need was the stabilization of rapidly changing segments of the economy.

The New York Stock Exchange, the oldest and largest exchange in the United States, began as an agree-ment among 24 brokers to trade with one another and to charge a uniform commission to their cus-tomers. On the other hand, the Minneapolis Grain Exchange, a commodity exchange, was organized in response to the need to provide farmers with stable prices for their products.

What follows is a listing of several of the key ex-changes located throughout the country. It's not a complete list; only those exchanges that have a presence on the World Wide Web are featured. The Web pages listed provide useful and interesting information about the mechanics of the individual exchanges and their histories.

 ON THE WEB

For a more comprehensive list of all the major U.S. exchanges, including those not on the World Wide Web, visit The Syndicate at:

> **http://www.moneypages.com/syndicate/
> finance/exchange.html**

Or, if you're an E*TRADE customer, visit their list of exchanges at

> **https://www.etrade.com/cgi-bin/cgitrade/
> webresources**

AMEX: American Stock Exchange

86 Trinity Place, New York, New York 10006-1881
(212) 306-1000
http://www.amex.com

The American Stock Exchange (see Figure 12.1) is made up primarily of companies that were too small to get listed on the New York Stock Exchange. Too small is not synonymous with insufficient or weak. Among the requirements for listing on the AMEX is a pre-tax income of at least $750,000 for the last fiscal year or in two of the last three years. Stockholders' equity must be $4 million and the *market capitali-zation*—the total value of its publicly traded stocks—must be at least $3 million.

CBOE: Chicago Board Options Exchange, Inc.

400 South LaSalle Street, Chicago, IL 60605
(312) 663-2222
http://www.cboe.com

The Chicago Board Options Exchange specializes in stock calls and puts. Trading at CBOE includes op-tions on New York Stock Exchange stocks, S & P 500, U.S. Treasury Bonds, Japan's Nikkei 300 Stock Index, CBOE Mexico Index, and CBOE Israel Index.

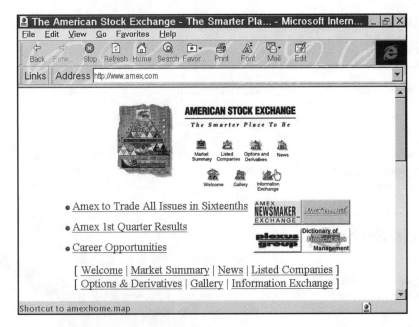

FIG. 12.1

The American Stock Exchange home page. The small icons link users to a market summary, an index of listed companies, a section on options and derivatives, market news, and more.

CBOT: Chicago Board of Trade

141 West Jackson Blvd., Chicago, IL 60604
(312) 435-3601
http://www.cbot.com

The Chicago Board of Trade is a leading futures and options exchange. It was founded in 1848 by a coalition of 82 merchants with the stated purpose of promoting commerce in the city by providing a place for buyers and sellers to meet to exchange commodities.

CME: Chicago Mercantile Exchange

30 South Wacker Drive, Chicago, IL 60606
(312) 930-1000
http://www.cme.com

The Chicago Mercantile Exchange is a major marketplace for futures contracts for commodities. After-hours trading is conducted via the GLOBEX electronic trading system.

CSCE: Coffee, Sugar & Cocoa Exchange, Inc.

4 World Trade Center, New York, NY 10048
(212) 742-6000
http://www.csce.com

The Coffee, Sugar & Cocoa Exchange specializes in futures and options for coffee, sugar, cocoa, milk, cheddar cheese, nonfat dry milk, and butter.

Minneapolis Grain Exchange

130 Grain Exchange Building, 400 South 4th Street, Minneapolis, MN 5514-1413
(800) 827-4746
http://www.mgex.com

The Minneapolis Grain Exchange is a commodities futures exchange specializing in grains and, more recently, shrimp. An average of 1 million bushels of grain is traded daily.

Nasdaq: National Association of Securities Dealers Automated Quotations

(212) 656-3000
http://www.nasdaq.com

Nasdaq (see Figure 12.2) specializes in the sale of over-the-counter (OTC) securities. Securities are bought and sold by securities brokers and dealers through online computer transactions. Securities traded over Nasdaq must meet predefined listing standards. Nasdaq is a virtual electronic marketplace. There is no fixed location for the exchange.

NYCE: New York Cotton Exchange

4 World Trade Center, New York, NY 10048
(212) 742–5050
http://www.nyce.com

The New York Cotton Exchange is the premier marketplace for cotton futures and futures options trading.

NYSE: New York Stock Exchange

11 Wall Street, New York, NY 10005
(212) 656–3000
http://www.nyse.com

Established in 1792, the New York Stock Exchange (see Figure 12.3) is the oldest and largest exchange in the United States. The NYSE is comprised of 1,366 members. The membership total is a fixed number. Persons wanting to become a member can do so only by purchasing an existing membership. (Plan on spending at least $1.25 million for this privilege.)

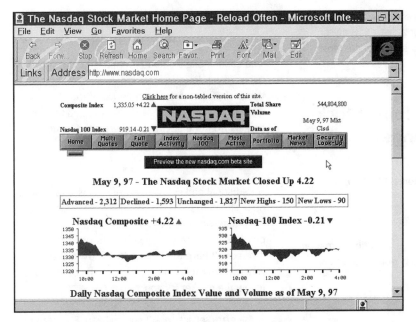

FIG. 12.2

The Nasdaq home page. Click the button bar for quotes, index reports, and a portfolio management tool.

FIG. 12.3

The New York Stock Exchange home page. Click the icons near the bottom of the page to find who's listed on the NYSE, a market summary, an annual report, educational materials, and more.

To be listed on the New York Stock Exchange, a company must have assets of at least $18 million and a pre-tax income of $2.5 million in the most recent year.

PHLX: Philadelphia Stock Exchange

1900 Market Street, Philadelphia, PA 19103
(215) 496–5404
http://www.phlx.com

The Philadelphia Stock Exchange is a primary market for the trading of stocks, equity options, index options, and currency options.

Brokers: Traditional and Discount

Your broker, whether traditional or discount, will be your agent for conducting trades on all the major markets. As the migration to the Internet continues, expect the line between a full-service traditional broker and a discount broker to become even less clear. This section will break them down and describe the differences between traditional and discount brokers. Although this book isn't titled "Hire a Full-Service Broker and Maximize Your Commission Payments," we are completely without bias. You have our word (sort of).

Traditional Broker

Traditional brokers operate from a large office with tall glass windows overlooking Wall Street, or from a tiny desk in the back of a crowded office. The primary characteristic that separates the traditional brokers from the discount brokers is the range of services they personally deliver to their clients and the cost.

A traditional broker will freely offer advice as to what he or she thinks you should buy or sell. Reports on individual companies or entire industries can be prepared specifically for you by your broker's analyst. If you don't have the time to follow the market yourself, your full-service broker will be delighted to follow the market for you.

These extra services don't come cheap. Expect to pay far more than you would at a discount broker. The extra cost incurred by commissions can be as much as 10 times that of a comparable trade placed with a discount broker.

Discount Broker

The discount broker works in a lifeless airless cube—or she could have a spacious office overlooking Wall Street. Discount brokers offer little in the way of frills: They won't conduct your research for you, and they won't offer personal investment advice.

On the other hand, most of the discount brokers do offer valuable resources to aid you in making your decisions. As you saw in Chapters 4 through 9, much of the information you'll need to make intelligent financial decisions is available, for free, online. In addition, customer-only resource areas from online discount brokers rival the information you'd get from a traditional broker. The big difference is that you must do the homework, and you'll have nobody to blame if your investments go south.

The cost? On a comparable trade from three brokers, we found prices ranging from nearly $150 to as little as $14.95. Same securities, same parameters. Other comparisons using other brokers generated wildly disparate transaction prices.

Additional savings can be found by shopping from among the discount brokers. Each commission-based discounter has its own unique way of calculating those commissions. Many use a secret algorithm that factors in such variables as volume, cost per share, and total value of the trade, making it virtually impossible to do a valid price comparison among the various brokers. Others, such as E*TRADE and e.Schwab, charge a flat rate (typically around $20) per transaction, regardless of the cost or volume (up to certain limits). Several organizations (The American Association for Individual Investors, for example, at **http://e.schwab**) have attempted to put together charts showing typical transactions in an attempt to aid in cost comparison.

Cash vs. Margin Trading

There are several ways to put investment money to work for you. In fact, we describe a variety of transaction and order types in Chapter 14. Here, the only concern will be whose money is doing the work.

Cash trading is the straightforward process. For a specified amount of cash, $1000 for example, you purchase an equivalent amount of stock.

Margin trading is the leveraged purchase of securities. Your $1000 goes in as cash equity. Your broker can then lend you an additional $1000, meaning you're leveraging 50 percent. This combined investment allows you to purchase up to $2000 of your favorite stock. The brokerage will charge you interest on the outstanding balance of what is, in effect, a loan. The draw? Ideally, the costs associated with the loan will be more than offset by money you earn from the appreciation of your stock.

Buying on margin has obvious costs when the value of the stock fails to rise; you're in some actual financial peril if the security experiences dramatic declines. When the equity in your account falls below a specified minimum amount, usually 25 to 30 percent, the brokerage will issue what's known as a *margin call*. Your phone will ring, and you'll be required to deposit funds in your account in an amount sufficient to bring you back within the established margin guidelines. Remember, if you get involved with margin trading, the brokerage has the right to either collect more cash from you or to sell a sufficient number of shares of the stock to maintain the *minimum maintenance requirement* within acceptable bounds. The minimum maintenance requirement is the minimum equity required in your account in

order to secure your leveraged purchase. The
amount required will vary depending on the type
of security purchased and the amount of money
borrowed.

13

Make an Online Trade

Finally. All your preparation, exploration, strategizing, and research are complete. Now it's time to open an account and actually buy something—online!

In this chapter, you'll do the most straightforward kind of trade—a simple stock purchase. To conduct this first transaction, we turn to the leading online brokerage: E*TRADE Securities. Chapters 14 and 15 will describe more complex trades and will briefly introduce you to other online brokers.

Why E*TRADE?

E*TRADE, with its simple, low-cost structure and in-depth information resources, is an ideal representation of what this book is about: taking charge of your own financial destiny. E*TRADE is easy to use, secure, and inexpensive, and is loaded with tools to help you invest smarter.

Noteworthy Features

Exceptionally low commission rates are an important part of the E*TRADE story but they're not the whole story. Customers have direct access to a wide array of information resources designed to help them invest with more confidence and intelligence:

- ◆ Personal Market Pages provide an instant snapshot of the markets as soon as you log on. Customize the main menu to display preferred market indicators, "Hot Stocks," financial news sources, and links to your favorite Web sites.

- ◆ Live market commentary and analysis from Briefing.com, the most widely read source of such information on the Web.

- ◆ Stock screening tools and direct access to 25 top-name research reports and advisory letters from INVESTools.

- ◆ Sophisticated Java routines enable you to chart specific stocks against other stocks, indexes, indicators, and mutual funds.

- ◆ Access fundamental analysis and earnings estimates from BASELINE financial services. Formerly, this service was only available to institutional investors.

- ◆ Easily track securities with Stock Watch. Create and store up to five lists with as many as 18 securities per list.

E*TRADE Security

Security is a topic that is always upfront in the minds of investors. Software providers and commercial online providers are constantly working to provide higher levels of security. Advanced data encryption methods allow for the transmission of data that is decipherable only to the intended parties.

In addition to data encryption, E*TRADE provides further protection through the use of unique user names, log-on passwords, and trading passwords. Passwords can be changed online at any time.

The assets in your account are protected by a combination of insurances. SIPC provides up to $500,000 of coverage (limited to $100,000 in cash claims), and an additional $9.5 million in coverage is provided through a member company of the American International Group. Of course, this protection does not cover fluctuations in the market value of your investment.

But don't take our word for it. See how the world views E*TRADE in a collection of E*TRADE-related articles from major publications. The collection can be found at **http://www.etrade.com/news/main.shtml**.

Opening Your Account

Before you can place your first trade, you must open an account with an online broker and, well, show them the money. This section explains how to sign up with E*TRADE. Go to another broker, and your mileage may vary.

In addition to its many other charms, E*TRADE happens to be one of the most accessible online brokerages. Here's how you get there:

◆ From the World Wide Web, go to E*TRADE's home page at **http://www.etrade.com** (see Figure 13.1).

◆ If you use America Online, log onto the AOL system, then enter the keyword **ETRADE**.

◆ CompuServe users, type **GO ETRADE**.

◆ Prodigy Internet users, go to the Business and Finance area, select Internet Invester and go to the Online Trading area.

◆ Many of the more popular financial sites on the Web, such as Microsoft Investor and Yahoo! Finance, feature direct links to E*TRADE's home page. Click the E*TRADE logo.

Access to the customer-only portions of E*TRADE requires Netscape Navigator or Microsoft Internet Explorer (version 2.0 or higher), or America Online 3.0.

The E*TRADE home page contains dozens of hyper-links to related pages: A log-on button (don't use it yet), demo, account registration, free quotes, a stock trading game, and more.

For Canadian investors, a hyperlink on E*TRADE's home page will take you to E*TRADE Canada, which caters to the needs of Canadian customers. Investors wanting to travel in a straight line can find E*TRADE Canada at **http://www.canada.etrade.com**.

First time visitors may find it worthwhile to take advantage of E*TRADE's demo program. It's an excellent way to see what E*TRADE has to offer,

FIG. 13.1

The E*TRADE home page, your starting point for online trading.

while at the same time learning to navigate the system. Playing the E*TRADE Game is also a great way to get your feet wet. To open a new account, click the Open an E*TRADE Account link near the middle of the page. The Open An Account page is displayed (see Figure 13.2).

In the Complete an Application Online box, select the type of account you want to open. The Registration and Trading Level boxes will present you with lists to select from. Check the method of funding—how you plan to get your money to E*TRADE—that you want to use. After these items are filled in, you can click the Click to Continue button.

An appropriate application will appear on your screen. Fill out the entire application online. Then just print the completed form, sign it, and mail to E*TRADE. If you prefer, click the Request by Mail button, and the full application packet will be sent to your home.

The completed forms have to be returned via regular mail. For your protection, an original signature is required. The minimum initial deposit you'll need to open an E*TRADE account is just $1,000 ($2,000 for margin accounts).

Bundle up your registration materials and send the whole package, including check, to:

E*TRADE Securities, Inc.
2400 Geng Road
Palo Alto, CA 94303-3317

In a few days, you'll receive by return mail a package of account information, including the *E*TRADE Trading Guide*. The package contains your unique user name and password, which you'll need to log on and place your trade.

FIG. 13.2

The Open an Account page at E*TRADE; apply for your account here.

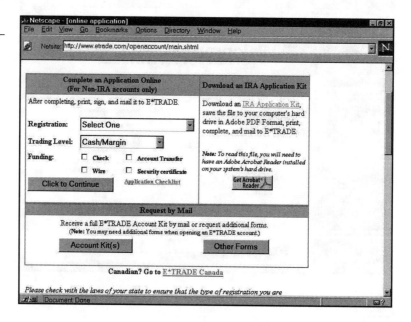

CHECK'S IN THE MAIL—NOT!

After your account is set up, there are basically five ways other than sending a check to get cash or securities into your account. E*TRADE accepts wired funds, securities deposits, account transfers from other brokers and mutual fund companies, and direct deposits and other forms of electronic transfers.

◆ *Wire Funds.* Ask your bank to wire money to:

Citibank, F.S.B.
260 California Street
San Francisco, CA 94111
ABA#321171184
For E*TRADE Securities Inc.,
account #601024235
For further credit to (your name, your
E*TRADE account)

◆ *Securities.* To deposit securities into your account, appoint E*TRADE Securities, Inc. as attorney, and sign your name exactly as it appears on the face of the certificate.

◆ *Transfer.* Fill out a Transfer Form to transfer specific securities or an entire account from another firm. Be sure to include a copy of your most recent statement. The transfer of funds takes at least 15 business days.

◆ *Direct deposit.* Arrange for payments you receive regularly—paychecks, government checks, mutual fund distributions—to be automatically deposited into your E*TRADE account. Contact E*TRADE by e-mail or on 1-800-STOCKS5 (1-800-786-2575) to request a form that will let you initiate the direct deposit with your employer, government agency, or mutual fund company.

◆ *Online Cash Transfer.* Sign up to transfer funds electronically from any account with check writing privileges. Using this method you can transfer as much as $10,000 per day to your E*TRADE account. If you submit your Cash Transfer request before 4:00 p.m. ET, your money will be available for investing in two business days. For transfers initiated after 4:00 p.m. ET, your money will be available for investing in three business days.

The First Timer Primer

The remainder of this chapter will guide you through a typical trading session on E*TRADE. For simplicity's sake, the types of user options explored in this section will be kept to a minimum. We explore the remainder in greater depth in Chapter 14.

Accessing Your Account

After you have your user name and password, reopen the E*TRADE Web site at **http://www. etrade.com**. You'll see the familiar E*TRADE home page. This time, though, you'll be looking for the Customer Log On button. Click this button, and enter your user name and password in the dialog box (see Figure 13.3).

Users of Microsoft Internet Explorer: Select the Save This Password check box, and click the OK button. The Save the Password check box will not appear to users of Netscape Navigator. The E*TRADE Customer Main Menu will appear (see Figure 13.4).

About the Customer Main Menu

The Customer Main Menu is divided into two segments: Navigation links are found in the left-hand column, and the large information area containing the E*TRADE bulletin, market indicator, user-selectable "hot stocks," and links to today's news is on the right. A new message will appear when E*TRADE has a message for you. At the bottom of the information area is a hyperlink that lets you customize the page and a toolbar with six operation buttons.

FIG. 13.3

Enter your user name and password in the pop-up dialog box.

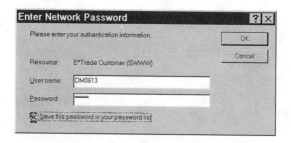

FIG. 13.4

The Customer Main Menu shows the navigation links and market information.

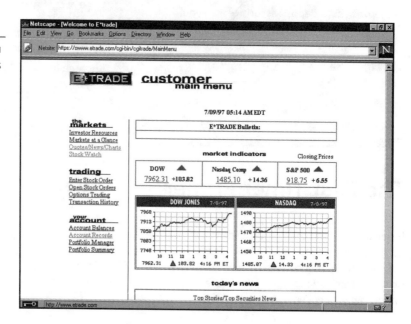

Customize the Main Menu

To personalize the Customer Main Menu page, click the Customize This Page hyperlink near the bottom of the Information Area. The Custom Options page appears (see Figure 13.5).

Choose up to three market indicators, decide which of two charts you'd like displayed, select 10 news providers, name six stocks you'd like tracked, and add the addresses of other Web pages you might want to visit regularly.

Click the OK button, and when your page is confirmed, click the main button to return to Customer Main Menu.

Last Minute Information Before You Buy

Before you actually execute the trade, you may want to review any last minute reports concerning the securities you plan to buy or sell. This section explains how to get a last minute status report on stock prices, company news, and other pertinent information.

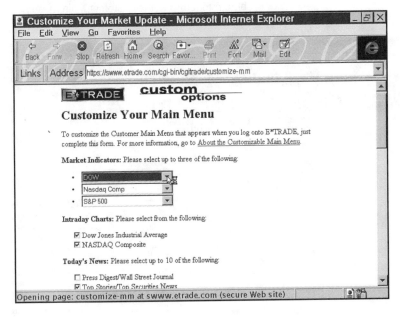

FIG. 13.5

From the Custom Options page, decide which information you'd like to have appear on the Main Menu.

Check the Price

Most investors want to check the price one last time. From the navigation links in the left column, select Quotes/News/Charts. The Quotes News Charts page appears (see Figure 13.6). (E*TRADE also gives you a free real-time quote the moment before you transmit your order.) The purpose here is a last minute review before sending your order to the market.

The Quotes News Charts page displays options for locating various kinds of quote-related information. If you want to look up a company but can't remember the stock symbol, type the company name in the Enter Company Name box, and click the Find Symbol button.

Quotes for options, indices, and funds can also be obtained from this page. See Chapter 6 for more on options, indices, and funds.

Enter the symbol in the Enter Stock Symbols box. Choose brief Summary or longer Full Quotes. Click the Get Quotes button to display the Quotes page (see Figure 13.7).

From the Quotes page, you can view 20-minute delayed quotes. You can also view current news (the 10 most recent news stories on that security) and charts by clicking the underlined stock symbol, and you can go directly to a prefilled order page by clicking the green box to the left of the symbol.

There's just one more item you might want to check—first: your balance. Use your browser's Back button to return to the Customer Main Menu.

FIG. 13.6

Use the Quotes News Charts page to check on a a price.

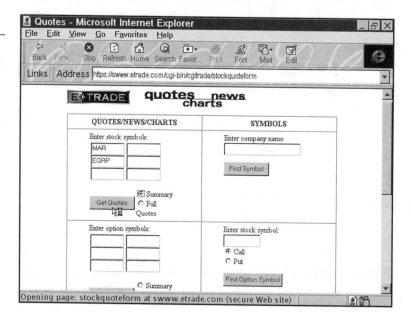

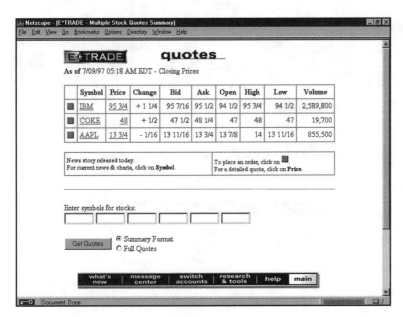

FIG. 13.7

The Quotes pages also deliver news and charts.

Check Your Balance

E*TRADE accepts orders up to the available buying power in your account. Before placing a trade, it's a good idea to check your balance. From the navigation links in the left column, select Account Balances. The Account Balances page appears (see Figure 13.8).

Your account balances are displayed here, along with hyperlinks to Account Positions (your securities, the price you paid, and the current value), Account Transactions (more accounting information about the status of your account), Current Yields (E*TRADE holds your uninvested cash in interest-earning money market funds; this page lists the current rates of interest), and Margin Rates (detailed in Chapter 14).

That's it. Time to go invest that deposit.

Purchase the Stock

Use your browser's Back button to return to the Customer Main Menu. If you're logging on after a break, go to the main E*TRADE screen at **http:// www.etrade.com** and click **Customer Log On** to get to the Customer Main Menu.

From the navigation links in the left column, click Enter Stock Order. On other E*TRADE pages, the navigation links are located at the bottom of the page. Same links, same order…just a different position. You can enter a stock order from any of them.

The Stock Order screen appears (see Figure 13.9).

FIG. 13.8

The Account Balances page gives you your available funds.

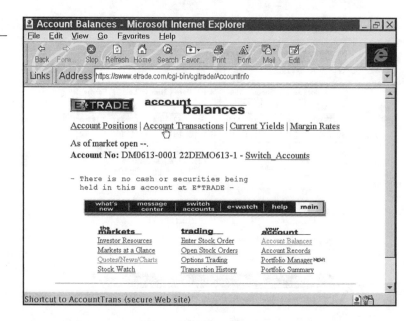

FIG. 13.9

The Stock Order page provides lots of trading options.

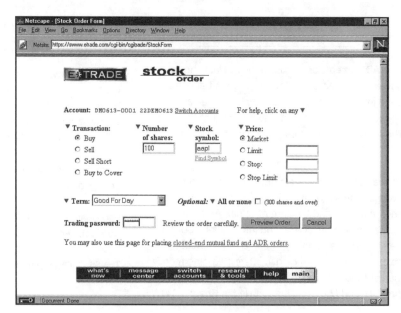

The Stock Order Page

The Stock Order page is replete with trading choices. In our sample trade, we're going to buy 100 shares of Apple Computer, with the company symbol AAPL. The following sections walk you through the items you'll need to complete for your stock order.

Transactions

To purchase the stock, select Buy in the Transaction column.

The other options in the Transaction column—Sell, Sell Short, and Buy to Cover—will be described in Chapter 14.

Number of Shares

Enter the total number of shares you want to purchase in the Number of Shares box. We entered the figure **100**.

Stock Symbol

Enter the company's ticker symbol in the Stock Symbol box. In our example, we enter the symbol **AAPL**.

If you have forgotten the symbol, or if you just jumped directly to this page, you can look up the symbol by clicking Find Symbol directly beneath the Stock Symbol box.

Price

In the Price column, select Market. E*TRADE always seeks the best market price available. The other Price selections—Limit, Stop, and Stop Limit—will be covered in Chapter 14.

Term

From the Term box, select the Good for Day option.

A Good for Day order is valid only for the day the order is entered. It will automatically expire at the end of the day's trading session. The other option in the Term box is Good-till-Canceled. A Good-till-Canceled order is valid for 60 days, or until the order is canceled.

The All or None Box

Because the number of shares selected for this demonstration is under 300, the All or None option is not available.

If you are trading more then 300 shares, you can use this option to request that your entire order take place as a single transaction. An order listed as All or None is also known as a *special order*. Special orders are placed after the regular limited orders are filled. What this means is that an order without the All or None designation gets preference over the All or None order. Also, the All or None order may be passed up entirely if the number of shares requested is unavailable.

The "All or None" order will guarantee that all of the shares in your order will be bought or sold at the same price, but it does not guarantee that the order will be able to be executed.

Trading Password

When you have finished entering all your trade information, enter your password in the Trading Password box. As an extra security measure, the trade will not be executed without a valid entry.

Preview

Click the Preview Order button to display the details of your order, including a free real-time quote.

Because this is a demonstration, click the Cancel button. This will cancel the order. Had this been an actual purchase, clicking the Place Order button would have completed the transaction. An order confirmation would have appeared, indicating your transaction number plus the date and time your order was placed. As soon as the order is executed, E*TRADE transmits an electronic trade confirmation through the E*TRADE message center e-mail. In addition, you will receive a hard-copy verification of your trade in the regular mail.

14

Advanced Trading Techniques

Have a dollar, buy a dollar's worth of goods. Life may have been that simple once, but not any more. In this chapter you'll learn the art of margin trading and—with complete disregard for the advice of William Shakespeare—both a borrower and a lender you'll be.

In our tour of securities trading, we'll once again step through the E*TRADE Stock Order page. This time, however, there'll be stops at every selection along the way, as we dig a little deeper to explain the many trading options offered by the E*TRADE trading system.

To begin, log on at **http://www.etrade.com**. From the Customer Main Menu, click Enter Stock Order. The Stock Order page appears. (See Figure 14.1.)

Selecting Transactions

To buy or to sell—now there's a question. Making trades can be as simple as exchanging cash for securities, and can be more convoluted than you'd ever imagine. We'll try to keep it simple, by breaking the transactions into three basic types:

◆ *Buy and Sell*. The most basic type of order you can give is to buy (covered in Chapter 13 "Make an Online Trade") or to sell. Both orders direct the broker to execute a transaction in the securities, type, and quantity you specify. (But even a simple buy or sell can give you lots of flexibility, as you'll see.)

◆ *Sell Short*. *Short selling* is the practice of selling securities you don't own for a potential profit that can't be realized until you replace the securities at a lower price. See the following section for a broader explanation of this type of transaction.

◆ *Buy to Cover*. As you'll discover in the following section, if you're going to sell short, you'll need to replace the borrowed stocks. Click Buy to Cover to replace securities you previously sold short.

A Closer Look at Short Selling

Investors sell short when they think the price of a stock will be going down. They borrow shares of the stock from their broker and immediately sell them, expecting that they can later *cover* the sale by buying replacement stock at a lower price. If this all sounds a great deal like borrowing from Peter to pay Paul, breathe easy. It's a legitimate form of trading and keeps the markets stable.

When you sell short, you do so with borrowed securities. In the giant ethersphere of Wall Street, though, all transactions take place in an electronic cloud. Don't sweat the details; keeping the books straight is the brokerage's job.

FIG. 14.1

Once again, the E*TRADE Stock Order Page.

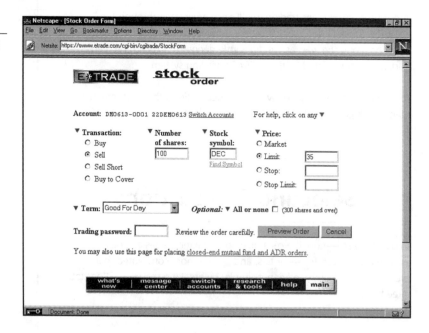

Typically, you'd sell short when you thought a particular stock—for our purposes, we'll short the badly out-of-favor Widget Corporation stock—had reached its peak.

Imagine that there are no Widget Corporation securities in your portfolio. The fact that you don't actually own the stock won't cause you to miss out on the opportunity to profit on the decline. You can still sell short 100 or more shares of Widget Corporation at $100 a share, generating an income of $10,000. That's not bad considering that before the sale you had nothing. (Don't plan on spending the money too quickly, however. Your broker will retain the proceeds until the deal is complete. There is still the matter of replacing the securities you just borrowed and sold.)

If your prophetic skills are functioning properly, the price of Widget's stock will soon drop through the floor, and you'll be able to replace the borrowed shares with an equal number of shares purchased at the new lower market price. If the new price is $75 a share, for example, you'll be able to replace the 100 borrowed shares for only $7,500. The original $10,000 you earned minus the $7,500 you use to cover your short, less the $14.95 commission on the initial short sale and the $14.95 commission on the cover, becomes your $2,470.10 profit. In light of the fact that you never owned the security, that's not a bad day's work.

Whoa! Slow down just a minute. There are dangers to selling short. Two, in fact.

Most importantly, there's always the chance that you're dead wrong, and the price of Widget Corporation is going nowhere but up—leaving you standing there dumbstruck, holding nothing but an empty sack and a promise to repay the ether-person you borrowed stock from. Your broker loves you, of course, and so won't force you to immediately *cover*

the short. You will, however, have to maintain a balance large enough to continue to carry this transaction—and the higher Widget goes, the more you need to maintain. Eventually, you may be required to pump more capital into your account, or even be forced to replace the stock at a higher price and simply absorb the loss.

Also, selling short is not as simple as jumping on a sinking ship and riding it to the bottom. The SEC and NASD have rules to prevent a small downward movement in a stock from becoming a full catastrophe. A short sale can be executed only after an *uptick* or *a zero-plus tick,* a last-reported price for the stock equal to or greater than the previous price. A sell-short order will not be executed unless this condition is met.

Additional useful information on short sales can be found at the following sites:

◆ *Equity Analytics Web*. The Short Sale of Stock page offers Equity Analytics' perspective on the subject. Equity Analytics, Ltd. provides research and analyses such as: portfolio modeling advisement, IPO assistance, individual company profiles, sector analysis, and hedging strategies with derivatives for institutions.

http://www.e-analytics.com/fp16b.htm

◆ *The Washington Post Business Glossary*. Get your financial vocabulary straight, as defined by the Washington Post. This is a straightforward listing with definitions of hundreds of words and terms often used by the financial community.

http://www.washingtonpost.com/wp-srv/ business/longterm/glossary

◆ *Pace University Library*. The text is certainly worthwhile, but it is the graphic representation of the short sale that makes this a site worth visiting. There's nothing flashy here, just a no nonsense clarity that helps to explain it all.

http://library.pace.edu/~viswanat/class/652/notes/shortsal.html

◆ *Rule 10b-21(T).* Short selling in connection with a public offering.

http://www.law.uc.edu/CCL/34ActRls/10b/rule10b-21T.html

Choosing the Price Parameters

In real life, there's more than one way to set a price. There's the sticker price, the discount price, the wholesale price, and, of course, the actual price. Why should the stock market be any different? Setting the type of order you want in the Price column will allow you to dictate as much control as is possible over the prices at which you will buy and sell. It is one of the best mechanisms available for assuring that ordered transactions are executed only when conditions are favorable for you. Select one of the following options from the Price list.

Market Orders

A market order is your most basic type of order. Issue a market order when you want to buy or sell a specified security as soon as possible after the order has been placed. This order will be executed at the best available price at the time the order is received in the marketplace.

The market price of a security is set by the forces of supply and demand. A bidding action moves the price either up or down until a transaction occurs. If buying a security, the trader representing you will bid up the price until he finds a seller. If selling, the trader decreases the offer price until he finds a buyer.

Limit Orders

With a limit order, you set the price requirements for the transaction.

If you're buying, you set the limit for the highest price you're willing to pay. For instance, Widget Corporation stock may be trading at $10 a share. You may want to purchase 100 shares, but you may not be willing to pay more than $8.50 a share. A limit order—provided the market is active enough to execute it—will assure you that you'll pay no more than the $8.50 a share that you designated. If the stock does not become available at $8.50 a share or less, the transaction will not be executed.

Similarly, if you're selling, you may want to sell your 100 shares but for no less than $11 a share. With a limit order your shares are offered for sale only if your minimum price or better can be obtained.

Stop Orders

A stop order—often called a *stop loss order*—is used to buy or sell a stock, or other securities, once they have reached a predetermined price, called the *stop price.* A stop order to sell is always set below the current market price; a stop order to buy is always set above the current market price.

At the predetermined price, the stop order become a regular market order. The order is executed at the prevailing market price. A stop order to sell is useful as a means of protecting against excessive losses, as well as offering partial protection of any paper profits you make while you own a particular security. Paper profits refer to the increased value your stock may have achieved but that you never cashed in. A stop order to buy can be used to protect a profit or limit a loss on a short sale.

Typically, a stop loss order is set 10 to 15 percent below the value of the stock. For example, imagine you own several shares of Widget Corporation stock, presently trading at $10 a share. You want to hang on to your investment, but you're not willing to risk a big loss if the price drops dramatically. To protect yourself, you set a stop order near the maximum loss you could comfortably absorb. In this case, $8.50 a share would be typical. As long as the value of Widget stock remains above the $8.50-a-share selling price, nothing happens. Should it reach the $8.50 minimum, the stop order becomes a market order to sell and is executed as quickly as possible. The actual price you receive per share will depend on the market price.

Stop Limit Orders

A stop limit is a combination of a limit order and a stop loss order. Like a stop order, a stop limit will begin to execute once the price of the security reaches a specified threshold. Unlike a stop loss order, however, a stop limit automatically becomes a limit order once the stop price is reached. This practice prevents selling off at a lower than expected price in a very volatile market.

As in the previous example, you might set an $8.50-per-share trigger price for your $10 Widget stock. Should the price drop to $8.50 a share, the stop limit is invoked, and your stock is offered for sale at that price. However, if the price of Widget stocks drops below $8.50, your lower limit is breached, and the execution of any further sales is halted.

Coming to Terms

Will the trader who placed a limit order for Widget stock today still want it in place tomorrow? Next month? For that reason E*TRADE will, like any other broker, let you select the time parameters of your limit order, your stop order, or your stop limit order. Go to the E*TRADE Stock Order page, and click the

Term drop-down list arrow. From there, select one of the following:

- *Good for Day Order*. A day order is good only on the trading day it is issued. If the order is not executed on the day it's given, the day order is allowed to expire.

- *Good-till-Canceled Order*. A Good-till-Canceled (GTC) order remains open for 60 days or until it is executed or canceled. You can check your open orders by clicking Open Stock Orders on the main menu or at the bottom of most pages.

All-or-None Order

An All-or-None order is a request to buy or sell 300 or more shares in a single transaction or not at all. (An All-or-None order is not valid for fewer then 300 shares.) Return to Chapter 13 for additional details about this option.

Put It All Together

As you did in Chapter 13, when you have finished entering all your trade information, enter your password in the Trading Password box. Click the Preview Order button to view your trade just before it's executed. You'll see a confirmation screen, along with a free real-time quote, and will have the option of placing or canceling the order.

Placing an Options Order

At times extremely risky and speculative and at times very conservative, options trading is not for the faint-of-heart or the inexperienced trader. In fact, inexperienced traders are not even not allowed to play. Would-be options traders are required to fill out special sections of the E*TRADE application. Only after proving they're sufficiently experienced will they be granted option trading authority. Without it, there is no accessing the Enter Option Order page used later on in this section.

Simply put, you buy an option if you want to lock in a certain price at a specified time in the future. A single contract will allow you to control 100 shares of the specified stock. Say, for example, you want the privilege of purchasing a stock at $100, at some point in the future—anticipating that the price will go up in the interim. Likewise, you can buy options to sell stock at a high price, expecting the price to drop before the option expires. If the stock price fails to move, you have the right to simply ignore the option and let it expire, unused. The price specified in the options contract is known as the *strike price*.

There are two types of options contracts, called *calls* and *puts*, either of which can be held in a long position or a short position (also known as *writing* an option). A *call* is an option to buy; a *put* is an option to sell.

To trade options, you'll go to a new screen. Log on as usual from the E*TRADE home page (**http://www.etrade.com**) to arrive at the Customer Main Menu screen. From there, select Options Trading from the Navigation Links in the left column. The Options Trading page will appear. Select the Enter

Option Order link to get to the Options Order screen. (See Figure 14.2.)

Placing Options Transactions

The radio button format of the Transactions area on the Options Order screen is similar to the selections on the Stock Order screen. Only the names and the functions have been changed. Here's a brief description of your options.

Buy Open

Select Buy Open to purchase a put or call option. Buy Open is the choice to make when you think you may want to purchase or sell a security at a specified price in the future.

As the purchaser of an option, you receive an agreement from the seller that she will buy, or sell, a specified security at a specified price on or before a specified date. You are under no obligation, however, to ever exercise your future rights if, when the option expires, you perceive you'll make no profit.

◆ *Call*. Investors who buy to open a Call option generally hope the security will increase in value above the contractual strike price. An upward movement lets them profit by purchasing below the market value.

◆ *Put*. Investors who buy to open a Put option are generally looking for the price of the underlying security to fall. The option would allow them to sell at the contractual strike price which is above the market price, regardless of market fluctuations.

◆ *Sell Close*. Sell Close counters the Buy Open order. Click Sell Close to close a long position by selling an equivalent contract.

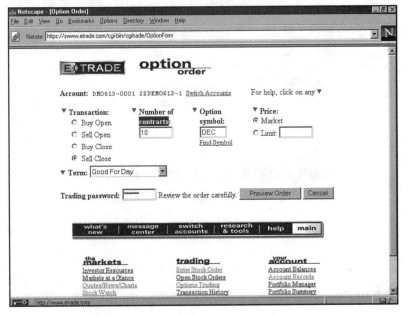

FIG. 14.2

The Options Order screen—the place to go when you want to transact options.

Sell Open

Select Sell Open to *write* a Call or Put option. As the writer of an option, you are agreeing to buy, or sell, a specified security at a specified price at any time during the life of the option.

- *Call.* Call writers are generally expecting the price of the underlying security (which they own) to stay steady or decline during the life of the option contract. Their profit is made when the purchaser fails to exercise the option, and they get to keep the proceeds of the option sale (the premium), as well as their underlying security.

- *Put.* Put writers are generally hoping the underlying security stays steady or increases in value above the contract price. The profit comes in when the buyer at the other end decides not to exercise the contract because the stock is trading above the strike price.

- *Buy Close.* Buy Close is the counterpoint to the Sell Open order. Click Buy Close to cover a short position.

When you've selected a Transaction type, move to the Number of Contracts box and enter the number of options contracts you want to buy or sell. Remember, one equity option contract lets you control 100 shares of stock.

Option Symbol

In the Option Symbol text box, enter the symbol of the option you want to purchase. If you do not know the symbol for the option you want to purchase, click Find Symbol. The Options Symbols page will appear. (See Figure 14.3.)

FIG. 14.3

Use the Options Symbols page to find the symbol of the option you want to purchase.

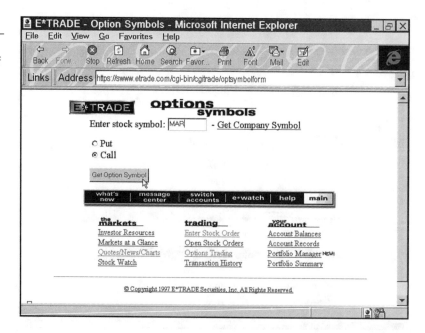

To use the Options Symbols page, enter the *underlying stock symbol*—the ticker symbol of the company whose stock you're looking to buy options on. MAR, for instance, is the symbol for the Marriott hotel chain. (If you're not certain of the stock symbol, click the Get Company Symbol link to look it up.)

After you've entered the stock symbol, go to the radio buttons and click either Put or Call. A put is an obligation (when you sell a put), or the right (if you're buying the put) to sell the security. A call is an obligation (when you sell the call), or the right (if you're buying the call) to purchase a security.

Click the Get Option Symbol button to see a list of the relevant options. (See Figure 14.4.)

Then click the Back button on your browser two times to return to the Option Order page.

Enter the name of the option in the Option Symbol box.

Selecting Price and Term Options

The Price list offers two options. The Market option is relatively straightforward. As you saw with the Stock Order page, a market order is issued when you want to buy or sell a given option as soon as possible, regardless of how the market changes. A market order is executed at the best available market price at the time of the transaction.

The Limit option requires a few more decisions, because it requires that you set the outside limits on the price you're willing to pay for an option and the term. To select Term options, choose one of these from the drop-down list:

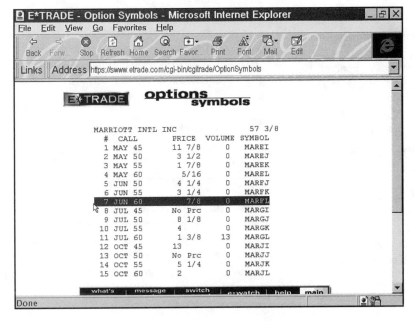

FIG. 14.4

Use the Options Symbols page to determine the name of the option you want to trade.

◆ *Day Order*. A day order is good only on the trading day it's issued.

◆ *Good-till-Canceled Order*. A (GTC) order remains open for 60 days, or until it is executed or canceled.

Preview Order

Prior to actually placing your order you can preview the order and check for any errors. If you're satisfied that all is correct, then place your order by clicking the Order button. Click Cancel to start over or to cancel your order.

Making a Margin Trade

Margin trading, as mentioned in Chapter 12, "Prepare to Invest Online," means borrowing your broker's funds to leverage your own assets. In any other arena, it would be called a loan. Your broker will charge interest for money used in making a margin trade.

Your fully paid-up marginable securities can be held as collateral for the margin loan, allowing you to, in effect, double your purchasing power.

It works like this: Normally, if you had $2,000 to invest, you might purchase 200 shares of Widget Corporation at $10 a share. If the price of the stock rose just $2, you could sell your shares for $2,400. That would be a profit of $400 or 20 percent.

If, on the other hand, you had exercised the full buying power of your margin account, you could still purchase the 200 shares with your $2,000, plus another 200 shares with your broker's money. Then, if the price of the stock rose $2, the resulting sale of the 400 shares would net you $4,800. Subtract the $2,000 you borrowed and the $2,000 of your own money that was invested and you'd have $800 profit or a 40 percent profit on your $2,000 investment. Even after paying interest and commission you'd come out ahead.

As with most things, there is a downside. If the value of the stock goes down $2 instead of up you would lose $800 plus interest and commissions. That's, of course, double what you would have lost if you hadn't borrowed.

The equity in your account determines how much you can purchase on margin. While the ratio of permissible margin spending to collateral doesn't change, the value of your securities might—meaning that you could find yourself with insufficient funds to cover your margin account if the value of your securities declines. When that happens, a *maintenance call* is issued. Maintenance calls are not nice things. They require you to increase the equity in your account to cover your margin requirements. Failure to do so could result in a market action by the broker.

To prevent the risk of receiving an inconvenient margin call, the best course of action is to borrow less than the maximum amounts permitted and avoid highly volatile securities.

Federal regulations require investors to deposit at least $2,000 to qualify for a margin account. E*TRADE also requires that the price of a single share of stock bought on margin be no less then $5.00. E*TRADE's additional margin account requirements are as follows:

◆ For stocks greater then $5.00 a share:

- The maximum loan value against collateral is 50 percent.

- The maintenance requirement is at least 30 percent.

◆ Non-money market mutual funds held more than 30 days:

- The maximum loan value against collateral is 50 percent.

- The maintenance requirement is 30 percent.

◆ Corporate bonds, A or better, $70 or more:

- The maximum loan value against collateral is 70 percent.

- The maintenance requirement is 25 percent.

◆ Convertible bonds, A or better, $70 or more:

- The maximum loan value against collateral is 50 percent.

- The maintenance requirement is 30 percent.

◆ Municipal bonds, A or better, $70 or more:

- The maximum loan value against collateral is 70 percent.

- The maintenance requirement is 25 percent.

◆ U.S. Treasury and government securities (bills, notes, bonds, GNMAs, zeros):

- The maximum loan value against collateral is 90 percent.

- The maintenance requirement is 10 percent.

15

Locate Other Internet Investment Tools

E*TRADE's a fine service that can easily handle the vast bulk of your online investing requirements. At some point, though, you're going to want to make a comparison with other online brokers, just to reassure yourself that you're still getting a great deal.

In this chapter, we stop by the online offices of various established brokerages, pick up a few brochures, and head off to lunch. Consider it a breather before the next section of this book, where investing gets a whole lot more serious.

Comparing Online Brokers

Across the board, online brokers have a few things in common:

◆ Low commission rates

◆ Electronic order placement

◆ 24-hour access to the Web site

These are the features that vary:

- Commission rates

- Minimum balance requirement

- Margin rates

- Research quality and quantity

- Other forms of access (A good broker might also offer touchtone telephone trading, for example.)

- Investment options (In addition to U.S. stocks, some brokerages offer mutual funds, bonds, and other securities.)

- Additional features (software tools, educational materials, and so on)

As a standard of comparison, E*TRADE offers commission rates of $14.95 for listed stocks and $19.95 for NASDAQ stocks, a minimum balance requirement of $1000 for cash accounts and $2000 for margin accounts, margin rates among the lowest in the industry, access to extensive market and company research and analysis, and a variety of valuable software tools. E*TRADE also offers a service called TELE*MASTER to place your trades by phone when your away from your computer.

Other Signs of Life

In keeping with the notion that an educated consumer is the best consumer, the following sections provide a rundown of some of the more popular online brokers, along with brief descriptions of what they have to offer.

AccuTrade

AccuTrade provides a wide range of investment options including stocks, bonds, options, mutual funds, and foreign securities (see Figure 15.1). Members have access to extensive research including market news, industry reports, top performers, daily earnings, price charts, and mutual fund news and reports.

Opening a new account requires an initial deposit of $5000. Trading fees are $28 per trade plus $.02 a share. Visit AccuTrade at **http://www. accutrade.com**.

American Express Financial Direct

American Express Financial Direct (see Figure 15.2) is associated with American Express Financial Advisors and other American Express groups. This service offers information about annuities, mutual funds, and money market funds.

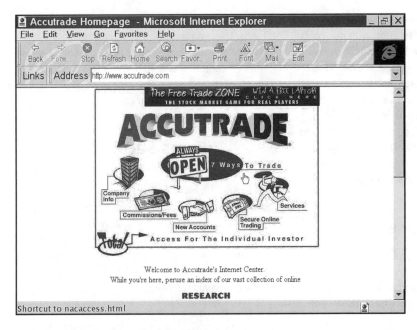

FIG. 15.1

AccuTrade: For a little variety check out AccuTrade's 7 Ways to Trade.

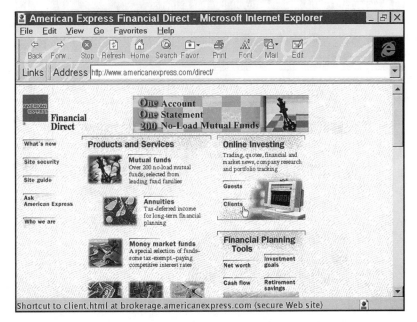

FIG. 15.2

The American Express Financial Direct offers a choice of accounts.

American Express offers two kinds of accounts. InvestDirect is a trading-only account, with no access to research. Commissions are $26.95 per trade, with no minimum deposit. The InvestDirect/Power Tools account includes news, research, and investment selection tools. Commissions are $34.95 per trade, with a $5000 minimum. The power tools/expert option, with maximum news, company research, and advanced search tools, is available for an additional $34.95 a month. The Financial Direct home page is **http://www.americanexpress.com/direct**.

Aufhauser

Aufhauser is notable for its innovative commission structure: A flat fee of $800 a year for up to 20 trades a month. See Figure 15.3. The company pro-

vides brokerage services for equities, options, and funds. The company also has some innovative international features, including toll-free telephone access from 39 countries, and equities trading in a variety of international securities. The Aufhauser page is found at **http://www.aufhauser.com**.

Ceres Securities

Ceres Securities is a discount broker offering online stock trading and quotes, albeit with limited tools and research (see Figure 15.4). A Web site commission calculator lets you know how Ceres' rates stack up against the competition's. Commission charges for Ceres are a flat $18 per trade. You'll find Ceres at **http://www.ceres.com**.

FIG. 15.3

Aufhauser provides international trading services and a flat-fee commission structure.

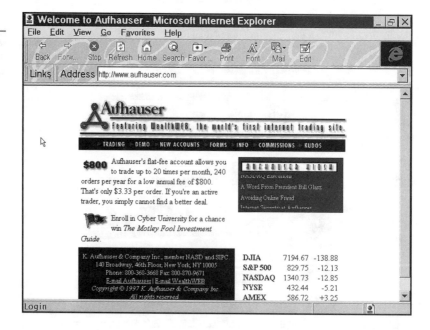

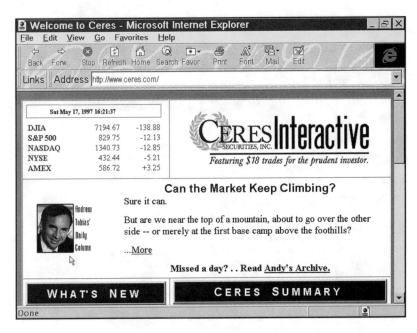

FIG. 15.4

Ceres Securities home page features advice from financial guru Andrew Tobias.

DATEK Online

DATEK is an online broker charging $9.99 for trades placed over the Internet (see Figure 15.5). As we went to press, trading was limited to equities on the New York Stock Exchange, NASDAQ, or American Stock Exchange; DATEK expects to add options soon. Higher rates apply for telephone trades. DATEK requires a $2000 minimum. It provides limited research resources. The DATEK page is located at **http://www.datek.com**.

eBroker

eBroker offers equity trades at a rate of $12 per trade (see Figure 15.6). The minimum deposit required to open a new account is $10,000. Additional accounts or related family accounts do not need to meet the minimum. eBroker provides no research and no tools. Go to **http://www.ebroker.com** to see what eBroker has to offer.

e.Schwab

e.Schwab offers real-time quotes, news and research, and stock trading (see Figure 15.7). e.Schwab's rates are $29.95 for stock trades up to 1000 shares and $.03 a share for trades over 1000 shares. e.Schwab requires a minimum deposit of $5000 for investment, custodial, or trust accounts. A minimum deposit of $2000 is required for IRAs. You can find e.Schwab at **http://www.eschwab.com**.

FIG. 15.5

DATEK Online's home page: Low rates, limited resources.

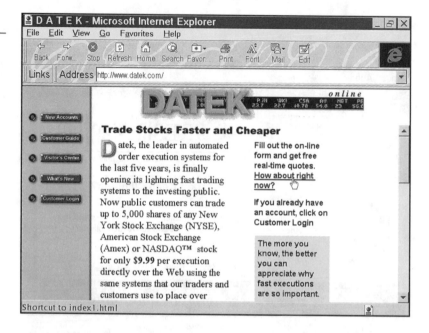

FIG. 15.6

eBroker epitomizes the no-frills approach to online trading.

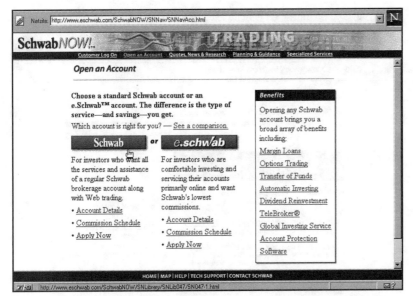

FIG. 15.7

e.Schwab's home page: Well-known discounter is available online.

Fidelity Investments

Fidelity offers online trading of stocks and bonds (see Figure 15.8). Special discounts are available to active traders. An *active trader* is defined as someone who trades 36 or more times per year. If qualified, the Spartan Active Trader Pricing program allows you to trade up to 1,000 shares online for $25 a transaction. To apply for Spartan Active Trader Pricing, you must have minimum of $20,000 in Ultra Service Account assets. Fidelity is located at **http://personal.fidelity.com/brokerage**.

PC Financial Network

PCFN trades in stocks, options, mutual funds, and Treasury products (see Figure 15.9). Members get real-time stock quotes, alerts on stocks of interest, reports from Standard & Poors, and Zacks Earnings Estimates. Research on mutual funds is available from Lipper Mutual Fund Profiles and PCFN Mutual Fund FundScan.

Standard commission rate is $39.95 a trade, plus 3 cents a share above 1,000 shares. Frequent traders get a slightly lower rate of $29.95 a trade, plus 2 cents a share above 1,000 shares. To qualify as a frequent trader, you need to generate about 25 trades per year ($1000 in commissions). PCFN is located at **http://www.pcfn.com**.

Wall Street Access Online

Wall Street Access Online allows you to place equity and options orders and access account information through its Web site (see Figure 15.10). Additional features include real-time quotes, the ability to view account positions and review your trading activity, and trading demos.

FIG. 15.8

Fidelity is a leading provider of financial services.

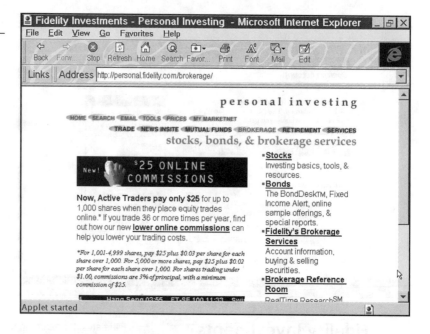

FIG. 15.9

PC Financial Network offers a discount to frequent traders.

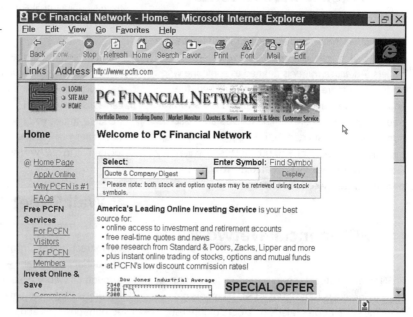

FIG. 15.10

Wall Street Access Online
provides free real-time
quotes with each trade.

At press time, rates for Wall Street Access are $25 for 1 to 4,999 shares, 2 cents a share for 5,000 or more shares. See the online schedule for bonds and options pricing. Active trader's may qualify for additional rebates. You'll find Wall Street Access at **http://www.wsaccess.com**.

Other Places to Look

The online broker scene changes weekly. Firms add options and modify rate schedules in an attempt to find what works best to attract customers. New brokers join the fray. Eventually, a few will opt out.

The usual warning: Before doing business with any online brokerage, be sure you're dealing with a legitimate, established organization. Anyone— *anyone!*— could create a brilliant Web page, call himself a broker, solicit your money, and use it to finance a one-way ticket to Brazil. (That's not a problem unique to the Web, of course; anyone could open a storefront in your neighborhood shopping mall and do the same thing. It's just a lot cheaper to build a Web page.) Be wise.

Now that you've been warned, here are just a couple of the places you could look to find the latest on online traders.

Daytraders

Daytraders is a site devoted, oddly enough, to day traders—that special breed of characters who trade all day, every day. They have an obvious interest in the goings-on of online brokering. Find a reviewed listing of online brokers at **http:// www.daytraders.com/brokers.html.**

Yahoo!

As one of the premier search engines, Yahoo! also has a vested interest in keeping its online brokers list up-to-date. It would, after all, like to remain a premier service. To find Yahoo's list of online brokers, click <u>Stock Quotes</u> on the main screen. Clicking the <u>Online Trading</u> selection in the left column will bring you to the current list. Check out the Web page at **http://www.yahoo.com**.

PART IV

The Postgame Show

16 Track Your Portfolio   207

17 Learn Analysis Techniques   215

18 Pick Your Analysis Tools   223

19 The Final Analysis   233

16

Track Your Portfolio

What was I worth before? How much am I worth now? And how much will I be worth if this continues?

The management tools we describe in this chapter will track your investment portfolio and answer all the questions you can raise about the value of your securities.

Track Your Investments with Portfolio Management

A portfolio management tool is any piece of software that aids in tracking the value of your securities.

There are many reasons you need this information. There is, of course, the obvious reason that you'd like to know your own worth. More importantly, though, you'll need to make investment decisions and tax decisions based on the changes in securities prices.

Portfolio trackers should provide a lot of information, and they should do it quickly, simply, clearly, and regularly. Fortunately, the Internet contains the tools to meet all these criteria. And even more fortunately, it's mostly free!

The larger your portfolio, the more important it is to take advantage of software tools that help manage your securities.

Among the items of information you should demand from your portfolio management software are current valuations, tax information, and price movements. At a minimum, every portfolio tracker will display:

◆ *The name or symbol for the security you trade*

◆ *The current or "last" price*

◆ *The change from the previous day's closing price*

◆ *The change in the dollar value of your portfolio*

◆ *The updated value of your portfolio*

The various tools described in this chapter also display some or most of the following additional information:

◆ *Trading Activity*

    Previous close

    Opening price

    Bid/ask prices

    Trading volume

    Day's price range

    Tick trends (price movements over time)

    52-week price range

    Previous high/low

    Average price

    Price/earnings ratio

    Earnings per share

    Latest dividend

    Company news

◆ *Portfolio History*

    Number of shares purchased

    Cost basis (purchase price)

    Commission paid

    Dates

    Notes

◆ *Portfolio Valuation*

    Total profit in dollars

    Total profit as a percentage of original investment

    Current value

Choosing a Portfolio Manager

You could hire a living, breathing portfolio manager to watch your investments for you. But if you prefer to cover your own assets, you'll want to use the power of your PC to keep track.

There are, quite literally, several hundred commercial portfolio management software packages on the market today. They cost as little as $39.95, and as much as $500. Some portfolio managers are even sold as subscription services at various prices.

The better portfolio managers are actually only a component of a larger investment software package. We describe many of these full-service investment analysis products in Chapter 19, "The Final Analysis."

To use any of these tools, you simply open the Web page, click the portfolio manager, and enter information as directed. To get started, you'll need to have at hand the name of your security, the number of shares you own, the purchase price per share, and the commissions and fees you paid. If you have the symbol (EGRP for E*TRADE, for example, and MAR for Marriott International), so much the better. If you don't have it, most of the tools include a clickable hyperlink or search box for finding the trading symbol.

Each of the tools permits you to enter existing investments, edit them if you make a mistake, and view the completed portfolio. For each security that has a recognized symbol, the portfolio tool automatically searches out a current price and displays it as part of your portfolio information.

The following sections describe some of the best portfolio managers on the Internet.

E*TRADE Portfolio Manager

Available only to E*TRADE customers, the Portfolio Manager is one of several account tracking tools provided by E*TRADE. The Manager automatically updates itself to reflect trading activity in your E*TRADE accounts. You can manually modify the information displayed, add additional items, and split out the investments into multiple portfolios. (See Figure 16.1.)

https://swww.etrade.com/cgi-bin/cgitrade/ manager

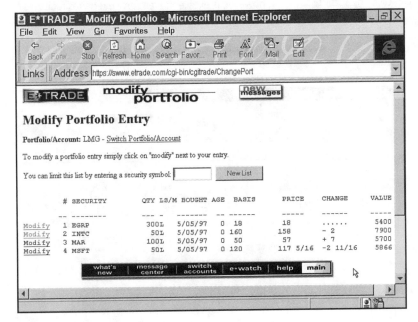

FIG. 16.1

Portfolio Manager automatically enters E*TRADE account activity.

Personal Portfolio

Track the status of up to 40 securities. Personal Portfolios features straightforward data entry, and a useful glossary of terms. The software is a free service from DBC Online. (See Figure 16.2.)

http://www.dbc.com/cgi-bin/htx.exe/core/dbc/ finarena.html?source=core/dbc

Excite Business and Investing

Manage 50 securities per portfolio. Initial data entry is a bit tedious, but the result is worth the effort: From the opening page, you can click any security in

your portfolio to see a list of news items relating to your investment. (See Figure 16.3.)

http://my.excite.com/channel/business/?a-chb-t

Galt NetWorth

Free portfolio manager tracks 50 stocks and funds from a Web site. It includes an option for downloading personal portfolio information to Quicken. Various views provide background information on each stock. We're not fond of the minimalist data entry form, which fails to break out basis by cost per share and commissions and fees. Instead, you enter only a total cost of the entire trade. The glossary help, however, is excellent. Free service requires registration. (See Figure 16.4.)

http://quotes.galt.com/cgi-bin/port

FIG. 16.2

Personal Portfolio is just one of the many information services on DBC Online.

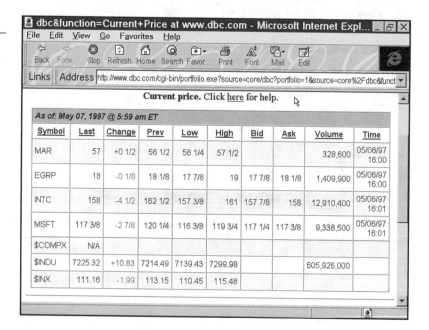

Current price. Click here for help.

As of: May 07, 1997 @ 5:59 am ET

Symbol	Last	Change	Prev	Low	High	Bid	Ask	Volume	Time
MAR	57	+0 1/2	56 1/2	56 1/4	57 1/2			328,600	05/06/97 16:00
EGRP	18	-0 1/8	18 1/8	17 7/8	19	17 7/8	18 1/8	1,409,900	05/06/97 16:00
INTC	158	-4 1/2	162 1/2	157 3/8	161	157 7/8	158	12,910,400	05/06/97 16:01
MSFT	117 3/8	-2 7/8	120 1/4	116 3/8	119 3/4	117 1/4	117 3/8	9,338,500	05/06/97 16:01
$COMPX	N/A								
$INDU	7225.32	+10.83	7214.49	7139.43	7299.98			605,926,000	
$INX	111.16	-1.99	113.15	110.45	115.48				

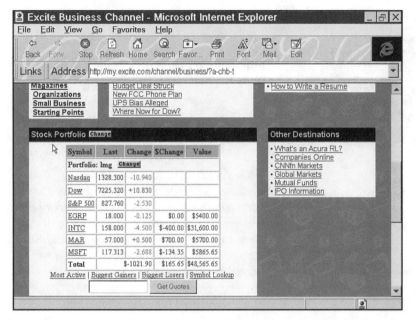

FIG. 16.3

View your portfolio from the front page of Excite's business channel.

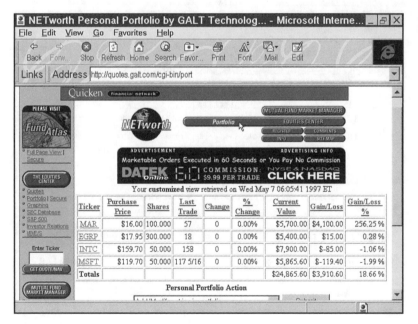

FIG. 16.4

Download Galt's portfolio, which updates directly to Quicken.

folio based on 20-minute delayed quotes. There is no charge, but it requires registration. (See Figure 16.5.)

http://infoseek.moneynet.com/infoseek/ content.mhtml?CONTENT=Portrack

InvestorsEdge

This is a personal portfolio service from InvestorsEdge. Create a personal portfolio of 15 stocks and 15 mutual funds, and monitor their performance. Download the updates to Quicken if you want. An end-of-the-day e-mail summary is available at no cost. The service is free, but it does require registration. (See Figure 16.6.)

http://www.irnet.com/pages/login.stm

Infoseek Investor

Track up to 300 stocks, mutual funds, and options. The Portfolio Tracker displays the value of your port-

FIG. 16.5

Clicking a company name calls up a detailed company report.

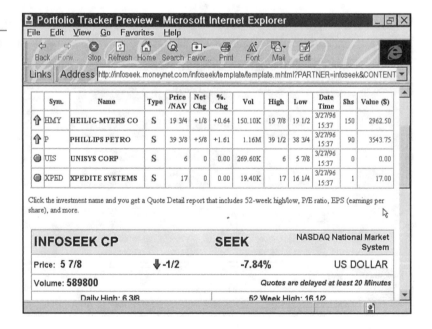

Sym.	Name	Type	Price /NAV	Net Chg	%. Chg	Vol	High	Low	Date Time	Shs	Value ($)
⬆ HMY	HEILIG-MYERS CO	S	19 3/4	+1/8	+0.64	150.10K	19 7/8	19 1/2	3/27/96 15:37	150	2962.50
⬆ P	PHILLIPS PETRO	S	39 3/8	+5/8	+1.61	1.16M	39 1/2	38 3/4	3/27/96 15:37	90	3543.75
◉ UIS	UNISYS CORP	S	6	0	0.00	269.60K	6	5 7/8	3/27/96 15:37	0	0.00
◉ XPED	XPEDITE SYSTEMS	S	17	0	0.00	19.40K	17	16 1/4	3/27/96 15:37	1	17.00

Click the investment name and you get a Quote Detail report that includes 52-week high/low, P/E ratio, EPS (earnings per share), and more.

INFOSEEK CP	SEEK	NASDAQ National Market System
Price: 5 7/8	⬇ -1/2	-7.84%	US DOLLAR
Volume: 589800		Quotes are delayed at least 20 Minutes
Daily High: 6 3/8	52 Week High: 16 1/2	

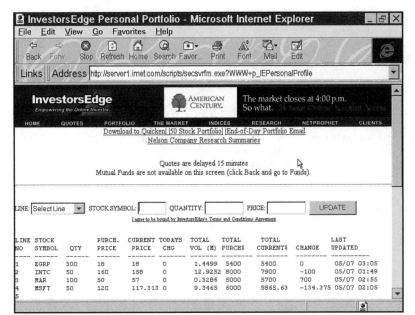

FIG. 16.6

Downloads and e-mail summaries are part of the InvestorsEdge service.

Market Watcher Version 1.10

Unlike the other items in this list, Market Watcher is not a Web site. It's a downloadable piece of portfolio management software that you install on your PC. It provides portfolio management with links to news and quotes directly from Stock Smart. Download the free version. The enhanced edition with more features costs $39.95. (See Figure 16.7.)

http://www.marketwatcher.com

Stock Smart

This is the most information you'll get for free. This portfolio manager tracks stocks, mutual funds, money markets, indices, options, and bonds. View the portfolio online, or receive an e-mail notification monthly, weekly, or daily. In addition to most of the information found on the other sites in this list, Stock Smart also provides charts and graphs for the industry, company contact information, a brief history of the offering, stock and index options, technical analysis, historical performance graph, and number of shares outstanding. (See Figure 16.8.)

http://www.stocksmart.com/portfolio.html

FIG. 16.7

Market Watcher is
downloadable to your PC.

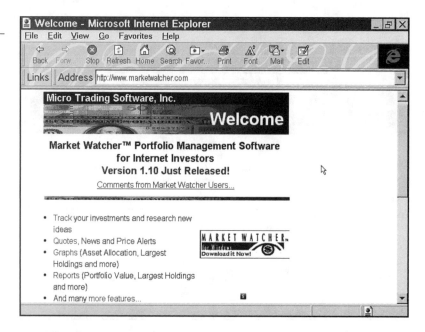

FIG. 16.8

StockSmart: The best all-
around site for monitoring
your portfolio.

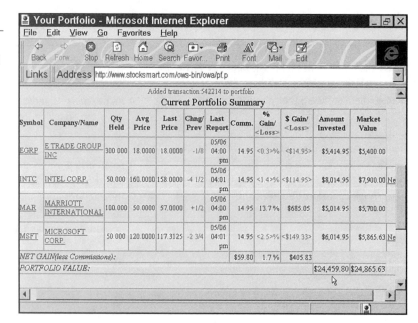

17

Learn Analysis Techniques

It's all a matter of personal style, really. Do you buy a stock and hold it forever? Or are you a day trader who trades on momentum and is in and out of the market seven, eight times a day?

There's another option of course: Become your own analyst, and make careful, rational choices about your trades. In this chapter, we examine the first of two schools of stock analysis: The Fundamentals. Chapter 18, "Pick Your Analysis Tools," looks at the other school of thought: The Technicals.

Before you get wet, though, take a moment to read some thoughts on becoming an active trader: *Why Buy and Hold May Not Be The Best Strategy*, an essay on how regular trading can provide superior returns to buying and holding. This essay can be found at **http://www. e-analytics.com/fs7.htm**

Fundamental Analysis

The basic goal of fundamental analysis is to determine whether a stock is under- or overvalued at the current price. Fundamental analysis looks closely at balance sheets and income statements of companies to determine whether they are fundamentally sound. It considers the relationships between earnings, revenues, liabilities, expenses, and many other pieces of financial data about the company.

Even traders who lean heavily toward technical analysis—which we explain in the next chapter—must have a firm grasp of the fundamentals. Every investor should know, at a minimum, how to read financial statements, and how to understand the simple analytical formulas that are derived from those numbers.

Fortunately, you needn't look very far to find this information. The numbers are all located in a single convenient place: the company's annual report.

Get an Annual Report

Beautiful cover, lots of pretty pictures, words of encouragement from the CEO…and some cheap paper at the back filled with lots of fine print. Wouldn't you just love to have an annual report of your own?

If you're willing to live without the glossies, the Web provides all the corporate financial information you'll ever need.

The best site on the Web for annual report data is indisputably the Wall Street Research Net's Company Research (WSRN) page. WSRN is so good, in fact, that it's worth a walk through.

At WSRN's opening page, **http://www.wsrn.com/home/companyResearch.html**, you'll find a few data entry boxes. Enter the company symbol (or follow the instructions on this site to look it up, if you don't already know it). WSRN returns a four-part report screen (see Figure 17.1).

All four of the following WSRN report areas are worth coming back to:

◆ *Company Links* takes you to the home page, investigates corporate filings with the Securities and Exchange Commission, and uses the Lycos search engine to hunt for other relevant links.

◆ *News Center* searches major news publications, *PC Quote*, the Yahoo! finance page, and a press release-reporting service for news about the company you are researching.

◆ *Graphs/Charts* is a good source for quotes and historical data.

◆ *Research, Reports & Summaries* is the gold vein you're looking for. In addition to the very useful descriptions, statistics, earnings estimates and profiles, you'll find a link to QuickSource: Fundamentals, Ratios & Earnings Estimates.

REPORT CARD

Want a paper-and-ink copy of an annual report? Visit the company's home page. (By the way, most corporate Web site URLs are intuitive. Before conducting a time-consuming search for the site URL, go to your browser and try entering **http://www.**companyname**.com**.) There you may find an investor relations-type link, with instructions for ordering a copy of the report, or you might locate a toll-free number so that you can call the company directly and request one.

Better yet, you might find a copy of the actual annual report online (see Figure 17.2). Click the Print button on your browser, and within moments you'll have your own paper copy of the annual report, suitable for framing.

◆

FIG. 17.1

The WSRN report screen creates links to data found in corporate annual reports.

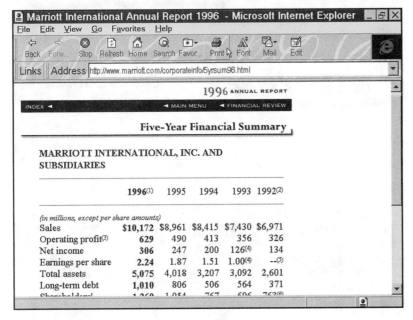

FIG. 17.2

Some corporate home pages publish their entire annual report online. Click the Print button to make your own copy.

Click the QuickSource: Fundamentals hyperlink to go to the Fundamental Data and Ratios page. (See Figure 17.3.)

On this page you'll find a compilation of vital stats from the company's annual report.

The Least You Should Know About Financial Statements

The annual report contains two basic financial statements: the balance sheet and the income statement. The combination of these statements gives a fairly accurate picture of the financial health of the company you're thinking of investing in.

A FREE INFORMATION ACT

If you want reports from several companies, check the Public Register's Annual Report Service (PRARS) at **http://www.prars.com/newform2.html**. This free service will send you corporate annual reports by request. PRARS categorizes companies into 55 industries. Choose an industry, and you can order multiple individual reports, or reports from all the companies in the entire industry. PRARS is by no means a complete listing, however. In the lodging industry, PRARS lists only 14 companies. Still, it's a fine place to get started, and the price is unbeatable!

FIG. 17.3

The Fundamental Data and Ratios come from corporate financial statements.

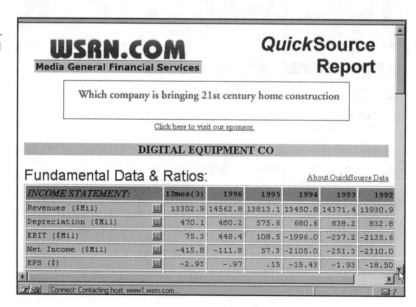

WSRN.COM
Media General Financial Services

*Quick*Source Report

Which company is bringing 21st century home construction

Click here to visit our sponsor.

DIGITAL EQUIPMENT CO

Fundamental Data & Ratios:
About QuickSource Data

INCOME STATEMENT:		12mos(3)	1996	1995	1994	1993	1992
Revenues ($Mil)		13302.9	14562.8	13813.1	13450.8	14371.4	13930.9
Depreciation ($Mil)		470.1	480.2	575.6	680.6	838.2	832.8
EBIT ($Mil)		75.3	448.4	108.5	-1996.0	-237.2	-2135.6
Net Income ($Mil)		-415.8	-111.8	57.3	-2105.0	-251.3	-2310.0
EPS ($)		-2.93	-.97	.15	-15.43	-1.93	-18.50

Connect: Contacting host: www1.wsrn.com...

The balance sheet describes where the company stood financially at a single point in time—in the case of an annual report, the last minute of the company's fiscal year. If you could line up the balance sheet numbers side by side for, say July 1, 1996 and July 1, 1997, you'd have a basis for determining how well the company did this year compared to last year.

Boiled down to basics, a balance sheet contains three figures: Assets (everything the company owns), Liabilities (everything the company owes), and Net Worth (assets minus liabilities). That Net Worth number goes by other names, most significantly, Stockholder's Equity. The Stockholder's Equity figure is comprised of the "value" of the outstanding stock—sort of. Actually, since stock prices fluctuate, the generally accepted accounting practice is to assign various classes of stock an arbitrary value, called par value, and retain that number on the balance sheet from year to year. The Equity column also includes items such as surplus capital and last year's retained earnings, the money left over after stockholders were paid dividends.

As a shareholder, you're hoping that the Net Worth figures grow from year to year.

The income statement, on the other hand, reads more like your checkbook register. It shows Income (money coming in from sales or other revenues), Expenses (created by manufacturing, selling, depreciation, and administrative costs), and Profit, which is the balance for the year. Interest and expenses are subtracted from that Profit figure to arrive at Net Income. The bottom line adds last year's Retained Earnings to this year's Net Income, then subtracts Dividends paid to shareholders, to arrive at this year's Retained Earnings.

As a shareholder, you like to see two things: a nice fat Dividend and a healthy amount of Retained Earnings.

Depending on what you're looking for, financial statements can tell many stories. The next section will examine some important financial statement ratios, but to get truly informed about financial statements, you'll first want to do a bit of extra-curricular reading at these Internet sites:

◆ *Financial Savvy*. Directed toward the owners of small businesses, it's nevertheless useful to investors who need a quick refresher on various financial statements.

A quick tutorial on balance sheets and net worth:

http://pathfinder.com/ @@jA*WxwYAlZXDFkHe/ money/features/savvy_0995/ savvynetworth.html

A simple balance sheet:

http://pathfinder.com/ @@jA*WxwYAlZXDFkHe/money/features/ savvy_0995/tablebalance.html

◆ *Financial Statements: A Look Behind the Numbers*. Spend some time learning about the qualitative nature of financial statement numbers.

http://www.aaii.org/stocks/fsnumber.html

◆ *Searching For Nonfiction In Financial Statements*. A *Fortune* magazine article analyzes the real value of balance sheets, noting that some companies inflate the value of intangibles to alter the company's perceived value.

http://pathfinder.com/ @@jA*WxwYAlZXDFkHe/fortune/1996/ 961223/fir.html

Ratio Analysis

Should you be happy with a dividend of 12 cents? Is a profit of $1.1 million good or bad? The numbers on the financial statements mean little all by themselves. What is significant, when you view the statements, is the comparison, or ratio, between numbers. Ratio analysis is used to show the mathematical relationship between two figures on the financial statements. The number is expressed in the form of a fraction, a percentage, or a decimal. Following is an introduction to some of the most important figures you'll find on a financial statement, along with an explanation of how to calculate the ratios.

As you calculate these simple ratios, compare them with the same ratios from a year ago, from two years ago, from another company in the same industry, and from the averages for a group of companies in the same industry.

Yes, that can be a lot of work. The reward, though, is worth the time if it allows you to find an undervalued gem of a company before the rest of the market clues in.

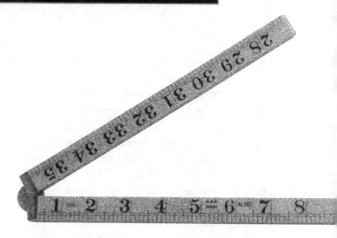

much stock on hand, and business probably isn't up to expectations.

You'll also want to keep an eye on accounts receivable turnover. If this number is high, bills are getting paid. If it's low, the company's having some collection problems. By themselves, these ratios have little significance. They're very significant if you find large changes from year to year, or if you find that the ratios for your company vary a great deal from the average ratio for the entire industry. In looking at the activity numbers, you'll want to make the following comparisons:

♦ *Inventory turnover ratio*: cost of goods sold divided by the cost of inventory

♦ *Accounts receivable turnover*: net credit sales divided by the average accounts receivable

♦ *Total asset turnover*: sales divided by the average total assets

Measurements of Activity

Activity ratios measure turnover. High inventory turnover, for example, indicates that the company has low inventory levels, which could conceivably cause it to miss out on sales opportunities. (Everyone should have such a problem.)

You'd be more concerned to learn that inventory turnover is low, meaning that the company has too

Measurements of Leverage

Leverage ratios measure how much a company relies on debt capital—politely referred to as *leverage*—

instead of equity capital to finance its operations. These ratios determine whether a company is in over its head when it comes into debt.

There are several ratios in this category. The debt-to-asset ratio measures debt in relation to total assets. Similarly, the debt-to-equity ratio is a measure of leverage. Higher ratios mean greater debt. The times-interest-earned ratio is a safety measure of how many times the company can cover its interest expense out of earnings (before interest and taxes). These are the figures you should look at when measuring leverage:

◆ *Debt to asset ratio*: total debt divided by total assets

◆ *Debt to equity ratio*: long-term debt divided by common stockholders equity

◆ *Times-interest-earned ratio*: (net income plus interest expense plus income tax expense) divided by interest expense

Measurements of Liquidity

A company can have all the net worth in the world, but if it can't cover payroll, it's in trouble. Liquidity measurements measure the likelihood of the company being able to pay its bills as they come due.

Liquidity ratios include *working capital*—the extra cash available to cover current expenses or to take advantage of business opportunities as they arise. The *current ratio* is a different way to measure working capital. When it gets below 2, the company may be having some difficulties. The *acid-test ratio*

(sometimes called the *quick ratio*) is a commonly used balance sheet test for short-term liquidity. The measurement you hope to see here is 1 or higher. Here are the calculations you'll perform to measure liquidity:

◆ *Working capital*: current assets minus current liabilities

◆ *Current ratio*: current assets divided by current liabilities

◆ *Acid-test ratio*: (current assets minus inventories) divided by current liabilities

Measurements of Profitability

Profit is, of course, what this entire exercise is all about. Use profitability ratios to measure the bottom line.

A company's earnings are most frequently described as *earnings per share*, which means the number of dollars generated for each share of outstanding stock. The *profit margin ratio* compares the earnings to net sales. This number is expressed as a percentage, and you want it to be high— really high! *Return on equity* is just a measure of the total return you get for each dollar you invest in a company. *Total return* refers to the entire increase or decrease in value of a security over a given period. This figure gives you a dollar value, rather than a ratio. When examining profitability, you'll want to make the following calculations:

◆ *Earnings per share*: earnings divided by number of shares outstanding

◆ *Profit margin*: net income divided by revenue

◆ *Return on equity*: earnings divided by common stockholders equity

◆ *Total return (stock)*: capital appreciation plus dividends

◆ *Total return (mutual funds)*: change in net asset value plus capital gains plus income distributions

Securities Ratios

Securities ratio measurements compare stock prices and values to determine whether the stock price is in line with the value of the company.

The most significant number you'll use is the *price/earnings ratio*. The P/E is the relationship between the price of a stock and its earnings per share. This ratio is critical because it indicates how many multiples of the earnings (double? triple?) investors are willing to pay to own a share.

Securities that are referred to as *growth stocks* tend to have lower earnings and higher P/E ratios. When a company has exceptional growth prospects, the market is willing to pay a premium price. Stocks that are expected to stay steady—big, well-established blue chips—and those that are unloved or unappreciated or unknown by the market tend to have lower P/Es. Low P/Es sometimes serve as a red flag; generally, though, they're viewed as more of an opportunity. Stocks with extremely high P/Es are those that the market considers potential winners. Of course, their level of risk is proportionally higher.

Typically, a stock with a P/E greater than 20 is considered riskier than a stock with lower growth, proven earnings, and a lower P/E. If the P/E ratio is greater than the growth rate, the security is considered to be overvalued; if the P/E ratio is less than the growth rate, the security is considered to be undervalued. Negative earnings—er, losses—throw off the measurement, and are considered not calculable.

Dividend payout describes how much of the company's earnings were paid to stockholders, rather than held in the company's coffers as *retained earnings*. Dividends are great, but a company that reinvests its earnings in new growth opportunities could pay off handsomely in the long-term.

The final ratio is *book value per share*. Shares are valued on the company books at an arbitrary number—generally a number such as $10 or $100. This ratio adds the book value and the company cash to determine what each share is worth on the books.

Another widely followed ratio is *price-to-book*, the comparison between the price of the security to the book value. Changes in this figure indicate how well the price of the security reflects the accountants' valuation of the company.

The following ratios describe the value of the security:

◆ *Price/earnings ratio*: current market price per share divided by earnings per share

◆ *Dividend payout*: dividends paid per share divided by earnings per share

◆ *Book value per share*: balance sheet value of common stock plus retained earnings plus cash surplus divided by number of shares outstanding

◆ *Price-to-book*: current market price per share divided by balance sheet value of common stock plus retained earnings plus cash surplus

18

Pick Your Analysis Tools

Instant wealth. Untold riches. It's all yours—if you can simply predict the direction of the stock market.

Technical analysis is all about foretelling the future. Charts, graphs, theories—all of them look for the story that explains where the market, and any individual security in the market, is headed tomorrow.

If the quantitative approach to analysis is about understanding the *cause* of price variations, the technical approach is all about understanding the *effect*. In this chapter, we look at both the theory and the practice of technical analysis.

Technical Analysis: The Theory

Technical analysis is, at its root, a belief system, a fiscal religious experience that holds to the following creed:

1. Stock prices are nine parts psychology, and one part reality.

2. The stock market is efficient—in other words, it quickly compensates for change.

3. Stock prices are persistent.

4. History is repetitive.

The obscure god of technical analysis is a long-dead Italian mathematician named Leonardo Fibonacci. Fibonacci observed a series of numbers and drew some fascinating conclusions about them. Each number in the Fibonacci Series is the sum of the two preceding numbers—1,1,2,3,5,8,13,21, and so on. Among the conclusions was this: That there is a naturally recurring pattern in the universe. (Interestingly, Fibonacci's numeric series applies to much more than investing. Give him credit for a large chunk of Western civilization. Fibonacci numbers were known to Greek and Egyptian mathematicians who devised a ratio known as the *Golden Mean*, a ratio that today informs disciplines as diverse as music, art, and architecture. Or give him even more credit. Natural patterns such as populations of rabbits and the spiral growth of leaves on some trees exhibit the Fibonacci series.)

In investing terms, Fibonacci gave mathematical support to the notion that there is a pattern in all human behavior. If human psychology causes people—investors—to repeat behavior, even when the behavior is less than rational, then perhaps it's possible to predict the direction of the market by simply observing the patterns of investor behavior.

If you hold to the creed, you behave quite differently from, say, a fundamental analyst, who believes that changes in the underlying value of a stock play the greatest role in its market price.

The Tao of Tau

You'll find on the Internet an endless supply of interesting background information about Fibonacci, the Golden Mean (designated by the Greek letter t, or Tau), and other amorphous mathematical thought that may give you an understanding of the philosophy of group psychologies.

Be cautious. Technical analysis varies from the really rational to the completely far out. The real value of a stock, in the end, is only what the market *says* it's worth—an evaluation based on an arcane blend of fundamental, economic, political, historical, and psychological factors, along with a dash of whimsy.

Not all of the following links are specifically investment-related, but they all illustrate the variety of thought that imbues technical analysis:

◆ *The Golden Section*. Simple explanation of the Golden Mean.

   http://www.zometool.com/deepzome/golden.html

◆ *Fibonacci and Natural Occurrences*. An exploration of Fibonacci numbers.

   http://www.mcs.surrey.ac.uk/Personal/R.Knott/Fibonacci/fib.html

◆ *AstroEcon*. The confluence of astrology and technical analysis.

   http://206.84.40.155

◆ *The Grand SuperCycle Peak*. The stock market, crop circles, Fibonacci, and astroharmonics. Here you'll discover what they all have in common.

   http://nw3.nai.net/~virtual/sot/peak.htm

◆ *Elliott Wave Principle*. This Fibonacci-based theory is complex, but it's worth understanding for its psychological insights.

http://oceania.org/mall/elliotw.html

Trend Watch

Investors tend to make investment decisions based on two factors: greed and fear. Perhaps you, personally, are an exception to this tendency, but for the most part, when a stock price is rising, investors want in. When it falls, investors fear losing their money and want out.

Technical analysts, or *technicians*, don't look for a cause behind price movements. They merely watch for trends in securities prices and attempt to predict the future course of those prices. Once a trend is established, the technician assumes that market psychology takes over, and the masses will behave, well, *en masse*.

To predict these mass movements, technical analysts have developed hundreds of modeling techniques, a few of which we'll examine in this chapter. New techniques arise from week to week; all of them evolve from the oldest technique, the *Dow Theory*.

The Dow Theory

Charles H. Dow, editor of the *Wall Street Journal* and a founder of Dow Jones & Company, began publishing stock market averages—the well-known Dow Industrial and, at the time, Railroad averages—in the 1880s. He noticed a certain synchronicity among the stocks in his averages; they had a tendency to move up or down simultaneously.

Out of this observation grew the Dow Theory, set forth in a series of editorials Dow published in the *Journal*. While his original hypotheses have been altered and reinterpreted over the years, the theory basically describes the signals that indicate the start of bull and bear markets.

The Dow Theory watches the behavior of the two averages—Industrial and now Transportation—for signs of similar behavior. The Theory's premise is that if both indicators move in the same direction, either a bull or a bear market is starting or confirmed. Confirmation needn't appear on the same day, but once both indicators are moving in synchronization, the trend is established.

Basically, a *bull market* exists as long as each successive rally's high is higher than the preceding high, and each low is higher than the preceding low. A *bear market* exists in the face of downward trends, where each decline has lower lows and lower highs than those of the previous movement.

The Dow Theory has additional rules where Fibonaccisms can be observed. One of the rules is the notion that each trend has Primary, Secondary, and Minor movements. Another is that primary trends last about a year, while opposing secondary trends last about two-fifths of a year. During those *retracements*, prices vary by one-third to two-thirds, but hover at 1/2.

Trends are considered to be in effect until there's an observable and persistent directional change in both averages. All the intermediate changes are viewed as normal corrections.

So how does one distinguish price movements that signal a major shift in direction from those that are merely normal corrections? Simply put, that's the whole point of the myriad of technical analysis tools that have grown out of the Dow Theory over the years.

Before jumping into an examination of some of the more popular technical tools, it might be worthwhile to visit some of the following Web sites for more background on the Dow Theory:

- *Charles Dow and the Dow Theory.* A brief history of the life of Charles Dow, and the conclusions drawn from his theories.

    http://www.e-analytics.com/cd.htm

- *Dow Theory.* Applying the theory to market movements.

    http://www5.interaccess.com/ luckowgroup/Dowthery.htm

- *Decoding the Dow.* Brief articles on where it came from, why it endures, and where it's headed.

    http://foxnews.com/news/features/dow

Technical Analysis: The Application

Once you get past the Dow Theory, technical analysis can suddenly become quite daunting. Don't let the terminology and charts scare you off. The theories often throw around a lot of algebraic equations, but in the end, you need understand only the basic principles, and know what to look for when you view a chart (see Figures 18.1, 18.2, and 18.3). Personal computers and the analysis software described in the next chapter, "The Final Analysis," make the mathematics merely a background operation.

Before leaping into the details of technical analysis tools, it will help to understand all you can about applying technical analysis.

If you learn nothing else, remember this: Each of the tools gives off *signals* to buy or sell. If you're wise, you'll never act on a single signal. Instead, you'll look for confirmation from other tools. Only when you're confident that the signals are in sync should you make your move.

FIG. 18.1

Over a period of time, prices move up and down. A line connecting the high points or the low points is called a *Trend Line*. Understanding trend lines is fundamental to reading technical analysis charts.

Trendlines

Trendlines are the most basic and the most valuable to the tehnician. It is to our benefit to establish trendlines as we can then most accurately time our points of entry or exit along that line.

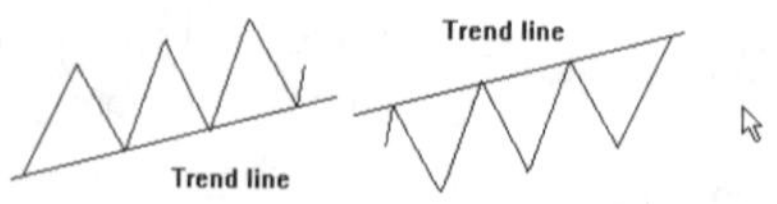

A trendline should not be confused with a moving average. A trendline is determined by drawing a line, which connects the "top of the inverted saucer" to the follow "tops" as is shown in the diagram above. Also, it can connect the "bottom of the following saucer" to the following "bottom".

Channels

A channel line is a line that runs parallel to the trend line and is often called a return line. It marks off the area in which a share is trading and the more often it is touched, the more valid it is.

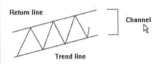

1. Failure to touch the return line can constitute a warning signal
2. Penetration of a return line is a sign that it will move further in the direction of its penetration

FIG. 18.2

Trend lines take a variety of configurations. Illustrated here is a channel configuration, where the price of a security bounces back and forth between a trend line and a return line. If the price crosses an established return line, it could signal a reversal.

Head and Shoulders

This is the best known of the reliable reversal patterns and provides the basic blueprint for the majority of all reversal patterns.

They manifest themselves in the shape of three well-defined peaks, where the middle peak is more pronounced that the two outside peaks - creating an image of a head flanked by two shoulders - hence, the name.

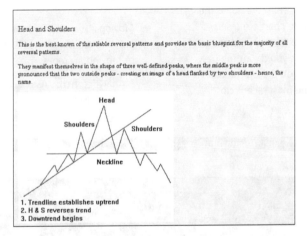

1. Trendline establishes uptrend
2. H & S reverses trend
3. Downtrend begins

FIG. 18.3

Complex technical analysis techniques look to Fibonacci sequences for confirmation of trends. Chartists say this configuration, a classic Head and Shoulders, demonstrates group psychology at work.

These Internet sites provide more general background on technical analysis:

♦ *Technical Analysis.* A thorough explication of trends, trend lines, and the meanings associated with various shapes. If you want to understand charts, this site is a must-read.

http://www.sharenet.co.za/sharenet/ Library/technica.htm

♦ *About Technical Analysis.* The good technical analyst looks at different indicators in different time periods. E-Analytics is an educational site

describing general theories of technical analysis. Follow the links for a thorough explanation of major technical indicators.

http://www.e-analytics.com/techdesc.htm

♦ *Glossary of Technical Terms.* An explanation, in glossary format, of major technical analysis terminology.

http://www.centrex.com/indicate.html

♦ *When to Buy and Sell.* An overview of technical indicators that signal it's time to make a change.

http://www.wallstreetcity.com/ OV_Buy_and_Sell.html

◆ *Syndicate*. Links to lots of charts.

**http://www.moneypages.com/syndicate/
finance/charts.html**

Moving Averages

If you were going to design your own chart, or draw a graph on paper, you'd start by plotting each day's closing price on a graph. (Dow called the closing price the most significant, because it's the one investors are willing to live with overnight.)

The moving average (see Figure 18.4) would be the next step in your progression. To chart a moving average, you'd plot the average of, say, 20 days' prices on a graph. The next day, you'd plot the new average, and so on. Each day, you'd drop the oldest price in the series, and add the most recent close.

■ **N O T E**

The charting software used to illustrate the remainder of this chapter is Alpha Chart, available at **http://www.alphachart.com**.

When you connect the averages, you create a trend line that illustrates the direction the stock price is heading. The moving average smoothes out daily fluctuations, and gives you a better picture of the real state of the price movement.

You can learn more about moving averages at these Web sites:

◆ *Moving Averages*. Each of these three Web sites provides a different point of view on the subject of moving averages.

E-Analytics: **http://www.e-analytics.com/
movavg.htm**

FIG. 18.4

The moving average shows price movements averaged over a period of days. The jagged line is daily prices. The bottom line shows a 120-day average. The middle line (arrow pointer) is a 20-day average.

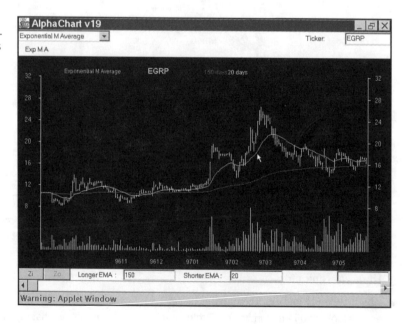

Optima: **http://www.oir.com/ techind.htm#MA**

Stocksmart: **http://www.stocksmart.com/ moveavg.html**

◆ *Charts.* Two charts demonstrating moving averages.

E-Analytics: **http://www.e-analytics.com/ chart104.htm**

Optima: **http://www.oir.com/images/ chart2.jpg**

Telescan on Bollinger Bands: **http:// univel.telescan.com/bbands.html**

Telescan on Envelopes: **http:// univel.telescan.com/envel.html**

◆ *John Bollinger's Capital Growth Letter.* Bollinger's home page.

http://www.tfc.com/bollinger

◆ *Chart.* Graphic illustration of Bollinger bands.

http://www.e-analytics.com/chart102.htm

Bollinger Bands

Trading bands create an *envelope* above and below the moving average. When prices are in the lower band, it's time to buy. When they're in the upper band, it's time to sell. Normally, trading bands are set a specific distance from the moving average, and never change.

An analyst named John Bollinger noted that the band widths are more meaningful when they reflect the volatility of the market. He proposed calculating the bands based on price movements, and setting them at two statistical standard deviations from the moving average. Hence, in quiet markets, the bands tighten. In volatile markets, the bands loosen.

The following Web sites introduce Bollinger bands:

◆ *Bollinger Bands.* In-depth explanations of Bollinger band plotting.

E-Analytics: **http://www.e-analytics.com/ bolinger.htm**

Stocksmart: **http://www.stocksmart.com/ bbands.html**

Moving Average Convergence/Divergence (MACD)

In the 1960s, a trader named Gerald Appel devised a different measure of moving averages. In Appel's view, it's possible to compare moving averages for different time periods to effectively predict price movements.

Appel's system is called *Moving Average Convergence/Divergence (MACD),* and involves, basically, three moving averages (see Figure 18.5). The first is a longer-term exponential moving average for a 26-day period. The second is a 12-day period. Appel then subtracts the long one from the short one to get his MACD trend line.

The third average is for a 9-day period, and it's called the *trigger line.* As markets *advance,* or rise, the shorter trigger line moves above the longer-term MACD line, signaling a buy. When the trigger line falls below the MACD line, it's a signal to sell.

These Web sites provide additional background information on MACD:

FIG. 18.5

In this illustration of MACD, the two significant trend lines are found at the top of the chart. The lighter line is the MACD line. The darker line (arrow) is the trigger, or signal line.

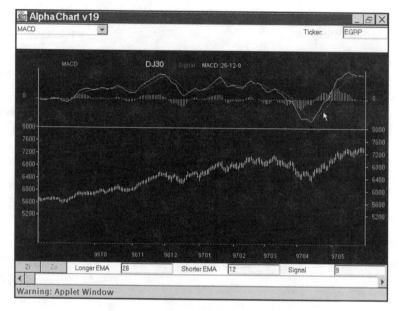

◆ *MACD.* Three explanations of Moving Average Convergence/Divergence.

E-Analytics: **http://www.e-analytics.com/ macd.htm**

Wall Street City: **http:// www.wallstreetcity.com/ OV_MA_and_MACD.html**

Optima: **http://www.oir.com/ techind.htm#MADO**

◆ *MACD Charts.* Graphical charts illustrating MACD.

E-Analytics: **http://www.e-analytics.com/ chart101.htm**

Optima: **http://www.oir.com/images/ chart4.jpg**

A Surfeit of Strategies

There are, quite literally, hundreds—maybe thousands—of other trading theories in use today. Some are inherently successful, some are accidentally successful, and some are completely worthless.

To get a feeling for some of the variety, and to educate yourself about other ways of viewing the market, stop by these Web sites. Contemplate their contents, and if something grabs your attention, try trading on paper for a while to see how you fare. Alternatively, try *back testing*, the theory using historical prices. Step back four or five years, and test the theory to see how well you would have performed if you'd invested early on. If you find a winner, consider yourself a technician!

◆ *Encyclopedia of Indicators.* Extensive list of both technical and fundamental indicators.

**http://www.univel.telescan.com/
indicators.html**

◆ *Top Stocks.* A statistical investing model based on periodic ranking of 3,000 stocks.

**http://www.fishnet.net/~topstock/
index.html**

◆ *The Dow Dividend Approach.* Motley Fool's own technical analysis technique. It's part six of The 13 Steps To Investing "Foolishly."

http://www.fool.com/School/StepSix.htm

◆ *Pristine Profit Plan.* Five rules based on price movements that the writer claims will make it mathematically impossible to lose money.

**http://www.regaldiscount.com/
article5.html**

◆ *Techniques.* Links to a variety of different analysis theories.

**http://www.wallstreetcity.com/
Learn_about_Investing.html**

◆ *Volatility.* Use stock volatility as a measure of market trends.

History: **http://www.stocksmart.com/
volhist.html**

Ratio: **http://www.stocksmart.com/
volratio.html**

19

The Final Analysis

Does the thought of running your securities through the 3 million or so technical analysis theories leave you catatonic? If you're part of that generation who can't remember math before the pocket calculator, stay awake. Help is here in the form of software specially designed to wade through the oceans of data for you.

Truthfully, you could perform most technical analysis with just a protractor and a slide rule. Of course, you'd be collecting Social Security long before you ever came to a meaningful conclusion. Identifying patterns and trends involves a lot of hard work and reams of data. In order to perform a meaningful analysis you'll want to examine several years' worth of historical data for any security that interests you and at least five years' worth of data in the industry category to which it belongs.

Fortunately, a contingent of enterprising software programmers, sensing that there would be a need for faster, more comprehensive security analysis, has come to the rescue. The software you need for data analysis is available for your personal computer and much of it is free directly from the E*TRADE Web site and elsewhere on the Web. It's not magic, exactly. You still have to interpret the analysis within the framework of your own risk tolerance and your own philosophies about investing. But securities analysis software does do all the tedious analytical work for you, leaving you free to spend your afternoons enjoying your wealth. In this chapter, we'll first introduce you to commercial suppliers of company information, and then we'll walk through the software that analyzes the information.

Data for Sale

Perhaps the hottest commodity available today is data—the information on historical stock prices, earnings, profitability, and all the other puzzle pieces that go into making a decision about buying stock. If data could be listed on a public exchange, it would soar to record highs. Because selling data is so profitable, you can expect to see even more vendors enter the business in the future. Normally more competition is good for consumers, and while it's certainly not bad, the increasing size of the vendor pool does mean increased deviation from traditional standards. Competitive pricing is always a prime consideration when choosing a data provider. However, the overriding factor must be the provider's ability to give you accurate, timely information that is 100 percent compatible with your analysis software.

Before signing on with a data supplier, consult the developer of the software you'll purchase. The product documentation will definitely offer an "A" list of providers they'd like you to deal with. Don't automatically eliminate providers that don't make the "A" cut. Consider the "A" list as your starting point. A little shopping around may net you a data provider that is cheaper, more convenient, and just as compatible.

The Data Store

OmniTrader, covered later in this chapter, and programs like it, are meaningless without a steady supply of fresh data. To get that data requires subscribing to a data provider. What follows is a list of a few of the leading commercial data providers.

- ◆ *Commodities Systems, Inc. (CSI)*. CSI is a low cost information vendor. CSI supplies daily summary data on New York Stock Exchange, American and NASDAQ stocks, and mutual funds. Daily updates on thousands of time lines are made available to subscribers at the close of each business day.

  http://www.csidata.com

- ◆ *Interactive Data (IDSI)*. IDSI Services is a central source of bulk U.S. and Canadian securities pricing, capital action, and descriptive information.

  http://www.intdata.com/idsi.htm

- ◆ *FutureSource*. FutureSource gathers information from exchanges and transmits data directly to subscribers by satellite, telephone, airwaves, or landlines.

  http://www.futuresource.com

Walking Through the Technical Analysis

The advent of high-speed 200MHz computers on the shelves of every discount store in the world has freed up programmers to add lots of bells and whistles to their software packages. Developers know that what would have been unbearably slow just a few months ago will now fly with the greatest of speed on the latest generation of computers.

The result is several good software packages that can reduce the time required for extensive technical analysis from days to minutes. While there are many great packages available today, they all tend to work pretty much the same way. This section focuses on just one package, OmniTrader from Nirvana, to demonstrate the power of securities analysis software. An OmniTrader demo can be found on the Investor Toolkit CD-ROM accompanying this book.

OmniTrader won't recommend your trades for you. That's not its intent. What it will do is calculate the results of around 150 different technical analysis methods. It then generates buy-or-sell suggestions based on a summation of the historical analysis of all the technical analysis methods. OmniTrader presents you with the numbers. The final decision is yours.

Overview

More then just a state of total bliss, Nirvana is also the producer of OmniTrader. OmniTrader is a technical analysis tool capable of running multiple analyses on your securities.

As mentioned in Chapter 18, there are hundreds (if not thousands) of technical analysis theories. Imagine applying a single technical analysis technique to a single security over a span of, say, five years. Now imagine tracking the historical success rate of your single technical analysis method on your particular security.

Then imagine applying that technical analysis tool to several securities representing the same industry. Compare the results. How did your security do against the industry average? How good of a job did your technical analysis method do predicting the results for your security? For the industry as a whole?

Now, armed with all that data, imagine repeating the process with a different technical analysis technique. Then take it one step further and compare the results of the first technical analysis method with the results from the second technical analysis method. Have you tracked a pattern yet?

If you can imagine going through this process about 150 times, then you'd have some idea about what it is that OmniTrader does.

The Quick Tour

The Quick Tour is a tutorial of sorts but its purpose is not to make you an OmniTrader pro. Rather, when you finish the Quick Tour, you should be able to understand what securities analysis software is, and what it does.

Normally the first step in performing securities analysis would be to open a portfolio. An OmniTrader portfolio contains a list of all your securities, as well as a record of all the OmniTrader settings that you set to analyze your securities. Theoretically OmniTrader has no limit as to the number of records it can maintain. Nor is there a limit to the number of securities that can be placed in a portfolio. The number of records you can store may be limited by the capacity of your computer; you could run out of space—but it's not very likely.

However, as stated earlier, this is the Quick Tour. There's no assumption being made that you own a copy of OmniTrader. Instead Quick Tour will highlight key points and leave the OmniTrader details for the demo software on the CD-ROM.

The Focus List

A key feature of OmniTrader is the Focus List (see Figure 19.1). It is the primary data management feature of OmniTrader. You build a Focus List by selecting the securities that will be included. This grouping is then analyzed either with OmniTrader's default setting or with criteria that you set.

Everyday users of OmniTrader must subscribe to a financial data service. A data service will supply you with up-to-the-minute information concerning your securities.

To Calculate

Clicking a To-Do icon, three horizontal bars with two check marks on the left side, puts OmniTrader to work on the securities present in your Focus List. OmniTrader runs through each of its 150 featured technical analysis systems for each security. A few minutes later, depending on the speed of your system and the size of your portfolio, it displays trends and information on every one of your securities.

Charting a Course

To display a detailed chart of a selected security, you would click the symbol for that security in your Focus List dialog box. (OmniTrader is capable of displaying more then one chart at a time. It can also synchronize the time scale of displayed charts. However, those features are beyond the scope of this quick tour.)

A chart would appear as shown in the sample (see Figure 19.2). Slide bars in the lower right corner of the of the screen enable you to control the last date displayed as well as the total number of days displayed on the chart.

Immediately below the chart area is a band containing green up arrows and red down arrows. This is the *Voting Line*. The green up arrows are the buy indicators, and the red down arrows are the sell indicators. These symbols are generated by OmniTrader, utilizing a process that polls the results of all the technical analysis methods employed and then analyzes the summation.

Detailed explanations of the buy and sell symbols can be obtained by clicking them. The Advisor information box gives the explanation, along with a recommendation rating of the buy, or sell, indication (see Figure 19.3). Think of the recommendation rating the same way you would a test score. A 79 is a weak score; a 99 is a strong score.

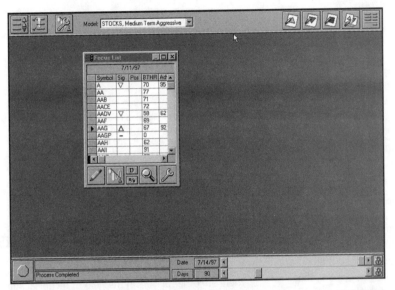

FIG. 19.1

The OmniTrader Focus List contains the names of the securities you want to manage.

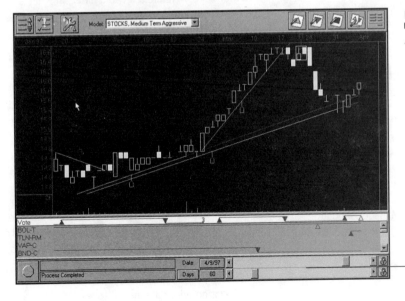

FIG. 19.2

An OmniTrader price chart.

A typical chart featuring days and date adjustment slide bars, and some of the technical analysis indicators

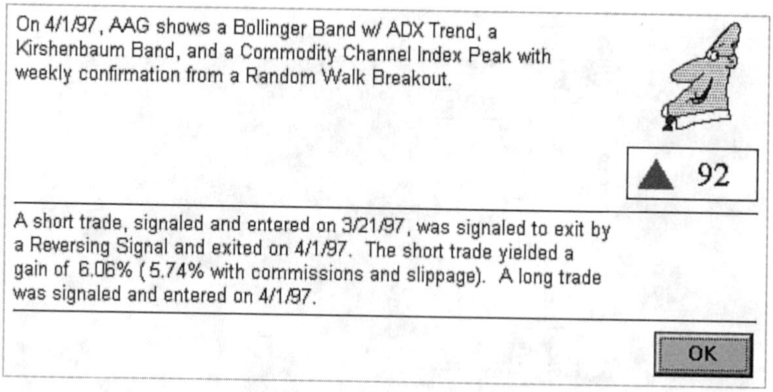

FIG. 19.3

The Advisor information box contains a buy or sell signal; the green up-arrow indicates buy, the advisor rating, 92, and the explanation of the rating.

On 4/1/97, AAG shows a Bollinger Band w/ ADX Trend, a Kirshenbaum Band, and a Commodity Channel Index Peak with weekly confirmation from a Random Walk Breakout.

▲ 92

A short trade, signaled and entered on 3/21/97, was signaled to exit by a Reversing Signal and exited on 4/1/97. The short trade yielded a gain of 6.06% (5.74% with commissions and slippage). A long trade was signaled and entered on 4/1/97.

OK

Below the Voting Line, the individual statistical methods and the results they produced are displayed. It's possible to see an overlay of any analysis method on the chart. Click the technical analysis symbol, the abbreviations on the left side of the screen. An explanation of the analytical methods used is also available by right-clicking the name.

The Quick Out

There's much more to OmniTrader than is shown in this chapter. The Quick Tour was just a glimpse at how OmniTrader could help you with your securities management decisions. Analytical methods can be tailored to your personal preferences. The default conditions may be too aggressive, or too conservative for your taste. Portfolio Manager, simulators, a trading game, and the ability to download live data are also a part of OmniTrader.

■ **N O T E**

For more information check OmniTrader's Web site at **http://www.nirv.com.**

Analyzing the Analysis

There are other players in the field of technical analysis software. Here are a few big hitters in what is likely to become a crowded field:

◆ *Investing FAQs: Tech Analysis.* What would a PC program do that a charting service doesn't?

Programs provide a wide range of technical analysis computations. AIQ StockExpert provides an "expert rating," suggesting buying long or going short depending on the rating.

**http://www.invest-faq.com/articles/
tech-an-basics.html**

◆ *Zacks.* Zacks offers Daily E-mail Alerts as a tool for discovering the secrets of when to sell. The Portfolio Alert sends you a daily e-mail portfolio update which summarizes relevant changes to the stocks in your portfolio: broker recommendation changes, earnings estimate revisions, closing price data, news stories, and company actions (such as declared dividends and expected earnings report dates).

**http://www.zacks.com/docs/Len/
buysell.htm**

◆ *Business Cycle Indicators*. This site features software that analyzes economic indicators.

http://www.globalexposure.com/ howbci.html#Special

◆ *Wall Street Software*. Wall Street Software is a seller of investment software, portfolio managers, and technical analysis featuring MetaStock and more.

http://www.fastlane.net/homepages/ wallst/wallst.html

◆ *Charting and Analysis Software*. A catalog of analysis software available from Investors Software, Inc.

Includes:

- *AIQ Trading Expert V3.0*. Expert rules identify when it's time to buy and sell.

- *Analyst Lite*. Macintosh-based market analysis tool at an affordable price.

- *Candlestick Forecaster*. Sophisticated recognition of more than 700 candlestick and oscillator price patterns.

- *Insider TA*. Better investing through box charting and volume analysis.

- *Instant Investor CD-ROM*. International data, shareware, and more.

- *MathCAD*. Popular technical calculations software.

- *Monocle*. Mutual fund analysis made simple.

- *Mutual Fund Expert*. Mutual fund charting and selection software.

- *Option Pro*. Explores options trading variable using built-in historical testing routines, trading models, and a historical database.

- *Options, Exotics, Yields, Zeros & Swaps*. Advanced financial market Excel spreadsheet libraries.

- *Personal Analyst*. Technical analysis for Macintosh-based investors.

- *Quickcharts*. Create hundreds of stock charts instantly.

- *The Technician*. Get a big-picture view of the market.

- *Telescan Investor's Platform*. Technical analysis, fundamental analysis, and historical database access in one package.

- *Wall Street Analyst Deluxe*. Powerful charting and analysis for the burgeoning new technical analyst.

- *Wall Street Investor*. Integrated portfolio management, charting, and analysis.

- *Windows On Wall Street Deluxe*. Fundamental and technical screening all in one.

- *Windows On Wall Street Personal*. Everything you need to be a stock market success.

http://www.invest-soft.com

◆ *E*TRADE's Options Analysis*. Stock option pricing, using Option leverage analysis and Black-Scholes price analysis. This feature is available to E*TRADE customers only.

https://swww.etrade.com/cgi-bin/cgitrade/ optanalysisform

◆ *StockSmart*. A tool for charting technicals. (Bollinger Bands and more)

http://www.stocksmart.com/ows-bin/owa/ ezgraphs.d?symbols=EGRP

◆ *Technical Analysis Software*. Use the search function to find links to dozens of programs designed to perform technical analysis on your PC.

http://www.wsdinc.com

◆ *Telescan Investor's Platform*. Fundamental and technical analysis. No portfolio management capabilities.

http://www.telescan.com

◆ *Worden TeleChart 2000*. DOS-based charting program. Free 30-day evaluation.

http://www.worden.com

◆ *Equis' MetaStock Professional*. A very popular charting- and system-testing program. Good for technical analysis, but no portfolio management capabilities. Not intended for beginners.

http://www.equis.com

◆ *MarketArts Window on Wall Street Deluxe*. Not for beginners, WOWS is good for technical analysis. Good graphing capabilities and market indicator alerts. Links to Quicken for portfolio management. A beginner's version is also available.

http://www.wallstreet.net

◆ *Omega Research's Wall Street* Analyst. Automated information retrieval, charts, trendlines, and historical data. Intended for those who already know how to perform technical analysis. The company also offers a deluxe version and an introductory version.

http://www.omegaresearch.com/ wsafree.htm

◆ *Omega Research's Super* Charts. Provides automation and testing of most technical indicators.

http://www.omega.com

◆ *E*TRADE's Interactive Charts.* A powerful charting and technical analysis tool available to E*TRADE customers free of charge.

https://swww.etrade.com/cgi-bin/cgitrade/ javaedition

Value Line

Longevity counts. Reputation counts even more. Value Line has both. Value Line Publishing can trace its beginnings back to 1931. Since that time, it has earned a reputation as an energetic and innovative organization in the investment community. The company is probably best known for The Value Line Investment Survey, the world's most widely read investment information service (see Figure 19.4). Other widely acclaimed services include Options and Convertibles Surveys, OTC Special Situations Service, The Value Line Mutual Fund Survey, The Value Line No-Load Fund Advisor, the Small-Cap Value Line Investment Survey Expanded Edition, and electronic data services for individual and institutional clients. For more details, visit the Value Line home page at **http://www.valueline.com**.

FIG. 19.4

The Value Line Products and Services Page provides links to the full range of Value Line services.

The Value Line Analyzer

Value Line's Analyzer is a software tool designed to help investors analyze and select mutual funds. Analyzer is a Windows-based application that is very similar in look and feel to other popular spreadsheet programs such as Excel, Lotus 1-2-3, and Quattro Pro. Data is organized into tables of rows and columns, as in a spreadsheet (see Figure 19.5). Analyzer allows all of the standard spreadsheet-like analytical functions such as sorting, querying, and graphing. Create reports on funds or groups of funds. Additional features enable you to view Value Line data in a format identical to print versions and connect directly to Value Line Online.

Value Line Online

Value Line Online is Value Line's proprietary online service. Just load it onto your computer. The software knows what number to dial. Once logged on to Value Line, you can download the latest data on Mutual Funds, ask technical support questions, search for fund news, review the latest copy of the Value Fund Advisor newsletter, or just get information on other services that Value Line has to offer. First time users of Value Line Online will be prompted to sign up for a user ID and password.

FIG. 19.5

The default view of Value
Line Analyzer presents data
in a familiar spreadsheet
format.

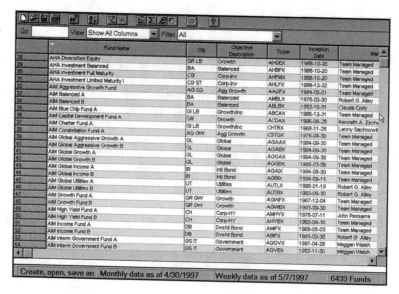

Index

Symbols

101 Investment Terms You Should Know 51

401(k) plans 50

A

A Crash Course on Discounted Paper 47

A Penny Saved 47

A.G. Edwards & Co. 121

AAII (American Association for Individual Investors)— Economic Indicators 117, 124

ABCs of Bonds 81

About Risk and Reward 59

About Technical Analysis 227

About the Net 141

accounts
   commercial online services 29
   E*TRADE
      balances 179
      opening 172–174

accounts receivable turnovers 220

AccuTrade 196

acid-test ratio 221

Active Futures Contracts 88

activity ratio turnovers 220

adapters, video 18

addresses, URLs 33

Advantage Newsletter 79

Advantage of No-Load Mutual Funds 84

AIG (American International Group) 14

All the Rest 100

all-or-none orders 188

Allocation Adjustment 75

allocation of assets 74–76

AltaVista search engine 149–150

America Online (AOL)
   communications software 26
   financial services 30
   IRCs 141
   Mailing List Directory 150
   Message Boards 134

American Association for Individual Investors (AAII) 124, 169

American Express Financial Direct 196–198

American International Group (AIG) 14

American Stock Exchange (AMEX) 121, 164

America's Job Bank 42

AMEX (American Stock Exchange) 121, 164

analysis
   economy 119
   industries 116
   software
      Equis' MetaStock Professional 240
      Interactive Charts 240
      Investing FAQs 238–239
      MarketArts Window on Wall Street Deluxe 240
      Options Analysis 239
      StockSmart 239
      Super Charts 240
      Technical Analysis Software 240
      Telescan Investor's Platform 240
      Wall Street Analyst 240
      Worden TeleChart 2000 240
   stocks
      back testing 230–231
      book value per share 222
      dividend yields 222

Dow Jones & Company 225–226
fundamental 215
growth 222
MACD 229–230
P/E ratio 222
price-to-book ratio 222
prices 222
securities ratios 222
trends 225
values 222

Analyzer 241

AND operator 147

Anderson Investors Software 22

annual reports
financial statements 219
locating 216

annuities, Web sites 85
Basic Look at Variable Annuity Contracts 85
FAQ about Annuities 85
List of Annuities 85

Answers to FAQs About Trading Commodities 87

apprentice investors 4, 101

archives, searching 96

Art of Collecting Animation Art 86

Assessing Your Risk Tolerance 60

Asset Allocation 74, 76

Assets 219

assets 51, 74–76

AstroEcon 224

astrology, stock analysis 224

AT&T WorldNet 32

Aufhauser 198

Australia, legal issues 142

authentication of data 13–14

B

Authoring, Web pages 41

averages
dollar-cost 47–48
moving 228–230

back testing stocks 230–231

BackWeb 106

balance sheets 219

bands, trading 229

Bank of America 22

banking, Web sites
Bank of America 22
FDIC 115
First City Bank & Trust Company 22
First National Bank 22
First National Bank of Baldwind County 22
Huntington Bancshares 22
Security First Network Bank 23
Signet Bank 23
Union Bank of California 23
Wells Fargo Bank 23
Wilber National Bank 23

Barron's Online 93, 96

Basic Investment Principles of Risk and Return 65

Basic Look at Variable Annuity Contracts 85

Basic Types of Investments 78

baud rate, modems 25

BBSs (bulletin board systems) 134

Become a Real-time Commodity Futures Trader 87

benefits, online investing 11

Benefits of Diversification 71

Benefits of Tax-free Investing 73

beta stock measurement 66

Birds in the Hand—Once Again, Junk Has Its Uses 90

Bloomberg Personal 102

Bob'z 129

Bollinger Bands 229

Bond Market Tutorial 80

Bond Professor Glossary 81

bonds 64, 213
brokers 196, 201
call options 79
capital gains 51
convertible 193
corporate 79–81, 193
diversification 70
guaranteed interest rates 80
inflation risks 79
interest payments 51
junk 61, 64, 90
maturities 70
mortgage-backed 92
municipal 72, 79, 193
rating services 61
savings (EE) 79, 82
T-bills 82
taxes 81
treasury bonds/notes 82
Web sites
ABCs of Bonds 81
Birds in the Hand—Once Again, Junk Has Its Uses 90
Bond Market Tutorial 80
Bond Professor's Glossary 81
Bonds as an Investment 51
Briefing.com 121
Building a Bond Ladder 80
Cash Flo 94
Check Free Investment Services 110
Closing Bell 113

Corporate Bonds 80
Current Municiapl Bond
  Yields 81
DBC Online 110
E*TRADE 110, 113–114
End of Day 113
Hoover's Online 114
InterQuote 112
Junk Bonds—They're
  Baaack 90
Making the Most of Zeros
  94
Market Watch 112
MarketSmart 112
Money Magazine 114
Moody's Investors Service
  80
Municipal Bonds 81
PC Quote 111
Quicken Financial Network
  111
Quote.Com 111
Research: Magazine 114
Silicon Investor 114
Standard and Poor's 80
StockMaster 111
TeleQuote Web 112
Thomson MarketEdge 115
Wall Street Journal's
  Briefing Books 114
Wall Street Research Net
  114
Why Invest in Fixed-Income
  Securities? 80
Yahoo! 112
Zack's EPS Surprises 115
zero coupon 79, 93-94

Bonds as an Investment 51

book value per share ratio 222

Boolean operators 147

Bos' Economic Forecasts 119

**Brief Guide to Closed-End
  Funds 84**

Briefing.com 121

**Brokered CDs: The Whys and
  Hows 86**

brokers
AccuTrade 196
American Express Financial
  Direct 196–198
Aufhauser 198
bonds 196, 201
browsing 32
Ceres Securities 198
DATEK Online 199
Daytraders 203
discount 168–169
E*TRADE 171–172, 195–196
  account balances 179
  accounts 172–174
  Canada 173
  Customer Main Menu 177
  Internet Explorer 176
  real-time quotes 178
  security 172
E*TRADE 4–5, 32, 173, 244
eBroker 199
equities 199, 201
e.Schwab 199
Fidelity Investments 201
funds 198
growth 4
locating 203–204
mutual funds 196, 201
options 196–201
PC Financial Network (PCFN)
  201
securities 196
stocks 196–201
traditional 168
treasury notes 201
Wall Street Access Online
  201–203
Yahoo! search engine 204
browsers, 149
brokers 32
files 36

Internet Explorer 27, 32
Netscape Navigator 27, 32
newsgroups 134
pull-down menus 36
scroll bars 36
toolbar buttons 34
see also search engines

Budget Counseling 43

Budget/Plan 40

budgeting investments 45

Building a Bond Ladder 80

**Building Toward an Investment
  Plan Starting From Scratch
  83**

**bulletin board systems (BBSs)
  134**

Bureau of the Public Debt 82

Business Cycle Indicators 118

Business Week 97

Bust the Tipster 130

buying 184
stocks 181
trading options 189

Byte Magazine 27

C

calculating
  investment returns 58
  net worth 45
  ratios activity 220
    leverage 221
    liquidity 221
    profitability 221
    securities 222, 236
  returns 47

call options 79

calls 188–191

Canada
E*TRADE 173
stocks 140

capital gains 51, 81

Capital Markets Commentary
121

Career Path 42

Cash Flo 94

cash flow 45

cash trading 169

CBOE (Chicago Board Options
Exchange) 164

CBOT (Chicago Board of Trade)
165

CD Rate Sheet 86

CD-ROMs 18

CDs (certificates of deposit)
early withdrawal 85
Web sites
Brokered CDs: The Whys
and Hows 86
Want to Make More
$$$??? Invest in a CD! 86
CD Rate Sheet 86

central processing units (CPUs)
18

Ceres Securities 198

certificates of deposit, *see* **CDs**

Charles Dow and the Dow
Theory 226

charting securities 236–238

chat rooms, *see* **IRCs**

Check Free Investment Services
110

Chicago Board of Trade (CBOT)
165

Chicago Board Options
Exchange (CBOE) 93, 164

Chicago Mercantile Exchange
(CME) 165

closed-end mutual funds
83–84

Closing Bell 112

CME (Chicago Mercantile
Exchange) 165

CMOs (collateralized mortgage
obligations) 92
derivatives 92
Web sites
CMOs 92
Collateralized Mortgage
Obligations 92
Experts' Corner 92
Who Wins from Derivatives
Losses? 92

CNBC 124–125

CNNfn Financial Network 102

Coffee, Sugar & Cocoa
Exchange, Inc. (CSCE) 166

collateral 192

Collateralized Mortgage
Obligations 92

collectibles, Web sites
Art of Collecting Animation
Art 86
Dave's Appreciation of
Numismatics 86

Colleges without Borders 41

combining word searches
147–148

commercial online services 27
accounts 29
America Online (AOL) 30,
134, 141
CompuServe 31, 134, 141
Delphi 31
e-mail 36
GEnie 31

IRCs 141
Microsoft Network 31
portability 30
Prodigy 31

commodities, Web sites
Active Futures Contracts 88
Answers to FAQs About
Trading Commodities 87
Become a Real-time Commod-
ity Futures Trader 87
Futures, Options, and
Commodities Trading 87
NY Precious Metals 88

Commodities Systems, Inc.
(CSI) 234

common stock 78

communications software
America Online 26
CompuServe 26
Procomm Plus 27

company reports 113–115

Compaq 18

comparison, *see* **ratios**

compounding interest 48–49

CompuServe
communications software 26
cost 31
Forums 134
IRCs 141

Computer Law: Defamation
Online 142

computers
cost 19
desktop 19
notebooks 26
selecting 18
upgrading 20
see also Macintosh; PCs

Conference Calls 130

configuration 18

connection
Internet 25
IRCs 141
modems 25

Considering Your Investment Horizon 71

consulting firms, Forrester Research 4

Consumer Credit Counseling Service 43

consumer price index 117

consumer protection
insurance 14
Netscape Secure Commerce Server 13
Web sites
Cyber-Investors and Cyber-Fraud 128
NASD Regulation, Inc. 128
National Fraud Information Center 127
What Every Investor Should Know 128
Wild, Wild Web 128
see also security

convertible bonds 193

copyrights 141

Corel Quattro Pro 24

Corporate Bonds 80

corporate bonds 79–81, 193
cost
annuities 85
CompuServe 31
computers 19
funds 83–84
ISPs 31
modems 26
stocks 78

CPUs (central processing units) 18

Credit and Interest Rate Risk 64

credit
cards 43
ratings 79
risks 61–63

CSCE (Coffee, Sugar & Cocoa Exchange, Inc) 166

CSI (Commodities Systems, Inc.) 234

currencies 88–89

Currency Risk 65

Current Municipal Bond Yields 81

current ratio 221

Current US Treasury Yields 82

Cyber-Investors and Cyber-Fraud 128

cyclical risks 63

D

data encryption 13

data providers 234

DATEK Online 199

Dave's Appreciation of Numismatics 86

Daytraders 203

DBC Online 110

debentures corporate bonds 80

debt
investments 77
reducing 43
securities 50
bonds 64–65
money-market funds 65
T-bills 65

debt to asset ratio 220

debt to equity ratio 221

Decoding the Dow 226

decreasing risk diversification 68–70

defamation 141

Defamation and Libel in Cyberspace 142

Defamation Law and Free Speech 142

Default Risk Web site 63

default risks, see credit risks

deferred
annuities 85
taxes 49–50

DejaNews search engine 150–152

delayed stock quotes 110–112

Dell 18

Delphi 31

derivatives 92

Description of Asset Classes 51

desktop computers 19

Determine Your Investment Strategy 75

Determining Your Investment Goal 58

Difference Between Investing and Gambling 59

directories 159

discount brokers 168–169

Diversification 71

diversification
bonds 70
industries 68
international economies 70
maturities 70
mutual funds 70
portfolios 63

stocks 70
Web sites
  Benefits of Diversification
  71
  Diversification 71
  Importance of Diversifica-
  tion 71
dividends, yields 222
Dollar-Cost Averaging 48
domains, security 13–14
**DOS personal finance software
21**
Do's & Don'ts Web site 58
Dow Dividend Approach 231
**Dow Jones & Company
225–226**
Dow Theory 226
downloading files 36
drives 18
Dun and Bradstreet 102

E

E*TRADE 4–5, 110, 171, 244
accounts
  balances 179
  opening 172–174
broker, 32, 195–196
Canada 173
Company Profiles 113
Customer Main Menu 177
Dividend & Split Data 114
Interactive Charts 240
Internet Explorer 176
margin trading 193
options
  buying 189
  selling 190
  trading 188–189
Options Analysis 239

Portfolio Manager 209
real-time quotes 178
Sector Ratings 116
security 14, 172
Stock Order page 181–182
Web Resources List 102
E-Analytics 228–230
e-mail
  Eudora 27
  mailing lists 36
  Pronto 96 27
**early withdrawal, certificates
of deposit (CDs) 85**
earnings
  dividend yields 222
  per share 221
  reinvestment 68
  stocks 222
Easing the Tax Burden 50
eBroker 199
economic indicators
  analysis 119
  consumer price index 117
  unemployment 117
  Web sites
    AAII-Indicators 117
    Bos' Forecast 119
    Business Indicators 118
    Economy 118
    Media Logic—Economics/
    Markets/Investments
    Index 118
    Money Magazine 119
    U.S. Credit Market 119
    USA Today's Economic
    Indicators 118
    What the Markets Will
    Watch, and Why 117
    Yahoo! List 118
economic news 117–118
**Economics By E-Mail Distribu-
tion List 140**
economies, international 70

Economist 97
Economy, The 118
EDGAR Online 102
**educational Web sites,
Colleges Without Borders 41**
EE savings bonds 79, 82
Efficient Frontier 59
electronic mail, *see* e-mail
Electronic Publishing 99
electronic-only publications
  Bloomberg Personal 102
  CNNfn Financial Network 102
  Dun and Bradstreet 102
  E*TRADE's Web Resources 102
  EDGAR Online 102
  Motley Fool 104
  MSNBC 104
  Pawws Financial Network 104
  Pristine Day Trader 104
  Quote.com 105
  Reuters Money Network 105
  Smart Money 105
  Stock Research Group 105
  Thompson MarketEdge 105
  Zacks Investment Research
  105
Elliott Wave Principle 225
employment Web sites
  America's Job Bank 42
  Career Path 42
  Job Bank USA 42
  Monster Board 41
  Resumes Online 41
  Yahoo! Employment
  Classifieds 42
encryption 13–14
Encyclopedia of Indicators 230
End of Day 113
Equis
  MetaStock Professional 240

equities 50, 64
  brokers 199, 201
  investments 77
  returns 222

Equities Are Performers 78

Equity Analytics Web 185

e.Schwab 199

estate taxes, life insurance 91

Ethical Investing—"Green" Money 73

ethical investment, *see* **socially-responsible investing**

etiquette
  newsgroups 135, 142
  spamming 142

Eudora 27

exchanges
  history 164
  rates 65
  stocks 164

Excite search engine 152
  Business and Investing 210

Experts' Corner 92

external modems 25

F

Fannie Maes 92

fax directories 159

FDIC 115

Federal Home Loan Mortgage Corporation (FHLMC) 92

Federal National Morgage Association (FNMA) 92

Fewer Boomers Save for Retirement 44

FHLMC (Federal Home Loan Mortgage Corporation) 92

Fibacci, Leonardo 224

Fibonacci and Natural Occurrences 224

Fidelity Investments 201

file transfer protocol (ftp) 33, 36

files
  downloading 36
  storing 36
  transferring 33
  uploading 36

filters, search engines 149

finances
  balance sheets 219
  income statement 219
  organizing 40
  salary 41
  Web sites
    A Crash Course On Discounted Paper 47
    A Penny Saved 47
    Assets 219
    Budget Counseling 43
    Budget/Plan 40
    Consumer Credit Counseling Service 43
    Expenses 219
    Financial Savvy 219
    Financial Statements 219
    Future Value of Lump Sum 47
    Getting Organized 40
    Getting Started 40
    Income 219
    Interactive Financial Tools 40
    Intuit 15
    Liabilities 219
    Managing Your Money 42
    Mathematics of Individual Finance 47
    Net Worth 219

    Overview of Financial Planning Process 40
    Personal Finance Center 58
    Profit 219
    Searching for Nonfiction in Financial Statements 219
    Spending Less 43
    Your Financial Profile 45
    Your User of Consumer Credit 43

Financial Planning 44

Financial Savvy 219

financial services
  America Online 30
  assets 51, 96

financial software
  banking 22–23
  personal 20–21
  TurboTax 23

Financial Statements 219

Financial Times 99

Financial World 97

Find Your Risk Tolerance 60

finding Web sites, *see* **search engines**

firewalls 13

First City Bank & Trust Company 22

First National Bank 22

First National Bank of Baldwin County 22

FNMA (Federal National Morgage Association) 92

Forbes 97

foreign currency, Web sites 89
  Foreign Currency Exchange Rates 88
  Right on Japan, Wrong on the Year 88

foreign securities 196

Forrester Research consulting firm 4

Forté Free Agent 27

Fortune 98

fraud, *see* consumer protection

Freddy Macs 92

Frequently Asked Questions About Annuities 85

ftp (file transfer protocol) 33, 36

fundamental stock analysis 215

funds
  brokers 198
  index 84
  money market 91, 213
  mutual 51–52, 82–84, 212–213
  risks 91
  see also money-market funds; mutual funds

Future Value of a Lump Sum 47

Futures, Options, and Commodities Trading Tutorial 87

FutureSource 234

G

Galt NetWorth 210

gatekeepers 134

Gateway 18

GEnie 31

Getting Organized 40

Getting Started 40

Getting Started as a Socially Responsible Investor 74

Getting Started: Investing with Mutual Funds 84

Ginnie Maes 92

Global Investing 89

Glossary (American Association of Individual Investors) 52

Glossary of Investment Terms 52

Glossary of Technical Terms 227

GNMA (Government National Mortgage Association) 92

Golden Section 224

good for day orders 188

good-till-canceled (GTC) orders 188, 192

Government National Mortgage Association (GNMA) 92

government securities 82, 193
  Web sites
    Bureau of Public Debt 82
    Current US Treasury Yields 82
    Department of Treasury 82
    Savings Bond Informer 82
    US Treasury Bonds 82
  zero coupon bonds 93–94

Grand SuperCycle Peak 224

grouping word searches 148

Groups 140

growth of online brokers 4

growth stocks, securities ratios 222

guaranteed interest rates 80

Guide to International Marketplace 89

Guide to Social Investing 74

H

hard drives 18

hierarchy, UseNet newsgroups 134

high-yield bonds, *see* junk bonds

history 164

Hoover's Online 104, 114

How to Avoid Estate Taxes on Life Insurance 91

Hulbert Financial Digest 100

Huntington Bancshares 22

hyperlinks 34

I

IBM Internet Connection 32

IBM-compatible computers 18

Identify Goals and Objectives 58

IDSI (Interactive Data) 234

immediate annuities 85

Importance of a Mix of Assets 75

Importance of Diversification 71

income statement 219

increasing salary 41

index funds 84, 213

Index Investing versus Active Investing 84

indicators, *see* economic indicators

individual retirement accounts (IRAs) 50

Individuals Should Focus on the Long-term 71

Industry Briefing 115

industry news 121
diversification 68
Web sites
E*TRADE's Sector Ratings 116
FDIC 115
Industry Briefing 115
PR Newswire 115
Where to Invest 116
Yahoo! on the Money 115

industry risks, *see* cyclical risks

Inflation Risk Web site 63

inflation risks 63–64

Infoseek search engine 152–153
Investor 212

InfoSpace search engine 153

initial public offerings (IPOs) 90–91

insurance
life 91
security 14
Web sites
How to Avoid Estate Taxes on Life Insurance 91
Insurance 91

Interactive Data (IDSI) 234

Interactive Financial Tools 40

interactive investments, Web sites
Bob'z 129
Bust the Tipster 130
Conference Calls 130
Join Our Discussion 129
Message Boards 128
Michael Campbell's Money Talks 129
Mutual Funds Online 130
Participate 129
Silicon Investor 128
Socialize 128
Talk to Other Investors 130

interest 46–47
bond payments 51
compounding 48–49
guaranteed 80
Power of Compounding 49
risks 64

Interest-rate Risk 64

Intermind Communicator 106

internal modems 25

International 90

international economies 140
diversification 70
investments 65, 89–90
Web sites
Global Investing 89
Guide to International Marketplace 89
International 90
International Equities 89
International Equity 90
Micropal 90
Traps for Unwary in Foreign Investing 90

International Equities 89–90

Internet
connection 25
Explorer 27, 32, 176
legal issues 141–142
newsgroups 134
regulating 127
spamming 142
see also ISPs

Internet Relay Chat FAQ 141

Internet Relay Chats, *see* IRCs

InterQuote 112

Intuit 15, 21–23

inventory
activity ratios 220–222
turnovers 220

Invest-o-rama 125–126

Investing 101: Risk and Reward 59

Investing FAQs 238, 239

Investing Glossaries on the Web 52

investment clubs
returns 130
Web sites
Investment Clubs on the Web 131
National Association of Investors Corporation (NAI 131
So You Want to Start an Investment Club? 131

Investment Goals 74

Investment Rules 75

Investment Talk 140

investments 4, 101
brokers 168–169
budgeting 45
currencies 88–89
debt 77
diversification 63
economies 70
industries 68
maturities 70
mutual funds 70
dollar-cost averaging 47–48
equities 64, 77, 221
inflation risk 79
interest 46, 48–49
international 65, 89–90
long-term 58, 71
mid-term 58
online 11
partnerships 64
real estate 64
retirement funds 58
returns 221
risks 59–60
credit 61–63
cyclical 63
decreasing 70
inflation 63–64
interest rates 64

liquidity 64–65
market 65
opportunity costs 66
price volatility 66–67
reinvestment rates 67–68
"safe" 59
short-term 57–58
social responsibility 73–74
tax-free
municipal bonds 72
yields 73
terminology 51–52
trading 169
Web sites
101 Investment Terms You
Should Know 51
Basic Types of Investments
78
Bob'z 129
Bust the Tipster 130
Conference Calls 130
Determining Your Invest-
ment Goal 58
Glossary 52
Glossary of Investment
Terms 52
Identify Goals and
Objectives 58
Invest-o-rama 125
Investing Glossaries on the
Web 52
Join Our Discussion 129
Message Boards 128
Michael Campbell's Money
Talks 129
misc.investFAQ 78
Mutual Funds Online 130
Participate 129
Setting Your Goals and
Objectives 58
Silicon Investor 128
Socialize 128
Talk to Other Investors 130
Types of Investments 78
INVESTools 101
Investor Education Center 84

Investor's Business Daily 99
Investors Newsletter Digest
101
Investors—Stock Market
Investment 140
InvestorsEdge 212
IPO Center (inital public
offerings) 90–91
IRAs (individual retirement
accounts) 50
IRCs (Internet Relay Chats)
140–141
ISPs (Internet Service Provid-
ers) 27
AT&T WorldNet 32
cost 31
e-mail 36
EarthLink 244
IBM Internet Connection 32
locating 32
MCI Internet Dial Access 32
newsgroups 134
software 31
speed 31
Sprint Internet Passport 32

J-K

Job Bank USA 42
John Bollinger's Capital
Growth Letter 229
Join Our Discussion 129
journeyman investors 4
junk bonds 61, 64, 90
Junk Bonds—They're Baaack
90

keywords 147–149
Kiplinger Online 98
Kiplinger TaxCut 24

L

laptops, see notebooks
LawCrawler search engine 154
legal issues
Australia 142
copyrights 141
defamation 141
Internet 141–142
libel 141
United States 142
Web sites
About the Net 141
Computer Law: Defama-
tion Online 142
Defamation and Libel in
Cyberspace 142
Defamation Law and Free
Speech 142
Legg Mason 120
leverage ratios
debt to asset 220
debt to equity 221
times-interest-earned 221
leveraged
assets 192
purchasing 169
see also margin trading
Liabilities 219
libel 141
Life Cycle Investing: Your
Personal Investment Pro 75
life insurance 91
limit orders 186
limited partnerships 64
linking Web pages 34
Liquidity 65
liquidity ratios
acid-test 221
current 221
government securities 82

risks 64–65
  working capital 221
Liquidity Risk 64
List of Annuities 85
listowners 138
ListServ mailing list manager 138
Liszt search engine 154
load mutual funds 83
locating
  annual reports 216
  ISPs 32
  online brokers 203–204
locating Web sites, *see* **search engines**
long-term investments 58
  Web sites
    Considering Your Investment Horizon 71
    Individuals Should Focus on Long-term 71
    Portfolio Maintenance Program/Long-Term Investor 47, 72
Look at Historical Investment Returns 75
Los Angeles Times 99
Lotus 1-2-3 24
low signal-to-noise ratio 134
Lycos search engine 156

M

MACD (Moving Average Convergence/Divergence) 231
  trigger lines 229
  Web sites
    E-Analytics 230
    MACD 230

MACD Charts 230
  Optima 230
  Wall Street 230
Macintosh 17
  CD-ROM drives 18
  configuration 18
  desktop 19
  hard drives 18
  monitors 18
  notebooks 19, 26
  operating systems 19
  processors 18
  RAM 18
  selecting 18
  software 21
  video adapters 18
Magellan search engine 156
mail, *see* **e-mail**
Mailing Lists 139
mailing lists
  Economics By E-Mail Distribution List 140
  Groups 140
  Investment-Talk 140
  Investors—Stock Market Investment 140
  listowners 138
  Mailing Lists 139
  managers 138
  Mutual Fund Discussion List 140
  participatory 140
  read-only 140
  Stock and Investment News Distribution List 140
  subscribing 139
  Tips for Newcomers 140
maintenance calls 192
Majordomo mailing list manager 138
Making the Most of Zeros 94

management of portfolios
  E*TRADE Portfolio Manager 209
  Excite Business and Investing 210
  Galt NetWorth 210
  Infoseek Investor 212
  InvestorsEdge 212
  Market Watcher Version 213
  Personal Portfolio 210
  selecting 208–209
  software 208
  StockSmart 213
Managing Your Money 21, 42
margin calls 169
margin trading 169
  collateral 192
  maintenance calls 192
  requirements 193
Market Commentary 120
Market Risk and Time 65
market trends, Web sites
  A.G. Edwards & Co. 121
  American Stock Exchange 121
  Capital Markets Commentary 121
  Legg Mason 120
  Market Commentary 120
  Merrill Lynch 120
  Prudential Securities 121
  Yahoo! Finance 120
Market Watch 112
Market Watcher Version 213
Market Arts Window on Wall Street Deluxe 240
markets
  orders 186, 191
  risks 65
  stock indexes 84
MarketSmart 112
master investors 4
Mathematics of Individual Finance 47

maturities
bonds 70
T-bills 82
treasury bonds 82
treasury notes 82

MCI Internet Dial Access 32

Media Logic—Economics/ Markets/Investments Index 118

memory 18

menus, pull-down 36

Merrill Lynch 120

Message Boards 128

messages 142–143

Michael Campbell's Money Talks 129

Microsoft
Investor 104
Money 97 21
Network 31
Windows, *see* Windows

mid-term investments 58

Minneapolis Grain Exchange 93, 166

mIRC 141

misc.invest FAQ 78, 84

modems 25–26

moderated UseNet newsgroups 134

money
saving 44
value 47

Money Magazine 114, 119

Money Market Data 91

money market funds, Web sites 65, 213
Money Market Data 91
Money Market Funds 91
Money Market Funds: Advantages, Risks, and Costs 91

Money Online 98

Money Talks 101

monitors 18

Monster Board 41

Moody's 61

Moody's Investors Service 79–80

More on Inflation Risk Web site 63

More on Interest-rate Risk 64

Morningstar On Demand 84

mortgage-backed bonds 92

mortgages, collateralized obligations 92

Motley Fool 104, 126

Moving Average Convergence/ Divergence (MACD) 229–230

Moving Averages 228

MSNBC 104

Municipal Bonds 81

municipal bonds 72, 79, 81, 193

mutual funds 51, 82, 99, 212–213, 241
activity 52
brokers 196, 201
closed-end 83–84
cost 83
diversification 70
load 83
no-load 83
non-money market 193
open-end 83
returns 84, 222
software 241
Web sites
Advantage of No-Load Mutual Funds 84
Brief Guide to Closed-End Funds 84
Building Toward an Investment Plan Starting from Scratch 83
Getting Started: Investing with Mutual Funds 84
Investor Education Center 84
misc.invest.funds FAQ 84
Morningstar On Demand 84
Mutual Funds 84
Mutual Funds as Investments 51
Mutual Funds Discussion List 140
Mutual Funds Online 83, 99, 130
Reading a Mutual Fund Listing 52
Top US Mutual Funds 84

N

NAIC (National Association of Investors Corporatio 131

NASD (National Association of Security Dealers) 14

NASD Regulation, Inc. 128

Nasdaq (National Association of Securities Dealers Automated Quotations) 166

National Association of Investors Corporation (NAIC) 131

National Association of Securities Dealers Automated Quotations (Nasdaq) 166

National Association of Security Dealers (NASD) 14

National Fraud Information Center 127

Net Abuse FAQ 143

Net Worth 219

net worth 45

Netiquette 142

Netscape
Navigator 27, 32, 134
Secure Commerce Server 13

**New York Cotton Exchange
(NYCE) 166**

**New York Stock Exchange
(NYSE) 166**

New York Times 99

news 52
economy 117–118
industries 115, 121
publications
All the Rest 100
Financial Times 99
Investor's Business Daily 99
Los Angeles Times 99
New York Times 99
San Jose Mercury News 99
USA Today/USA Today
Financial Marketplace 99
Wall Street Journal
Interactive 99
readers, Forté Free Agent 27

news.newusers.questions 138

newsgroups
American Online (AOL)
Message Boards 134
CompuServer Forums 134
etiquette 135, 142
hierarchy 134
Internet Explorer 134
ISPs 134
low signal-to-noise ratio 134
messages 142–143
moderated 134
Netscape Navigator 134
searching 135
spamming 142
threads 135
UseNet 36, 134–138

Web sites
Net Abuse FAQ 143
news.newusers.questions
138
Newsgroups of Interest
138
Roadmap for the Informa-
tion Superhighway 143
UseNet News 138
User Guidelines and
Netiquette 143

Newsgroups of Interest 138

newsletters
Hulbert Financial Digest 100
INVESTools 101
Investors Newsletter 101
Money Talks 101
Stock Manager's Investment
Report 101
stock analysis 100–101
Zacks Online Magazine 101

newspapers, *see* **news
publications**

no-load mutual funds 83

**non-money market mutual
funds 193**

NOT operator 147

notebooks 19, 26

**NYCE (New York Cotton
Exchange) 166**

**NYSE (New York Stock
Exchange) 166**

O

odd lots 78

Omega Research
Super Charts 240
Wall Street Analyst 240

OmniTrader 235
Focus List 236
securities 236–238
To Calcuate 236

Online 241

online brokers
AccuTrade 196
American Express Financial
Direct 196–198
Aufhauser 198
Ceres Securities 198
DATEK Online 199
Daytraders 203
E*TRADE 171–172, 195–196
account balances 179
accounts 172–174
Canada 173
Customer Main Menu 177
Internet Explorer 176
real-time quotes 178
security 172, 182
eBroker 199
e.Schwab 199
Fidelity Investments 201
growth 4
locating 203, 204
PC Financial Network (PCFN)
201
Wall Street Access Online
201–203
Yahoo! search engine 204
see also brokers

online regulation, *see* **consumer protection; security**

online services
annual reports 216
commercial
accounts 29
America Online 30
CompuServe 31
Delphi 31
GEnie 31
Microsoft Network 31
Prodigy 31

open-end mutual funds 83

opening accounts with
E*TRADE 172–174

operating systems 19

Opportunity Cost Risk 66

Opportunity Costs 66

Optima 229–230

options 92–93, 212–213
  brokers 196, 198, 201
  trading 188–189
    buying 189
    calls 188–191
    market orders 191–192
    previewing 192
    puts 188–191
    selling 190
    symbols 190–191
  Web sites
    Barron's Online 93
    Chicago Board Options
      Exchange 93
    Minneapolis Grain
      Exchange 93

OR operator 147

orders
  all-or-none 188
  good for day 188
  good-till-canceled (GTC)
    188, 192
  limit 186
  market 186
  stop limit 187
  stop loss 186–187

organizing finances 40

OS/2 Warp 19

over-the-counter (OTC)
securities 166

Overview of Financial Planning
Process 40

ownership of newsgroups
messages 143

P

P/E ratio 65, 222

Pace University Library 185

Participate 129

participatory mailing lists 140

partnerships 64

pass-throughs 92

Pawws Financial Network 104

payments 51, 85

PC Card 26

PC Financial Network (PCFN)
201

PC Quote 110

PC World 20

PCs 17
  CD-ROM drives 18
  configuration 18
  desktop 19
  hard drives 18
  monitors 18
  notebooks 19, 26
  operating systems 19
  OS/2 Warp 19
  processors 18
  RAM 18
  selecting 18
  software 21
  video adapters 18
  Windows 19–20

PCs (personal computers) 17

Pentium 18

periodicals, see publications

permanent life insurance 91

personal computers, 17–18

Personal Finance Center 58

personal financial 20–22,
40–41

Personal Portfolio 210

Philadelphia Stock Exchange
(PHLX) 168

Physical & Financial Assets 51

physical assets 51

PitBull Investor 66

planning
  finances 40
  investment portfolios 57–58

PointCast 107

"pointing finger" 34

portability
  commercial online services 30
  modems 26

Portfolio Maintenance
Program for the Long-term
Investor 47, 72

portfolios
  asset allocation 74–76
  creating 57–58
  diversification 63
    economies 70
    industries 68
    maturities 70
    mutual funds 70
  equities 64
  investments
    bonds 64
    clubs 130
    limited partnerships 64
    long-term 58, 71
    mid-term 58
    money-market funds 65
    penny stocks 64
    planning 57–58
    real estate 64
    retirement 58
    short-term 57
    socially-responsible 73–74
    stocks 63
    T-bills 65
    tax-free 72–73

management
  E*TRADE Portfolio
    Manager 209
  Excite Business and
    Investing 210
  Galt NetWorth 210
  Infoseek Investor 212
  InvestorsEdge 212
  Market Watcher Version
    1.10 213
  Personal Portfolio 210
  selecting 208–209
  software 208
  StockSmart 213
risks 59–60
  credit 61–63
  cyclical 63
  decreasing 70
  inflation 63–64
  interest rates 64
  liquidity 64–65
  market 65
  opportunity costs 66
  price volatility 66–67
  reinvestment rates 67–68
Web sites
  Allocation Adjustment 75
  Asset Allocation 74–76
  Determine Your Investment
    Strategy 75
  Importance of a Mix of
    Assets 75
  Investment Goals 74
  Investment Rules 75
  Life Cycle Investing 75
  Look at Historical Invest-
    ment Returns 75
  Right Investment Mix 74
  Sample Investment
    Portfolios 74
  What to Do with Different
    Levels of Investable
    Money 76
posting messages 142
Power of Compounding 49

PR Newswire 115
preferred stock 78
previewing options trading
  192
price volatility risks 66
price-to-book ratio 222
price/earnings ratio, see P/E
  ratio
pricing stocks 186–187, 222
Pristine Day Trader 104
Pristine Profit Plan 231
processors 18
Procomm Plus 27
Prodigy 31
profit margins 221
profitability ratios 221–222
promissory notes, see bonds
Pronto 96 27
Prudential Securities 60, 121
publications
  Barron's Online 96
  Business Week 97
  Byte Magazine 27
  Economist 97
  Electronic Publishing 99
  Financial World 97
  Forbes 97
  Fortune 98
  Kiplinger Online 98
  Money Online 98
  Mutual Funds Online 99
  PC World 20
  Washington Post Business
    Glossary 185
  see also electronic-only
    publications
pull-down menus 36
purchasing stocks 179
  see also buying
Push Technology 106–107
puts 188–191

Q

Quarterdeck Procomm Plus 27
Quicken Deluxe 21
Quicken Financial Network
  111
Quote.Com 105,
quotes
  real-time 178
  stocks 96, 112–113

R

RAM (random access memory)
  18
ratios 221–222
read-only mailing lists 140
Reading a Mutual Fund Listing
  52
Reading a Stock Listing 52
real estate 64
real estate investment trusts
  (REITs) 93
real-time
  chat 140–141
  quotes 112, 178
receiving, see downloading
reducing
  cyclical risks 63
  debt 43
regulating the Internet, see
  consumer protection
reinvestment rate risks 67–68
REITs (real estate investment
  trusts) 93

reports
companies 113–115
financial 96

requirements, margin trading 193

Research: Magazine 114

Resumes Online 41

Retire Right 58

retirement
401(k) plans 50
individual retirement accounts (IRAs) 50
tax deferrals 49–50
Web sites
Fewer Boomers Save for Retirement 44
Financial Planning 44
Retire Right 58
Women Need to Save More Than Mend Do for Retirement 44

returns
calculating 47
equity 222
investment club 130
mutual funds 84, 222
total 46–47, 222
Web sites
About Risk and Reward 59
Difference Between Investing and Gambling 59
Efficient Frontier 59
Investing 101: Risk and Reward 59
Moody's 61
Prudential Securities 60
see also yields

Reuters Money Network 105

Right Investment Mix 74

Right on Japan, Wrong on the Yen 88

risks
bonds 79
credit 61–63
cyclical 63
decreasing diversification 70
inflation 63–64, 82
interest rates 64
investments 59–60
liquidity 64–65
market 65
money market funds 91
opportunity costs 66
P/E ratio 222
price volatility 66–67
reinvestment rates 67–68
securities 82
stocks 222
Web sites
About Risk and Reward 59
Assessing Your Risk Tolerance 60
Basic Investment Principles of Risk/Return 65
Battle Against Inflation 64
Credit and Interest Rate Risk 64
Currency Risk 65
Default Risk 63
Difference Between Investing and Gambling 59
Efficient Frontier 59
Find Your Risk Tolerance 60
Inflation Risk 63
Interest-rate Risk 64
Investing 101: Risk and Reward 59
Liquidity 65
Liquidity Risk 64
Market Risk and Time 65
Moody's 61
More on Inflation Risk 63
More on Interest-rate Risk 64

Opportunity Cost Risk 66
Opportunity Costs 66
PitBull Investor 66
Prudential Securities 60
Reinvestment Rate Risk 68
Reinvestment Risk 68
Standard and Poor's 61
Volatility 67
Volatility Risk 67
Ways to Group Stocks 63

Roadmap for the Information Superhighway 143

round lots 78

Rule 10b-21(T) 186

S

"safe" investments 59

salary, increasing 41

Sample Investment Portfolios 74

San Jose Mercury News 99

savings (EE) bonds 82

Savings Bond Informer 82

scams, *see* **consumer protection; security**

scroll bars 36

search engines 145–146
AltaVista 149–150
America Online Mailing List Directory 150
Boolean operators 147
DejaNews 150–152
Excite 152
Infoseek 152–153
InfoSpace 153
keywords 147
LawCrawler 154
Liszt 154
Lycos 156

Magellan 156
SEARCH.COM 157
Starting Point 157
WebCrawler 159
word searches 147–149
    wildcard characters 149
WorldPages 159
Yahoo! 160, 204

**SEARCH.COM search engine
157**

searching
newsgroups 135
publication archives 96

**Searching for Nonfiction in
Financial Statements 219**

secured corporate bonds 80

securities 210
calculating 236
charting 236–238
debt 50, 65
derivatives 92
equities 50
government 193
    liquidity 82
    T-bills 82
    treasury bonds/notes 82
    zero coupon bonds 93–94
leveraged purchasing 169
mutual funds 51
over-the-counter (OTC) 166
ratios 222

**Securities Investor Protection
Corporation (SIPC) 14**

security
domains 13–14
    E*TRADE 14, 172
firewalls 13
insurance 14
Netscape Secure Commerce
    Server 13
online brokers 182
see also consumer protection

Security APL 110

**Security First Network Bank
23**

selecting
computers 18
portfolio managers 208–209

selling 184
options trading 190
short 184–186

sending, *see* uploading files

**Setting Your Goals and
Objectives 58**

shares
book values 222
stocks 181

short selling 184–186

short-term investments 57–58

Signet Bank 23

Silicon Investor 114, 128

Simple Money 2.1 21

**SIPC (Securities Investor
Protection Corporation) 14**

small-capitalization stock 79

Smart Money 105

**So You Want to Start An
Investment Club? 131**

Socialize 128

**socially responsible invest-
ments, Web sites**
Ethical Investing 73
Getting Started as Socially
    Responsible Investor 74
Guide to Social Investing 74

software
analysis 238–239
banking 22–23
chat 28
communications 26–27

e-mail 27
ISPs 31
mutual funds 241
personal finance 20–22
portfolio management 208,
    213
Push Technology, 106–107
spreadsheets 24
taxes 23–24, 240–241

spamming 142

specialists 164

speed 26, 31

Spending Less 43

spreadsheet software 24

Sprint Internet Passport 32

**Standard and Poor's
61, 68, 79–80**

**Starting Point search engine
157**

statements, financial 219

**Stock and Investment News
Distribution List 140**

Stock as an Investment 51

**Stock Manager's Investment
Report 101**

Stock Research Group 105

Stockholder's Equity, *see* Net
Worth 219

StockMaster 111

stocks 51, 210–213
analysis 224–225
    back testing 230–231
    Dow Jones & Company
        225–226
    fundamental 215
    Investing FAQs 238–239
    MACD 229–230
    moving averages 228–230
    newsletters 100–101

prices 222
trading bands 229
trends 225
values 222
Worden TeleChart 2000
  240
beta measurement 66
brokers 196–198, 201
buying 181–183
Canada 140
common 78
cost 78, 181
diversification 63, 70
dollar-cost averaging 47–48
earnings per share 221
exchanges 164–166
growth 222
initial public offerings (IPOs)
  90–91
international 140
liquidity ratios 221
market indexes 84
odd lots 78
orders 186–188
preferred 78
pricing 186–187
profit margins 221
profitability ratios 221
purchasing 179
quotes 52, 96
  delayed 110–112
  real-time 112, 178
risks and returns 222
round lots 78
securities ratios
  book value per share ratio
    222
  dividend yields 222
  P/E 65, 222
  price-to-book 222
selling 183–186
shares 181–182
small-capitalization 79
symbols 190–191
terms 181
ticker symbols 181

trading 78, 182, 215
undervalued 79
Web sites
  About Technical Analysis
    227
  Advantage Newsletter 79
  AstroEcon 224
  Bollinger Bands 229
  Briefing.com 121
  Charles Dow and the Dow
    Theory 226
  Check Free Investment
    Services 110
  Closing Bell 113
  DBC Online 110
  Decoding the Dow 226
  Dollar-Cost Averaging 48
  Do's & Don't's 58
  Dow Dividend Approach
    231
  Dow Theory 226
  E*TRADE 110, 113–114,
    239–240
  E-Analytics 228–230
  Elliott Wave Principle 225
  Encyclopedia of Indicators
    230
  End of Day 113
  Equis' MetaStock Profes-
    sional 240
  Equities Are Performers 78
  Equity Analytics Web 185
  Fibonacci and Natural
    Occurrences 224
  Glossary of Technical Terms
    227
  Golden Section 224
  Grand SuperCycle Peak
    224
  Hoover's Online 114
  InterQuote 112
  John Bollinger's Capital
    Growth Letter 229
  MACD 230
  MACD Charts 230
  Market Watch 112

MarketArts Window on
  Wall Street Deluxe 240
MarketSmart 112
Money Magazine 114
Moving Averages 228
Optima 229, 230
Option's Analysis 239
Pace University Library 185
PC Quote 111
Pristine Profit Plan 231
Quicken Financial Network
  111
Quote.Com 111
Reading a Stock Listing 52
Research: Magazine 114
Reuters 245
Rule 10b-21(T) 186
Silicon Investor 114
Stock as an Investment 51
StockMaster 111
Stocks & Commodities 78
StockSmart 213, 229, 239
Super Charts 240
Syndicate 228
Technical Analysis 227,
  240
Techniques 231
TeleQuote Web 112
Telescan 229, 240
Thomson MarketEdge 115
Top Stocks 231
Traditional Formula Plans
  for Buying and Selling
  Stocks 48
US Stocks 79
Volatility 231
Wall Street 230
Wall Street Analyst 240
Wall Street Journal's
  Briefing Books 114
Wall Street Research Net
  114
Ways to Group Stocks 63
When to Buy and Sell 227
Why Buy and Hold May
  Not Be Best Strategy 215

Why Invest in Equities? 78
Worden TeleChart 2000 240
Yahoo! 112
Zack's EPS Surprise 115

Stocks & Commodities 78

StockSmart 213, 229, 239

stop limit orders 187

stop loss orders 186–187

storing files 36

subscribing to mailing lists 139

surfing, *see* **browsers; search engines**

symbols, stocks 190–191

Syndicate 228

T

T-bills, *see* **government securities**

Talk to Other Investors 130

Tax Logic 24

Tax-Deferred and Tax-Free Investing 50

tax-free municipal bonds 72–73, 81

taxable equivalent yields 50

taxes
capital gains 81
deferrals 49–50
estate 91
software
Kiplinger TaxCut 24
Tax Logic 24
TurboTax 23
Web sites
Benefits of Tax-free Investing 73
Easing the Tax Burden 50

Kiplinger TaxCut 24
Tax Logic 24
Tax-Deferred and Tax-Free Investing 50
TurboTax 23

Technical Analysis 227

Technical Analysis Software 240

Techniques 231

telephone directories 159

TeleQuote Web 112

Telescan Investor's Platform 240

Telescan on Bollinger Bands 229

term life insurance 91

terminology for investing 51–52

Thompson MarketEdge 105, 115

threads 135

ticker symbols 181

times-interest-earned ratios 221

Tips for Newcomers 140

toolbar buttons 34

Top Stocks 231

Top US Mutual Funds 84

total asset turnovers 220

total returns 46–47, 222

trading
bands 229
cash 169
margin 169, 192–193
options 188–189
buying 189
calls 188–191
market orders 191–192
previewing 192

puts 188–191
selling 190
symbols 190–191
stocks 78, 182, 215

traditional brokers 168

Traditional Formula Plans for Buying and Selling Stocks 48

transactions 183–186
buying 184
selling 184–186

transferring files 33

Traps for the Unwary in Foreign Investing 90

treasury bills, see government securities

treasury bonds/notes
brokers 201
maturities 82
see also government securities

trends
analysis 225
markets 120–121

trigger lines 229

TurboTax 23

turnovers

Types of Investments 78

U

U.S. Treasury Bonds 82

undervalued stock 79

unemployment 117

Uniform Resource Locators, *see* **Web sites**

Union Bank of California 23

United States, legal issues 142

upgrading computers 20

uploading files 36

URLs, *see* Web sites

US Credit Market 119

US Index Movers 84

US Stocks 79

USA Today
Economic Indicators 118
Financial Marketplace 99

UseNet News 138

UseNet newsgroups 36
American Online (AOL)
Message Board 134
CompuServe Forums 134
etiquette 135
hierarchy 134
Internet Explorer 134
low signal-to-noise ratio 134
moderated 134
Netscape Navigator 134
searching 135
threads 135

User Guidelines and
Netiquette 143

V

Value Line 240
Analyzer 241
Online 241

values 47, 222

video adapters 18

Volatility 67, 231

Volatility Risk 67

W

Wall Street 201–203, 230

Wall Street Journal Interactive
99

Wall Street Research Net 114,
216

Wall Street Journal's Briefing
Books 114

Want to Make More $$$???
Invest in a CD! 86

Washington Post Business
Glossary 185

Ways to Group Stocks 63

Web sites
addresses 33
annual reports
Company Links 216
Graphs/Charts 216
News Center 216
Research, Reports &
Summaries 216
annuities
Basic Look at Variable
Annuity Contracts 85
Frequently Asked Questions
About Annuities 85
List of Annuities 85
assets
Description of Asset Classes
51
Physical & Financial Assets
51
Authoring 41
banking
Bank of America 22
FDIC 115
First City Bank & Trust
Company 22
First National Bank 22
First National Bank of
Baldwin County 22
Huntington Bancshares 22
Security First Network Bank
23
Signet Bank 23
Union Bank, California 23
Wells Fargo Bank 23
Wilber National Bank 23

brokers
American Express Financial
Direct 198
Aufhauser 198
Ceres Securities 198
DATEK Online 199
Daytraders 203
E*TRADE 14, 32, 102,
116, 173, 244
eBroker 199
e.Schwab 199
Fidelity Investments 201
PC Financial Network
(PCFN) 201
Wall Street Access Online
203
browsers
Internet Explorer 27, 32
Netscape Navigator 27, 32
pull-down menus 36
scroll bars 36
toolbar buttons 34
certificates of deposit
CD Rate Sheet 86
Brokered CDs: The Whys
and Hows 86
Want to Make More $$$??
Invest in a CD! 86
collateralized mortgage
obligations
CMO's 92
Collateralized Mortgage
Obligations 92
Experts' Corner 92
Who Wins from Derivatives
Losses? 92
collectibles
Art of Collecting Animation
Art 86
Dave's Appreication of
Numismatics 86
commodity futures
Active Futures Contracts
88
Answers to FAQs About
Trading Commodities 87

Become a Real-time
Commodity Futures
Trader 87
Futures, Options, and
Commodities Trading
Tutorial 87
connection 25
consumer protection
Cyber-Investors and Cyber-
Fraud 128
NASD Regulation, Inc. 128
National Fraud Information
Center 127
What Every Investor Should
Know 128
Wild, Wild Web 128
diversification
Benefits of Diversification
71
Diversification 71
Importance of Diversifica-
tion 71
e-mail
Eudora 27
Pronto 96 27
economic indicators
AAII-Economic Indicators
117
Bos' Economic Forecast
119
Business Cycle Indicators
118
Economy 118
Media Logic—Economics/
Markets/Investments
Index 118
Money Magazine 119
U.S. Credit Market 119
USA Today's Economic
Indicators 118
What the Markets Will
Watch, and Why 117
Yahoo! List 118

education, Colleges without
Borders 41
employment
America's Job Bank 42
Authoring 41
Career Path 42
Job Bank USA 42
Monster Board 41
Resumes Online 41
Yahoo! Employment
Classifieds 42
exchanges
AMEX 164
CBOE 164
CBOT 165
CME 165
CSCE 166
Minneapolis Grain
Exchange 93, 166
Nasdaq 166
NYCE 166
NYSE 166
PHLX 168
finances
A Crash Course on
Discounted Paper 47
A Penny Saved 47
Boot Your Broker 244
Budget Counseling 43
Budget/Plan 40
Consumer Credit Counsel-
ing Service 43
Financial Savvy 219
Financial Statements 219
Future Value of a Lump
Sum 47
Getting Organized 40
Getting Started 40
Interactive Financial Tools
40
Intuit 15
Managing Your Money 42

Mathematics of Individual
Finance 47
Overview of Financial
Planning Process 40
Personal Finance Center
58
Searching for Nonfiction
219
Spending Less 43
Your Financial Profile 45
Your Use of Consumer
Credit 43
foreign currencies
Foreign Currency Exchange
Rates 88
Right on Japan, Wrong on
the Yen 88
government securities
Bureau of Public Debt 82
Cash Flo 94
Current U.S. Treasury Yields
82
Making the Most of Zeros
94
Savings Bond Informer 82
U.S. Treasury Bonds 82
Zero Coupon Bonds 94
hyperlinks 34
index funds
Index Investing versus
Active Investing 84
U.S. Index Movers 84
industry analysis
FDIC 115
Industry Briefing 115
PR Newswire 115
Where to Invest 116
Yahoo! on the Money 115
inflation
Battle Against Inflation 64
Inflation Risk 63
More on Inflation Risk 63

initial public offerings (IPOs) 90–91

insurance 91

interactive investments
  Bob'z 129
  Bust the Tipster 130
  Conference Calls 130
  Join Our Discussion 129
  Message Boards 128
  Michael Campbell's Money Talks 129
  Mutual Funds Online 130
  Participate 129
  Silicon Investor 128
  Socialize 128
  Talk to Other Investors 130

interest, Power of Compounding 49

international
  Global Investing 89
  Guide to International Marketplace 89
  International 90
  International Equities 89
  International Equity 90
  Traps for the Unwary in Foreign Investing 90

Internet etiquette, User Guidelines and Netiquette 143

investment clubs
  Investment Clubs on the Web 131
  National Association of Investors Corporation (NAIC) 131
  So You Want to Start an Investment Club? 131

investment planning
  American Association for Individual Investors 169
  Basic Types of Investments 78
  Benefits of Tax-free Investing 73
  Bloomberg Personal 102

Determining Your Investment Goal 58

Getting Started as a Socially Responsible Investor 74

Identify Goals and Objectives 58

Invest-o-rama 125

misc.investFAQ 78

Motley Fool 104

Setting Your Goals and Objectives 58

Types of Investments 78

Zacks Investment Research 105

IRCs
  Internet Relay Chat FAQ 141
  IRC Help 141

ISPs
  AT&T WorldNet 32
  IBM Internet Connection 32
  MCI Internet Dial Access 32
  Sprint Internet Passport 32

legal issues
  About the Net 141
  Computer Law: Defamation Online 142
  Defamation and Libel in Cyberspace 142
  Defamation Law and Free Speech 142

life insurance
  How to Avoid Estate Taxes on Life Insurance 91
  Insurance 91

long-term investments
  Considering Your Investment Horizon 71
  Individuals Should Focus on the Long-term 71
  Maintenance Program for the Long-term Investor 72

Portfolio Maintenance Program for the Long-Term Investor 47

mailing lists
  Groups 140
  Mailing Lists 139
  Tips for Newcomers 140

market trends
  A.G. Edwards & Co. 121
  American Stock Exchange 121
  Basic Investment Principles of Risk and Return 65
  Capital Markets Commentary 121
  Currency Risk 65
  Legg Mason 120
  Market Commentary 120
  Market Risk and Time 65
  Merrill Lynch 120
  Prudential Securities 121
  Yahoo! Finance 120

money market funds
  Money Market Data 91
  Money Market Funds: Advantages, Risks, and Costs 91

Motley Fool 126

mutual funds
  Advantage of No-Load Mutual Funds 84
  Brief Guide to Closed-End Funds 84
  Building Toward an Investment Plan Starting from Scratch 83
  Getting Started: Investing with Mutual Funds 84
  Investor Education Center 84
  misc.invest.funds FAQ 84
  Morningstar On Demand 84
  Mutual Funds 84
  Mutual Funds as Investments 51

Mutual Funds Online 83
Reading a Mutual Fund
    Listing 52
Top U.S. Mutual Funds 84
news
    BackWeb 106
    CNNfn Financial Network
        102
    Dun and Bradstreet 102
    EDGAR Online 102
    Forté Free Agent 27
    FreeLoader 106
    Hoover's Online 104
    Intermind Communicator
        107
    MSNBC 104
    Pawws Financial Network
        104
    PointCast 107
    Quote.com 105
    Reuters Money Network
        105
    Smart Money 105
    Thompson MarketEdge
        105
newsgroups
    Net Abuse FAQ 143
    news.newusers.questions
        138
    Newsgroups of Interest
        138
    Roadmap for the Informa-
        tion Superhighway 143
    UseNet News 138
online services
    America Online (AOL) 30
    CompuServe 31
    Delphi 31
    GEnie 31
    Microsoft Network 31
    Prodigy 31
options
    Barron's Online 93
    Chicago Board Options
        Exchange 93

portfolios
    Allocation Adjustment 75
    Asset Allocation 74, 76
    Determine Your Investment
        Strategy 75
    E*TRADE Portfolio
        Manager 209
    Excite Business and
        Investing 210
    Galt NetWorth 210
    Importance of a Mix of
        Assets 75
    Infoseek Investor 212
    Investment Goals 74
    Investment Rules 75
    InvestorsEdge 212
    Life Cycle Investing: Your
        Personal Investment Pro
        75
    Look at Historical Invest-
        ment Returns 75
    Microsoft Investor 104
    Personal Portfolio 210
    Right Investment Mix 74
    Sample Investment
        Portfolios 74
    StockSmart 213
    What to Do with Different
        Levels of Investable
        Money 76
price volatility
    Volatility 67
    Volatility Risk 67
publications
    All the Rest 100
    Barron's Online 96
    Business Week 97
    Byte Magazine 27
    Economist 97
    Electronic Publishing 99
    Financial Times 99
    Forbes 98
    Fortune 98
    Hulbert Financial Digest
        100

INVESTools 101
Investor's Business Daily 99
Investors Newsletter Digest
    101
Kiplinger Online 98
Los Angeles Times 99
Money Online 98
Money Talks 101
Mutual Funds Online 99
New York Times 99
PC World 20
San Jose Mercury News 99
Stock Manager's Invest-
    ment Report 101
USA Today/USA Today
    Financial Marketplace 99
Wall Street Journal
    Interactive 100
Washington Post Business
    Glossary 185
Zacks Online Magazine
    101
real estate investment trusts
    (REITs)
    REIT Fever Cools as
        Analysts' Ardor Fades 93
reinvestments
    Reinvestment Rate Risk 68
    Reinvestment Risk 68
retirement
    Fewer Boomers Save for
        Retirement 44
    Financial Planning 44
    Retire Right 58
    Women Need to Save More
        Than Men Do for
        Retirement 44
risks and returns
    About Risk and Reward 59
    Assessing Your Risk
        Tolerance 60
    Credit and Interest Rate
        Risk 64
    Default Risk 63
    Difference Between
        Investing and Gambling
        59

Efficient Frontier 59
Find Your Risk Tolerance
  60
Interest-rate Risk 64
Investing 101: Risk and
  Reward 59
Liquidity 65
Liquidity Risk 64
Moody's 61
More on Interest-rate Risk
  64
Opportunity Cost Risk 66
Opportunity Costs 66
PitBull Investor 66
Prudential Securities 60
search engines
  AltaVista 150
  America Online Mailing List
    Directory 150
  DejaNews 152
  Excite 152
  Infoseek 153
  InfoSpace 153
  LawCrawler 154
  Liszt 154
  Lycos 156
  Magellan 156
  SEARCH.COM 157
  Starting Point 157
  WebCrawler 159
  WorldPages 159
  Yahoo! 112, 160, 204
socially responsible
  Ethical Investing—"Green"
    Money 73
  Guide to Social Investing
    74
software
  Anderson Investors
    Software 22
  Corel Quattro Pro 24
  Kiplinger TaxCut 24
  Lotus 1-2-3 24
  Managing Your Money 21
  Microsoft 21, 24, 244

Procomm Plus 27
Simple Money 2.1 21
Total Access 244
Turbo Tax 23
stocks and bonds
  ABCs of Bonds 81
  About Technical Analysis
    227
  Advantage Newsletter 79
  AstroEcon 224
  Birds in the Hand—Once
    Again, Junk Has Its Uses
    90
  Bollinger Bands 229
  Bond Market Tutorial 80
  Bond Professor Glossary 81
  Bonds as an Investment 51
  Briefing.com 121
  Building a Bond Ladder 80
  Charles Dow and the Dow
    Theory 226
  Check Free Investment
    Services 110
  Closing Bell 113
  Corporate Bonds 80
  Current Municipal Bond
    Yields 81
  DBC Online 110
  Decoding the Dow 226
  Dollar-Cost Averaging 48
  Do's & Don'ts 58
  Dow Divident Approach
    231
  Dow Theory 226
  E-Analytics 228-230
  E*TRADE 110, 113–114
  Elliott Wave Principle 225
  Encyclopedia of Indicators
    230
  End of Day 113
  Equities Are Performers 78
  Equity Analytics Web 185
  Fibonacci and Natural
    Occurrences 224

Glossary of Technical Terms
  227
Golden Section 224
Grand SuperCycle Peak
  224
Hoover's Online 114
InterQuote 112
John Bollinger's Capital
  Growth Letter 229
Junk Bonds—They're
  Baaack 90
MACD 230
MACD Charts 230
Market Watch 112
MarketSmart 112
Money Magazine 114
Moody's Investors Service
  80
Moving Averages 228
Municipal Bonds 81
Optima 229–230
Pace University Library 185
PC Quote 111
Pristine Day Trader 104
Pristine Profit Plan 231
Quicken Financial Network
  111
Quote.Com 111
Reading a Stock Listing 52
Research: Magazine 114
Reuters 245
Rule 10b-21(T) 186
Silicon Investor 114
Standard and Poor's
  61–64, 68, 71, 74, 80
Stock as an Investment 51
Stock Research Group 105
StockMaster 111
Stocks & Commodities 78
StockSmart 229
Syndicate 228
Technical Analysis 227
Techniques 231
TeleQuote Web 112
Telescan 229
Thomson MarketEdge 115

Top Stocks 231
trading 215
Traditional Formula Plans
   for Buying and Selling
   Stocks 48
U.S. Stocks 79
Volatility 231
Wall Street 230
Wall Street Journal's
   Briefing Books 114
Wall Street Research Net
   114
Ways to Group Stocks 63
When to Buy and Sell 227
Why Buy and Hold May
   Not Be the Best Strategy
   215
Why Invest in Equities? 78
Why Invest in Fixed-Income
   Securities? 80
Zack's EPS Surprise 115
taxes
   Easing the Tax Burden 50
   Tax-Deferred and Tax-Free
      Investing 50
technical analysis
   E*TRADE's Interactive
      Charts 240
   Equis' MetaStock Profes-
      sional 240
   MarketArts Window on
      Wall Street Deluxe 240
   Option's Analysis 239
   StockSmart 239
   Super Charts 240
   Technical Analysis Software
      240
   Telescan Investor's Platform
      240
   Wall Street Analyst 240
   Worden TeleChart 2000
      240
terminology
   101 Investment Terms You
      Should Know 51

Glossary 52
Glossary of Investment
   Terms 52
Investing Glossaries on the
   Web 52
URLs 33
Web page construction
**WebCrawler search engine
   159**
Wells Fargo Bank 23
**What Every Investor Should
   Know 128**
**What the Markets Will Watch,
   and Why 117**
**What to Do with Different
   Levels of Investable Money
   76**
When to Buy and Sell 227
Where to Invest 116
**Who Wins from Derivatives
   Losses? 92**
whole life insurance, *see*
   permanent life insurance
**Why Buy and Hold May Not Be
   the Best Strategy 215**
Why Invest in Equities? 78
**Why Invest in Fixed-Income
   Securities? 80**
Wilber National Bank 23
**wildcard characters in search
   engines 149**
Wild, Wild Web 128
Windows 19–20
**Women Need to Save More
   Than Men for Retirement 44**
word searches 147–149
Worden TeleChart 2000 240
working capital 221
WorldPages search engine 159

**WSRN (Wall Street Research
   Net's Company Research)
   216**

Y

**Yahoo! search engine 42, 112,
   160**
   broker listings 204
   Employment Classifieds 42
   Finance 120
   List 118
   on the Money 115
yields 46–47
   dividends 222
   investments 73
   taxable equivalent 50
   see also returns
Your Financial Profile 45
**Your Use of Consumer Credit
   43**

Z

Zack's
   EPS Surprise 115
   Investment Research 105
   Online Magazine 101
zero coupon bonds 79, 93–94